Methodology of Educational Research

Published by
Lotus Press Publishers & Distributors

Methodology of Educational Research

KANWARJIT SINGH
Professor in Education
Rayat-Bahra Group of Institutes
Sahauran, Kharar (Mohali)

Lotus PRESS
4735/22, Prakash Deep Building,
Ansari Road, Dariyaganj,
New Delhi - 110002.

Lotus Press Publishers & Distributors
Unit No. 220, Second Floor, 4735/22, Prakash Deep Building,
Ansari Road, Darya Ganj, New Delhi-110002
Ph.: 011-23280047, 32903912
E-mail: lotuspress1984@gmail.com
www.lotuspress.co.in

Methodology of Educational Research

ISBN: 978-81-8382-294-7 (H/B)

Published by: **Lotus Press Publishers & Distributors** New Delhi - 110002
Printed at: **Bharat Offset Works,** *Delhi*

Preface

Methodology of Educational Research has been written as an introductory text for students pursuing master's level degrees in Education, Psychology and allied fields. The contents of the book are based on syllabi prescribed for this level by Indian Universities.

The book has been written in a simple language for comprehension by students who have difficulty with the English language. An attempt has been made to explain the statistical techniques through easy to understand examples, not requiring tedious calculations. Dependence on calculator has been minimized. Common conceptual difficulties experienced by students, when they work on their dissertations, have also been kept in view.

This book has been possible because of unconditional and total support of the following well wishers to whom the author is beholden.

- Shri Gurvinder Singh Bahra, Chairman Rayat-Bahra Group of Institutes.

- Principal Indu Rehani and the staff of Rayat-Bahra College of Education, Sahauran (Kharar), Dist. SAS Nagar, Punjab.
- His family–wife Aradhna and children Aditya and Sirat.

The author is indebted to all those authors whom he has cited in this book.

(KANWARJIT SINGH)

Contents

1

Nature of Educational Research

1.1 WHAT IS RESEARCH?

Research is a purposeful and systematic activity directed towards the solution of problems. It may lead to some kind of discovery, invention, and explanation of an event or phenomenon.

The dictionary meaning of research is that it is the systematic study of materials and sources in order to establish facts and new conclusions. It may reject, revise or modify the existing knowledge and beliefs in the light of new evidences.

Research is based on observation and experience. It develops its viewpoints on the basis of observations, and verification of its findings. Observation leads to some kind of information in the shape of data. The data are organized and then analysed to arrive at some conclusions. The hallmark of research is that it is objectively conducted. It is free from the biases and personal values of the researcher. Its findings can be verified by others. Nothing is concealed.

1.2 WHAT IS EDUCATIONAL RESEARCH?

Educational research is a systematic study of the problems in education. According to Anderson (1998:6), "educational research is a disciplined attempt to address questions or solve problems through the collection of primary data for the purpose of description, explanation, generalization and prediction".

For Ary and his colleagues (2006:19), "educational research is the application of the scientific approach to the study of educational problems".

Thus, we may conclude that educational research deals with problems in education in a systematic and orderly way. It describes, explains, generalises its findings and makes predictions in the discipline of education.

1.2.1 Characteristics of Educational Research

There is a popular though wrong belief that research in education is far more easier than in physical or natural sciences. By and large educational research is focussed on human behaviour in educational settings. Human behaviour is difficult to understand. There are individual and intra-individual differences. An individual may behave differently in similar situations. Observers may differ in their observations of the same phenomenon. Tools used to study and collect data are far less precise than those in the physical or natural sciences. This is true for the social sciences vis-a-vis physical sciences. All these difficulties create problems for replicating results obtained in educational research, especially when human behaviour is being studied. Lack of confirmation for the findings leads to limited generalizations in education. However, educational research follows the steps entailed in scientific research. The characteristics of educational research are as follows:

- Educational research is empirical.
- Educational research is systematic.
- Educational research is reliable.

- Educational research is valid.
- Educational research may take a variety of forms.

Empirical nature of educational research implies that all knowledge is based on sense experience that comes from observation. Experience takes the form of information or data. The data are organised and analysed to produce information. Therefore, knowledge obtained in research is information or data based.

As a systematic process, educational research is systematic and not haphazard. It is a planned, stepwise and a sequential process. But, at times, there may be some overlap or change in the order of the steps. The typical order of the steps is 1. Identifying problem, 2. Literature review, 3. Deciding about the method, 4. Collection of data, 5. Analysis of data and 6. Reporting and evaluating.

Educational research is valid. It is based on fact and evidence. Internal validity refers to the extent to which results can be interpreted accurately. External validity is concerned with the extent to which the results can be generalised to populations from which the samples for research were taken.

Educational research is reliable. This refers to consistency of the research and the extent to which it can be replicated. Internal reliability refers to the extent to which data collection, analysis and interpretation are consistent under same conditions.

External reliability concerns whether the study will lead to same or similar results when redone or replicated under same conditions. Validity and reliability provide credibility to research.

Finally, educational research can take a variety of forms, approaches and methods which have been taken up in the following section.

1.3 CLASSIFICATION OF EDUCATIONAL RESEARCH

Educational research may be classified on the basis of the nature of the problem, method used, and approach.

1.3.1 Basic, Applied, and Action Research

Basic educational research is more general in nature. It attempts to discover laws and principles of education. On the other hand, applied research aims at providing solutions to some immediate or practical problems. *For example*, technology is a consequence of the applied research.

E.L. Thorndike's theory of learning is an example of basic or pure research. Its application in effective learning is the applied aspect of basic research, in classroom situations.

Piaget's theory of cognitive development is basic research. The application of the developmental stages in school curriculum is applied research.

The main purpose of basic or pure research is extension of knowledge whereas applied research makes use of this knowledge in solving problems that confront the human race. One is not inferior to the other.

Action research is applied research with its focus of finding an immediate and practical solution at the local level. The focus is not on generalizing the findings at a bigger level. *For example*, a school may wish to find out the causes and remedy for high incidence of absenteeism among the school students. The information is generated for use at the classroom, school or local level.

1.3.2 Classification by Methods

Different methods and their variants are available for conducting educational research. The choice of the method depends upon the nature of the problem, resources and expertise available. Commonly, the methods used are as follows:

Research Method	*Focus*
• Historical Research	Past, implications for the present and future.
• Survey Research	Present, existing status.
• Experimental Research	Future, existing status.
• Case Study	In-depth study of one single case, institution.

1.3.3 Classification by Approach

This includes quantitative and qualitative research. Quantitative research relies on scientific approach, attempts to study causal relationships, generates numeric data which are analysed through statistical techniques. Quantitative research uses standardised tools and large samples. *For example*, the researcher may conduct a study on the relationship between anxiety and achievement among adolescents. He would take a large sample of adolescents usually school children. He would try to establish correlation between their anxiety and achievement scores obtained on standardised anxiety and achievement tests.

Qualitative research makes use of naturalistic settings, conducts in-depth study of a phenomenon, makes use of narrative description and interpretation of data. *For example*, the above relationship may be studied through in-depth study of a number of individual cases separately.

Qualitative research may be converted to quantitative but not *vice-versa.*

1.4 SOURCES OF KNOWLEDGE

1.4.1 Experience

It is practical contact with or personal observation of facts, events or phenomenon. Knowledge gained through experience passes on from one generation to another. We need not go through an experience to gain information if it is readily available. Smoking causes cancer. We need not experience or verify it on ourselves.

Experience as a source of knowledge has its limitations. The same situation may be experienced differently by different persons. Further, the same experience may be reported differently by different persons because of communication barriers. Finally, there are limits to experiencing. A researcher cannot count all the elementary children in India. To gain this information he will have to depend on some authentic, knowledgeable source.

1.4.2 Authority

An authority in a particular area may provide knowledge. However, the question arises how does the authority know? More often than not, people believe that the authority is right because of its position, status or divine powers. Traditionally, kings and religious heads were acknowledged as authority. Ptolemy's belief was that the Earth was the centre of universe until Copernicus, in 1543 refuted this belief and said that the Sun was the centre of the universe. Assertions of authority and belief by way of tradition or folk culture may be erroneous.

1.4.3 Deductive Reasoning

Aristotle and his followers introduced this approach for obtaining knowledge. Deductive reasoning is a thinking process in which one moves from general to specific knowledge through the use of logical argument. A major kind of deductive reasoning is syllogism. It consists of a major premise, a minor premise which is followed by a conclusion. *For example,*

Man is mortal.

A is a man.

Therefore, A is mortal.

Deductive reasoning has its weaknesses. To reach a valid conclusion, one must begin with a true premise. The conclusion drawn cannot exceed the major premise on which it is based. The premise must be a universal truth. Universal truth of many statements is difficult to establish.

1.4.4 Inductive Reasoning

During the Middle Ages (AD 476 to AD 1453), it became customary to use dogma and superstition in place of true premise. This resulted in deduction of invalid conclusions. Arrogant assertions of the day were taken as absolute truth.

Francis Bacon (1561-1626) gave a new approach to knowing called inductive reasoning. Bacon said that conclusions should be drawn on the basis of direct observation of events or phenomena. He advised the knowledge seeker to rid his mind of preconceptions and prejudices. Inductive reasoning approach is reverse of the deductive reasoning approach. In it, specific events of a particular class are observed over a period of time. On the basis of these observations, inferences are drawn and generalizations made for the whole class of events. *For example,*

A is mortal.

B is mortal.

A and B are men.

Therefore, man is mortal.

Thus, induction is the process by which it is concluded that what is true of certain individual cases is true of all the cases of the class. What is true at certain times will be true under the same circumstances at all times.

1.4.5 The Scientific Approach

The fundamental characteristic of this approach which differentiates it from the other approaches is its objectivity. Objectivity implies that the scientist by keeping aside his expectations, preferences and values, carefully perceives and faithfully records all the observations and facts of his investigation.

During the 19th century, inductive and deductive approach with hypothesis in between was given the name of scientific approach. A hypothesis is a tentative statement of the relationship among variables in an event. The investigator moves inductively from his observations to hypothesis and then deductively from the hypothesis to logical implications of the hypothesis. Hypothesis is tested by gathering empirical data. On the basis of the evidence obtained, it is either accepted or rejected.

1.5 WHAT IS SCIENCE?

Science is a study of truths that can be demonstrated. It also means a study dealing with observable phenomena.

Certain characteristics differentiate science from non-science. These are as follows and may also be given the name of characteristics of science.

- Science is empirical: it relies on experience.
- Science is objective: Observations are objective and recorded as such.
- Science is parsimonious: It prefers a simpler explanation to a complicated one, of the observed phenomenon. If we have to choose between two equally valid explanations, the simpler one is chosen.

- Science is self correcting: It updates its findings on the basis of new evidences. There is no absolute truth, no final word in science. Its explanations are in probable terms and not in terms of certainty.
- Science is concerned with theory building: It integrates isolated facts and information in order to explain and predict a phenomenon. It is an organized body of knowledge.

1.5.1 Assumptions in Science

- All events or happenings are ordered, lawful and with preceding causes.
- Reliable information can be obtained only through direct and objective observation.

1.5.2 Limitations of Scientific Approach

The scientific approach has limited success in education and the social sciences. This is not because of lack of expertise but the very nature of the subject matter, that is, human behaviour in education and the social or behavioural sciences. Human behaviour is difficult to understand. Physical or natural sciences, usually deal with phenomena many of which have limited number of variables. These variables are relatively easier to manipulate and measure. Human behaviour is unique, that is, individuals differ in their behaviour. When under observation, human behaviour changes. Then the tools used for measurement in education and social sciences are less consistent and precise than the tools and instruments used in natural sciences. Because of variability in behaviour among and within individuals, it becomes difficult to replicate findings in education and the social sciences. Identical conditions are difficult to recreate. Therefore, verification and generalization of findings in education and the social sciences becomes difficult. Since it is not possible to conduct studies under strictly controlled conditions as in physical science, therefore, generalisation of results of education experiments becomes limited.

1.6 LANGUAGE OF EDUCATIONAL RESEARCH

Every science makes use of specific language and terminology to describe its observations. Usually words from the everyday language are borrowed and context based specific meanings are given to these words.

1.6.1 Variable

A variable is a concept or a characteristic that can take on different values. It may vary in the individual from time to time, and among individuals and groups at the same time. *For example,* height, weight, gender, income, intelligence and achievement are the frequently encountered variables in education. Variables may be categorical, independent, dependent, intervening, stimulus and response.

A categorical variable is divided in two or more exclusive categories. *For example,* male-female, living-dead, rich-poor are categorical variables. A continuous variable has continuity in its unit of measurement. It can have infinite values within a range. Examples of continuous variables are height, weight, age, time and income.

The variable which can be manipulated, changed or controlled is called the independent variable. *For example,* intensity of illumination, the number of practice trials, reward and punishment can be manipulated by the experimenter. These are independent variables. Dependent variable is the variable which is caused or in which change occurs because of the independent variable. In typical psychology experiments variables are known as the stimulus (independent) and the response (dependent) variables. Intervening variables are a kind of independent variables.

They are controlled by the experimenter or they may influence the relationship between the independent and the dependent variable. In an experiment to test the relative efficacy of methods of teaching, the methods will be independent variables. The performance of the subjects will be the dependent variable. Teacher competency in teaching with the particular method will be the intervening variable. Another kind of independent variables is the attribute variables, for example, drug-addicts, males, females.

In relationship studies the independent and the dependent variables can interchange positions. When studying the relationship between academic achievement and adjustment, the first could be the independent variable and adjustment the dependent variable, or adjustment could be the independent variable. That is, one may be the cause of the other.

1.6.2 Constant

The opposite of variable is constant. Within a study or in an experiment it has a fixed value. *For example*, if a study is being conducted on 8th class students then class is a constant, only 8th class students are being taken. If the study pertains to 8th class boys then boys would be the another constant.

1.6.3 Construct

A construct is an abstraction, or an internal human process that cannot be touched, seen or measured directly. It can be inferred from its visible results. If an individual likes meeting new people, is fond of going to parties, and indulges in outdoor activities then we infer from these actions that he is extrovert. A person with profuse sweating, shallow breathing and speech incoherence would be inferred as under acute anxiety attack.

Intelligence, creativity, motivation, academic achievement are examples of constructs. Constructs have constitutive meaning (general definition) and operational or working definition.

1.6.4 Theory

The goal of science is theory building. A theory is a set of interrelated facts, or propositions that explain a phenomenon or relationships between observations. We may say that a theory is a generalization or a series of generalizations which enable us to explain some phenomenon in a systematic way. *For example*, Spearman's two factor theory of intelligence enables us to explain intelligence as consisting of a general factor which is pervasive in all intellectual activities, and a number of specific intelligences for specific tasks. E.L. Thorndike's theory of learning explains learning by way of the role of the effect of the response, repetition of the response and the readiness to respond.

A theory may give a complete or part explanation of some phenomenon. It may stand the test of time, be modified or refuted altogether. Theory serves a number of function such as organisation of isolated facts and empirical observation. It tries to explain and predict phenomena. It builds on weak points, gaps and inconsistencies existing in its explanation and findings. *For example*, E.L. Thorndike revised his law of exercise by including the importance of feedback in learning.

A sound theory should have the following characteristics:

- It should be consistent with the observed facts.
- It should be able to explain its observations and findings in the simplest possible way.
- It should provide means for its verification by others.

1.7 STEPS IN EDUCATIONAL RESEARCH

Educational research is a systematic activity which involves a series or sequential steps. A brief description of the steps in educational research is as follows:

- **Problem Identification:** The choice of a research problem may arise from some felt difficulty, expert suggestion, or just out of curiosity. Review of literature helps in focussing on some problem of interest.
- **The Research Hypothesis:** Review of literature and objectives of the study provide clarity for formulation of hypothesis(es). A hypothesis is a tentative answer to the research question.
- **Method of Research:** This entails how research would be conducted. It includes the research design, the sampling technique, tools for data collection and the statistical techniques for data analysis.
- **Collection of Data:** Information is collected in the shape of data which may be quantitative or qualitative. It may be based on observations, documents, or narratives.
- **Analysis and Interpretation:** The data obtained are analysed and results obtained. The results are interpreted in the light of existing information and evidence. Finally, conclusions are drawn.
- **Reporting:** A detailed report of the entire research activity is prepared and compiled as per prescribed standards.

1.8 AREAS OF EDUCATIONAL RESEARCH

Issues, problems and challenges in education have multiplied since 1990 when liberalization of economy began in India.

Broadly, the areas of educational research may be classified as follows:

- ***Segments of Education:*** Early childhood, elementary, secondary and higher education.
- ***Kinds of Education:*** General, vocational-technical, professional, nonformal and continuing education.
- ***Modes of Education:*** Regular face-to-face, distance and open learning.
- ***Persons involved in Education:*** Students, teachers, parents, school administrator, bureaucracy and public at large.
- ***Aspects of Education:*** History, philosophy, psychology, sociology and economics of education; curriculum; methodology; evaluation; capital and human resources; systems management.
- ***Key areas of Education:*** Inclusion and diversity, gender issues; minorities education; education for equity; marketing of education; environment and sustainable development.

National Council of Educational Research and Training in its Sixth survey of research in Education (1993-2000) of 2006 has classified educational research studies in India in twenty areas as follows: Philosophy of education; Teacher and teaching; Language teaching strategies; Science education; Physical education; Health education, Sports science; Vocational education; Educational technology; Distance education and Open learning; Inclusive education; Women's studies in education; Guidance and Counselling; Population education; Psychological dimensions of education; Curriculum and teaching mathematics; Education of the Scheduled Castes, Scheduled tribes and minorities; History of education; Management of elementary education; Value education; Sociology of education.

1.9 PRIORITY AREAS OF EDUCATIONAL RESEARCH IN INDIA

Education is a social process and related to the needs, values and aspirations of the society. As society undergoes change so does education. It has to adapt to the needs of the society. Being dynamic, it has its problems some of which are readily apparent and pressing.

1.9.1 Elementary Education

Universalization of elementary education in India has been a serious problem since independence. Right to Education Act became operative on April 1, 2010. There is a need to take a stock of implementation of this Act till date. What are the problems and difficulties–lack of resources, socio-cultural impediments, lack of will and motivation etc., need research. Studies are needed for one time and recurring per unit cost of elementary education. Existing status of elementary education with reference to the various demographic variables requires research. The problems of first generation learners need to be identified along with their solutions.

Sarv Shiksha Abhiyan was launched in mission mode in 2002. What have been its successes and failures in terms of its impact on enrolment, retention, progression and inclusion needs follow up and evaluation research studies. Micro and macro level studies need to be conducted by independent researchers.

1.9.2 Secondary Education

Increase in enrolment in elementary education will lead to a greater demand for secondary education. *Rashtriya*

Madhayamik Shiksha Abhiyan has been launched. Its policy perspective and implementation guidelines should be based on research evidence so that meagre resources are optimally utilized. Vocationalization of secondary education was envisaged in the NPE (1986), but its implementation has been very poor with only 6-7 percent of the secondary students enrolled in vocational stream as against the target of 50 percent. Focussed research is needed on the problems of this stream.

1.9.3 Higher Education

This segment has witnessed phenomenal growth. At present there are around 702 universities including institutes of national importance and 36000 colleges. According to the National Knowledge Commission (2007), India needs 1500 universities for enrolment of 25 percent of the relevant age group 18-23 years. New campuses, on account of private investment, have mushroomed in haphazard manner with reference to location, catchment areas and the courses offered. There is an acute shortage of qualified faculty which leads to unethical practices. Research should be conducted regarding existing status of educational standards, problems of faculty and students in these institutions. That higher education is a marketable commodity needs a fresh look. Liberal arts higher education is less favoured as compared to professional education, which is causing distortions in higher education. How to make liberal arts education meaningful is a question for research in higher education. None of the universities in India finds place in the top 200 univerities of the world. This implies that there is a dearth of quality education in India. This aspects needs research.

1.9.4 Educational Technology

Newer technologies of access to knowledge are replacing the traditional classroom teaching through 'chalk and talk'. Research studies need to be conducted with reference to the interface between the learner and technology, and integration of technology at all levels of education.

1.9.5 Curriculum Development

In the light of the national curriculum framework (2005) for school education and the advances in science and technology there is a need for updating curriculum at all levels of education. The school curriculum should strike a balance in contents with reference to national goals, local needs and future trends. Curriculum and study materials should be developed in line with the maturation level, developmental characteristics of the learner and according to the principles of learning. Content relevance and its difficulty level should be assessed on the basis of research evidence. Updated curriculum which is attuned to the needs of the society has a bearing on quality of education curriculum development should be based on research.

1.9.6 Education of Special Categories (Inclusive Education)

Education of weaker and economically backward sections, minorities, handicapped children and those with learning disabilities needs special attention and research.

Educational research in the area of learning is emerging. Evidence based approach to the services offered to people with disabilities is becoming a popular subject, according to Jena (2013:3).

Much educational research has been and is being done. Unfortunately it remains confined to library bookshelves or restricted to academic bodies. There is an urgent need of dissemination of educational research for the policy and programme implementation level to the classroom level. Meta analysis of studies in specific areas of educational research should be carried out to arrive at generalizations of the findings which have a bearing on theory and praxis of education. There is a need to conduct well designed micro and macro level research studies.

EXERCISES

1. Justify the need of educational research in elementary education.
2. Teacher plays a pivotal role in the educational process. In the light of this statement which aspects of teacher education need educational research?
3. Give a brief overview of the need of educational research in your state.

2

The Research Problem

The research process begins with the selection of a problem for investigation. Because of lack of experience it is a difficult step for the beginning researcher.

An example of the hierarchy from the research area to specific research questions is as follows.

Research Area: Adolescent depression

Research Topic: Factors associated with adolescent depression

General Question: What is the relationship between family background and adolescent depression?

Specific Research Questions:

- What are the depression rates for adolescents from intact and broken families?
- What are the depression rates for adolescents from high, average and low income families?

2.1 SELECTING A RESEARCH PROBLEM

The first step in the selection of a problem is to choose a general problem area. This requires some familiarity with that area. This is followed by the researcher's interest in that area. *For example,* the researcher may be interested in the area of "Personality Characteristics". After a broad area has been chosen, he narrows down his focus. *For example,* he may wish to investigate personality characteristics of students, and this subarea may be further narrowed down *for example* to "personality characteristics of habitually late coming students". A school head may wish to find out the impact of remedial classes on the performance of weak students.

After having narrowed down the focus, the researcher formulates specific statement of the research problem or question. This is one of the most difficult tasks in the research process.

2.1.1 Sources of Problems

These may include experience, interaction with knowledgeable persons, deductions from a theory, and study of related literature.

- **Experience**

  Personal experiences of the researcher as a teacher, parent, administrator or educational practitioner may help in deciding about the problem. A teacher may wish to identify causes of performance decline among students, after the summer break. An educational planner may wish to work out indicators for allocation of funds to schools. A school head may wish to find out the causes of lack of motivation among his teachers. Therefore, difficulties experienced become a source of problem selection.

- **Interaction with knowledgeable person**

  This a frequent cause of selection of a research problem though not formally acknowledged. Usually, students pursuing their degree, seek the help of their advisers, mentors and well wishers including fellow students in deciding about a problem.

- **Deductions from theory**

  To make use of this source is relatively difficult for the first time researcher. A theory attempts to explain a phenomenon by formulating principles that accounts for what causes the phenomenon. The general principles developed through a theory are applied to specific educational problems to see their usefulness in problem-solving. *For example*, the researcher may apply operant conditioning principles in classroom situations.

- **Study of the Related Literature**

  Review of the published material and literature on the problem area helps in the selection of a problem. The researcher may wish to do again or replicate the findings of a reviewed study. He may wish to use the same research design but on a different sample. This helps in better generalizations of the findings that already exist about that problem.

Study of literature helps in identifying the gaps and limitations in the previous studies. Old studies might need fresh investigation because of the changes in the socio-cultural environment, or context.

- **Non-education sources**

  These may include popular literature, newspapers and magazines of general interest. *For example*, school hours in the context of longer time to travel to the schools in urban areas; employers requirement of skills from fresh graduates.

2.2 CRITERIA FOR EVALUATING A RESEARCH PROBLEM

The significance of a research problem is dependent on fulfilment of a number of criteria.

- **Suitability of the problem**

  The level of complexity of a problem cannot be similar for a beginner and an experienced researcher. The beginning researcher should have entry level skills and motivation with interest to work on that problem. Sometimes, the problem is chosen out of excitement to be abandoned later on.

- **Feasibility**

  It should be possible to work on a problem within the given time frame and the resources available. The researcher has to be realistic from this aspect. The steps involved in the research process – collection and analysis of data, supportive evidence and compilation of the report is a time consuming affair. In how much time would be the data available? Whether subjects would be available? How much time would it take to construct the tools? etc., are some of the questions that arise in every study.

- **Problem Statement**

  The words and terms used in the statement of the problem should have generally agreed upon meanings. They should be free from ambiguities. Value laden terms such as 'good', 'bad' or 'poor' are to be avoided. Formulation of operational (working) definitions of the terms should be possible.

- **Contribution of the Study**

  Study of the problem should contribute to the existing body of knowledge. It should improve upon the existing information by removing gaps, inconsistencies and limitations. The problem should not be trivial, *for example*, the brands of shoes students wear.

- **The problem should be researchable**

  The study should be based on observable events. *For example*, the effect of feedback on student performance is visible. Philosophical or meta-physical issues are difficult to work on for a beginner.

- **Ethically appropriate problem**

  The research study should not cause physical or psychological harm to the subjects or violative of their privacy. Informed consent should be obtained from them by explaining the purpose and the procedure of the investigation. Human right activists will not allow little Albert's experiment today. Parental consent should be obtained in case of subjects who are minor, or children.

2.3 PROBLEM STATEMENT

The statement of the problem gives an exact clarification of what is being studied? The variables in the study are specified. Their working or operational definitions are given, that is, how the researcher proposes to measure them. *For example*, the researcher wants to study the relationship between anxiety and adjustment among adolescent students. The variables involved are anxiety, adjustment and adolescent students. Through working definitions he will explain how he intents to measure anxiety and adjustment. *For example*, for anxiety measurement he may use some anxiety scale scores of students, adjustment may be measured through teachers' ratings of the students; adolescent students may be boys and girls studying in class VIII to X of government schools.

The statement of the problem can be in declarative form or question form. In question form it will be "how is anxiety related to adjustment among adolescent students?" or "what is the relationship between anxiety and adjustment?" In the declarative form the statement could begin as "the present study attempts to study the relationship between anxiety and adjustment".

In some cases the declarative form of the statement is followed by the question form. Some researchers prefer to use the question form because it is straight forward and easy to understand for the layman.

The second criterion for the problem statement is that it should be put up in such a way that it allows for research into the problem. One must be able to collect data through observation. Such abstract terms as are not possible or difficult to be operationalised should be avoided.

According to Ary et al. (2006:59), "the development of a workable problem is an evolutionary process involving many attempts to sharpen concepts, define operations and consider ways of data collection".

Thus, the statement of the problem will include the research question, the objectives of the study, hypotheses formulated, underlying assumptions, and operational definitions, that is, how the variables will be measured. Quite often the beginning researcher confuses the statement with the title of the problem which is an aspect of the statement.

After the research problem has been formulated, the next step is the second phase of the study.

2.4 PLANNING THE RESEARCH STUDY

Formulating a research problem is the first step in the research step. It tells what we intend to investigate, research, or study. After this we decide about the plan for conduct of the research.

2.4.1 The Research Design

The main purpose of the research design is how we propose to find answers to our research question(s). The research design gives a detailed account of the methods to be used, that is, the study design, the measurement procedures, the sampling procedure, the analysis procedure and the time frame. Research design should not be confused with the study design. Research design is more comprehensive and includes all the above procedures including the study design. The study design explains whether the study will be experimental, ex post facto, correlational, historical or survey.

2.4.2 The Research Tools

The means of collecting information are called tools or instruments. These include questionnaire, inventory, interview schedules or rating scales. The researcher may use his own constructed tool, or those available in the market, or already constructed by some another investigator. However, the tool must have certain qualities, that is, reliability, validity, norms, and usability. Many a time, already constructed tools are adapted or modified for local use.

When the researcher wants to establish reliability and validity of his tools, he must use sample similar to the population on which he is going to use his tools. But this sample will not be a part of the study sample from which data or information is to be collected for analysis.

2.4.3 Selecting a Sample

The accuracy of the study depends on the way the subjects or the samples are taken for the study. The objective of any sampling technique is to minimise cost, labour and change in behaviour over an extended period of time. The sample should be a representative of the population which we wish to study.

After having decided about the research problem, the objectives, the research design, the tools and the sample, the next step is writing a research proposal.

2.4.4 Writing a Research Proposal

The research proposal is a sort of detailed operational plan which tells about what we propose to investigate. It is a kind of a blue print of the proposed investigation in which various steps are detailed.

More specifically, the research proposal seeks to answer the following questions:

(a) What is the proposal research about?
(b) What is being tried to fund out?
(c) How is it being found out?
(d) Why is it being found out?

Universities, institutions and sponsoring organisations may have different requirements regarding the style, format and contents of the research proposal. There may be some variations from problem to problem, supervisor to supervisor or discipline to discipline. The proposal should contain relevant information, that is, statement of the objectives of the problem, hypotheses (if formulated), the study design, the tools, the sample, data processing procedures, chapters outline, delimitations of the study, and time frame. If it is a funded research, then cost analysis should also be given.

The next phase is the collection of information or data.

2.5 CONDUCTING THE STUDY

The conduct of the study involves the following:

2.5.1 Collection of Information

Information or data are collected from the subjects or participants. This may include interviews, observations, measurement of some traits, characteristics or qualities. Ethical issues must be taken care of while collecting data.

2.5.2 Processing of Information

Quantitative and qualitative informations or data are processed or analysed by various methods. For quantitative analysis we may need the help of descriptive and inferential statistical techniques. In qualitative studies, field notes and content studies are analysed manually. Quantitative data, these days, is computer analysed. However, the beginning researcher should have an understanding of the underlying statistical techniques. He should be able to interpret the information obtained after data processing.

2.5.3 Writing the Research Report

The research report is written in the style manual approved by the institution for which the research is being conducted. It is divided into different chapters and sections.

2.6 REVIEW OF LITERATURE

In quantitative research, the search and review of related literature is completed before the actual conduct of the study. This provides a background and context that support the study. In qualitative research the review may be carried out before and during the study. *For example*, observation of an event may lead the researcher to modify or develop the tool for data collection such as a schedule or a questionnaire. The purposes of literature review are as follows:

- **Helps in defining the boundaries of Research**

  A study and knowledge of related literature enables the researcher to decide and fix the boundaries or limits of his study. *For example*, the researcher may say, "So much has been done and explored in the problem being studied. These are the gaps or missing links. I can build upon these in the following way."

- **Meaningful linkage with Previous Research**

  A review enables the researcher to link his research question(s) to the existing body of knowledge in a meaningful way so that there is a coherent addition to the accumulated knowledge. A study not linked to accumulated knowledge will be like a free floating radical with hardly any significant contribution to the field.

- **Choice of Methodology**

  Review of literature enables the researcher to know about the methods and techniques that were employed in the precious studies. Newer and refined research techniques of data collection and analysis are developing. The researcher may be able to identify relative strengths and weaknesses of techniques on the basis of the review.

- **Defining the variables in the Study**

  A review of literature helps in classifying the meanings of variables or constructs and their measurement. The researcher can improve upon the working or operational definitions of the terms. In research studies intelligence, creativity, achievement, anxiety, stress and motivation etc., are constructs or abstractions that need operational or working definitions.

- **Formulation of Hypotheses**

  A careful review helps in formulation of hypotheses regarding the relationships among the variables in a study.

- **Explanations for Contradictory Results**

  Review of literature enables him to explain inconsistent and contradictory findings which may be due to different procedures, different context or certain limitations.

- **Avoiding Unnecessary Replication**

  A review of literature may reveal that exhaustive research or a very large number of research studies have been conducted on a problem in which the researcher is interested. Thus, he can avoid unnecessary replication. More often than not, a beginning researcher feels that his problem is new or unexplored until he reviews the literature to find that much research has been done on the problem.

2.7 SOURCES OF INFORMATION

There are many sources from which information regarding research in the area of interest can be obtained. Periodical literature includes professional journals, abstracts, handbooks and yearbooks, both in the hard copy and online information. Some of the sources, both Indian and foreign (U.S.) are listed below.

2.7.1 Indian Sources

- Abstracts: Indian Educational Abstracts; Indian Psychological Abstracts; Indian Sociological Abstracts.
- Journals: Indian Educational Review; Journal of Indian Education; Science Education; Indian Journal of Teacher Education; Journal of Educational Planning and Administration; Perspectives in Education; Experiments in Education; Journal of Educational Research and Extension; Asian Journal of Psychology and Education; Progress of Education; Indian Journal of Adult Education; Indian Journal of Population Education; University News; Journal of Applied Psychology; Journal of Psychological Researches; Psychological Studies; Contemporary Education Dialogue.
- Theses: NCERT Surveys of Research in Education.
- Surveys: All India Educational Surveys (NCERT).

- Popular literature: Economic and Political Weekly; Seminar; Yojna.
- Handbooks: Training Instruments for HRD and OD (Udai Pareek); Handbook of Value Attitude Interest Measurement in India (NCERT); Handbook of Psychology in India (Misra).

Internet Sources: w.w.w.educationinindia.net

http:/n_list.inflibnit.ac.in

http:/www.ejournal.aiaer.net

2.7.2 Foreign Sources

- Abstracts and Indexes: Psychological Abstracts; Child Development Abstracts; Educational Administration Abstracts; Education Abstracts; Educational Index (All U.S.).
- Journals: Review of Educational Research; Review of Research in Education; Educational Researcher; American Educational Research Journal; Journal of Educational Psychology; Journal of Educational Measurement; Journal of Research in Science Teaching; British Journal of Educational Psychology.
- Theses and Dissertations: Dissertation Abstracts International.
- Handbooks: Handbooks of Research on Teaching(1963 onwards); Handbook of Research on Educational Psychology; Keogh's Advances in Special Education; Buros Mental Measurements Yearbooks.
- Encyclopedias: Encyclopedia of Educational Research (AERA); Corsini's Encyclopedia of Psychology.

- ERIC: It is the acronym for the 'Educational Resources Information Centre' of the U.S. government. It is an internet based digital library of educational research and information. It is a clearing house of a wide range of information on education related journals, articles, papers, books, reports and other education related materials(www.eric.ed.gov)
- Dictionaries and Style Manuals: C.V. Good's Dictionary of Education; Oxford Dictionary of Education; Oxford Dictionary of Psychology; Publication Manual of the American Psychological Association (2009).

  Open access journals: http://aera-crasu.edu/index.html

2.8 SELECTION OF STUDIES FOR REVIEW

Practically in every area and on any topic plenty of research literature is available. How many studies should be reviewed depends on time and resources available. There is no hard and fast rules as to how many studies should be reviewed. A few guidelines are as follows:

- Primary and secondary sources: An article written by the person who has conducted research and reported the results in the Journal is a primary source. The researcher should try to access a primary source and cite it in his review. A secondary source is at least one step removed from the primary or original source. X is cited by Y in his work. Z cites X from the work of Y. This is an example of a secondary source. Had Z cited X from X's work then it would have been a primary source. Further, the original communication may get distorted as it passes from one researcher to the other. Therefore, efforts should be made to cite information from primary sources.

- Most recent researches on the topic should be reviewed first. As they are current, they represent present thinking on the topic under study.
- The reviewer may come across contradictory results in some studies related to the topic. This requires careful handling. The contradictory results may be due to different contexts, differences in sampling techniques and methods of research. The study under review may be deficient in some respect.
- The number of the studies to be reviewed depends on the purpose of the review. A dissertation requires a more comprehensive review than a journal article. The review should contain 8 to 10 recent or latest studies related to the topic. Usually the review is carried out by moving backwards from the current studies. References in the current studies provide bibliography of previous studies.

Review of related literature may be stopped when no new information is being obtained or a saturation point has been reached.

2.9 SUMMARIZING INFORMATION

After having located and read the references, the researcher decides whether the information is relevant or not relevant to his research problem. If not then the information is dropped. Relevant information needs summarising and proper storage in a usable form for future use.

First of all bibliographic entry of the retained article should be ensured. A bibliographic entry contains the following information: author(s) name(s), the title of the article or report, facts about the publisher, edition (in case of a book), volume and number (in case of a periodical), the inclusive page numbers. Many universities and research journals have their own referencing styles. In the discipline of educational research a standard style of referencing is as per the Publication Manual of the American Psychological Association (2009). An example of the referencing style for a journal article is as follows.

Nadler, R.B. & Marrow, W. R. (1959). Authoritarian attitudes toward women and their correlates. *Journal of Social Psychology*, 49, 113-23.

2.9.1 Preparing Abstract or Summary

The reviewed article has to be abstracted, condensed or summarised. An abstract is a summary that contains relevant information from a report or an article.

The following elements are to be ensured in an abstract:

Bibliographic Entry, Statement of the Problem, Subjects or Sample, Procedure or Methodology, Results and Conclusions.

2.9.2 Organizing Information

Similar studies should be grouped together so that a logical continuity of thought is maintained. While writing the review, the literature should have the following structure, according to Wiersma and Jurs (2009:69).

- An overview of the research problem and the objectives of the review of the literature.
- Historical development of the issues or theories that are considered.
- Major categories of articles (by school of thought, by variable, by context, by research paradigm, or some other categorization).

- Critical review of articles.
- Differences and similarities of positions and findings.
- Current status of understanding, including gaps in knowledge.

Summing up, it may be said that a review provides information on what has been done, the gaps in the existing knowledge, inconsistencies in the available information. It provides information about the research design, sampling and instrumentation.

EXERCISES

1. How will you decide that the research topic chosen by you is suitable for research? Explain.
2. Describe in brief the need of review of literature in the conduct of a research study.
3. What is the difference between an abstract and a journal? Give names of two abstracts and five journals related to educational research.
4. While summarizing a research report what information would you include in the summary or abstract?

3

Sampling

3.1 SAMPLING

Sampling is the process of selecting a few individuals, objects, or events from a bigger group. The bigger group is called the sampling population.

A sample is a portion or subgroup of the population we are interested in.

3.2 SAMPLING TERMINOLOGY

A well defined class of people, objects, or events is called the population or study population. It is denoted by 'N'. A list identifying each individual, object, or event of the study population is called the sampling frame. The number of individuals, objects, or events that have been selected from the population or the sampling frame is called the sample and is denoted by 'n'. The way the sample is selected from the population is called the sampling design or the sampling strategy. The finding based on the information obtained from the sample is called sample statistics. From the sample statistics we make an estimate about the population. The estimate obtained is called the population parameter.

Let us say we have a population of 2000 class VIII boys. We are interested in their mean height. Through a sampling design we take a sample of 200 students from this population N=2000. We measure height of each of the 200 students and find average height of the sample to be 152 cms, which is sample statistics. The estimate arrived at from the sample statistics will be the population parameter.

3.3 NEED OF SAMPLING

If the population is finite and not scattered, then all the members of the population can be taken up for study, that is, for information collection.

When the population is large, scattered and not easily accessible then the researcher takes a sample from that population. *For example*, the researcher is interested in studying adjustment of class VIII pupils, in Punjab. The number of such pupils will be very large. Therefore, he will go in for some kind of sampling design to get a representative sample of class VIII pupils. Taking a representative sample would save upon his time, money and effort as it would be impossible to study every unit of the population. If his sample suffers from some bias or is not a true representative of the population, his findings based on observations made on this sample would not be accurate.

3.4 PRINCIPLES OF SAMPLING

Suppose we have four boys A, B, C, and D whose ages are 4, 5, 6, and 7 years respectively. The average age of this group is 5.5 years. We pick up two boys at a time to estimate the age of the group. Of two boys, there would be six possible combinations whose average ages would be as follows:

A+B = 4.5 years

A+C = 5 years

A+D = 5.5 years

B+C = 5.5 years

B+D = 6 years

C+D = 6.5 years

Out of these, four samples differ in average age from the group average of 5.5 years. The difference between the sample mean and the population mean is called the sampling error. This leads to the first principle of sampling which is "in a majority of samplings, the sampling statistics and the population parameter will differ". This difference is due to the selection of the cases in the samples.

In the above example we take samples each of size three. The samples would be

A+B+C = 5 years

A+B+D = 5.33 years

A+C+D = 5.67 years

B+C+D = 6 years

The gap between the minimum and the maximum average ages of these four subgroups is one year. In the earlier situation, the gap between the six subgroups was two years. This leads us to the second principle "the larger the sample size, the more accurate the estimate of the population parameter".

Let us say that the ages of the four boys are 4, 6, 8, 10 years. The range or variability of this group is 10-4 = 6 years whereas in the first situation it is 7-4 = 3 years. If we take samples of size two at a time, the minimum and the maximum average ages of sample would be 5 and 9 years. If three cases are taken in all the possible samples, the minimum and the maximum age ranges would be 6 and 8 years. The gaps between the minimum and maximum ages for sample sizes two and three are 4 and 2 years respectively. The average

age of the group is 7 years. This leads us to the third principle "the larger the difference in the variable under study in a given population, the larger the difference between the sample statistics and the population parameter".

From the above it may be concluded that two factors influence the degree of certainty of the inferences drawn from a sample: (*a*) the sample size and (*b*) the heterogeneity of the variable in the population. If the population is more variable (heterogeneous) with respect to the variable under study, the greater would be the uncertainty for a given sample size.

3.5 SAMPLE DESIGNS

The sampling designs are: probability sampling design, and nonprobability sampling design.

3.5.1 Probability Sampling Design

In this design each element of the population has an equal and independent chance of being selected in the sample. The choice of an element in the sample is not influenced by other considerations. Suppose we have a population of one hundred students and want to have a sample of twenty students from this population. While choosing twenty units the investigator can have no personal preferences. Let us say 30 students refuse to be a part of the sampling process. The sample of 20 students from the remaining 70 students will not represent the population of 100 students. Let us take another situation. There are three fast friends in the population. One of them is selected in the sample, but refuses to participate in the study because his fast friends have not been selected in the sample. This would affect the representativeness of the sample. On his insistence his fast friends are also selected in the sample. Again, this would affect representativeness of the sample. The acceptance or rejection of an element should not depend on selection or rejection of another element.

For practical purposes, refusal of a small number of cases say 2 or 3 cases out of a population of 100 will not make the sample non representative.

3.6 TYPES OF PROBABILITY SAMPLING TECHNIQUE

The techniques of probability sampling are:

- Simple Random Sample
- Systematic Sample
- Stratified Random Sample
- Multistage Cluster Sampling

3.6.1 Simple Random Sample

This is the most basic method of probability sampling. Each element of the population has an equal probability of being selected in the sample. Suppose we wish to study parents education level of students enrolled in a college. There are 3000 students in the college and we desire to have a random sample of 300 students. The probability of any student being selected in the sample is

$$\frac{300}{3000} = 1 \text{ in } 10$$

This is known as sampling fraction. The steps in random sampling are:

- Define the population i.e. 3000 students enrolled in the college.
- Select or devise a sampling frame. Enrolment particulars can be obtained from the college office. Assign numbers 1 to 3000 to these students.
- The sample size is $n = 300$.
- Using random number tables or computer program, generate 300 different random numbers that fall between 1 to 3000.

- The 300 students would constitute a simple random sample.

Simple random sampling technique is suitable when the population is finite, not scattered or widely dispersed.

3.6.2 Systematic Sample

This method is a variation of the simple random sampling technique. In this method, we select elements directly from the sampling frame, that is, without using the table of random numbers.

In the above example (3.6.1) we know that we have to select 1 student in 10. We would pick up any number randomly from the numbers 1 to 10. Suppose this number is 6. This means that the sixth element on the sampling frame is our first element in the sample. Thereafter, every tenth element would be picked up and the series would be 6, 16, 26, 36, 46 and so on.

This method is less cumbersome as it eliminates the need of assigning numbers to the names of 3000 students, then picking up 300 randomly, followed by the identification of the names. Before using systematic sampling it should be ensured that there is no inherent ordering of the sample frame. *For example*, alphabetically listed names should be rearranged or shuffled.

3.6.3 Stratified Random Sampling

Suppose the 3000 students are a mixed population of urban and rural students, 2000 students are from urban or city areas, and 1000 students are from villages or rural areas. This urban-rural dichotomy has a bearing on parents' education level. Therefore, we wish that our sample of 300 students should have proportionate number of urban and rural students. Our stratification of the population would be as urban and rural students. The urban students sample will be of the size 200 and rural students will be of the size 100. This means that urban and rural students are in the same proportion in the sample as they are in the population. From the sampling frame, 200 urban and 100 rural students will be randomly picked up to study their parents education level.

When a comparative analysis of the parents education level is to be made for urban and rural students, then equal number of cases, that is, 150 for each can be selected randomly.

Stratified random sampling is useful when the population is heterogeneous. This heterogeneity is likely to have an impact on the variables under consideration.

In education and social sciences, usually the stratification is on the basis of age, gender, residence, income, occupation, achievement, kinds of school, geographical location and social class.

3.6.4 Multistage Cluster Sampling

Suppose we have to obtain a sample of B. Ed. students from the sampling population of the B. Ed. one year regular students in Punjab. First of all we will obtain the names of the universities in the state which offer one year regular B. Ed. Course. For each of the identified university, a list of affiliated B. Ed. Colleges would be obtained. From such lists of the colleges, required number of B. Ed. Colleges will be selected through proportionate random sampling technique. All the students of a selected B. Ed. College would be a part of the sample, or one section picked up at random from each of the colleges could be the unit of sampling.

In cluster sampling, a group or a naturally occurring group with identifiable characteristics is the element or unit of sampling. This technique is used when the population is spread over a wide area. It saves on time and travel.

3.7 TYPES OF NON-PROBABILITY SAMPLING TECHNIQUE

These techniques do not follow the rules of probability in the choice of elements from the sampling population. When the number of elements in a population is not known then these techniques are used.

3.7.1 Convenience Sampling

A convenience sample is one that is available to researcher because it is accessible. Suppose an investigator wants to study parents' attitude towards homework. He can access those parents who visit schools. While carrying out preliminary analysis of a questionnaire or tool, this technique is useful for getting respondents.

3.7.2 Purposive or Judgemental Sampling

Here the researcher makes use of his judgement to decide as to who would be able to provide best information to achieve the objectives of the study. *For example*, we wish to study the impact of mid-day meal on classroom hunger. School children and their parents will be the best source to give information. More often than not, this sampling technique is used in qualitative research.

3.7.3 Expert Sampling

In this technique the person providing information or who is a part of the sample, is an expert or authority in the field of interest to the researcher.

3.7.4 Snowball Sampling

In this technique the sample is selected on the basis of networks. *For example*, we wish to conduct a study on drug deaddiction rehabilitation effects. Information is obtained from a rehabilitated person. He is then asked to identify or give names of persons who have been rehabilitated. Information is collected from such identified persons until no new information is coming forward or when a saturation point has been reached.

3.7.5 Quota Sampling

Quota sampling is similar to stratified random sampling except for that the sampling of units in the quota is not done on random basis. Once the sampling population has been stratified into categories and the number of persons within each category or quota decided, the researcher selects people who fit into these categories. The categorisation or quota may be on the basis of gender, occupation, social class, age etc.

Sometimes probability and nonprobability sampling may be combined. *For example*, the researcher may choose an institution for its convenience or some special quality. Then random samples may be taken from this institution.

Sampling involves a compromise between the researcher's desire to make it representative and the difficulties because of shortage of time, money, and lack of access. However, the investigator should be transparent in his reporting the ways and means of selecting the sample. He should describe all the characteristics of the sample studied. This would facilitate the context in which the findings can be applied or deciding about the limits to generalisation of the findings.

3.8 SAMPLING WITH REPLACEMENT

When we select a sample in such a way that each selected element in the sample is placed back into the sampling population before selecting the next element, this is called sampling with replacement. In case the replaced element is selected again it is discarded and the next one is selected.

Theoretically, this is done to provide an equal chance of selection to each element so as to adhere to the theory of probability to ensure randomisation of the sample.

3.9 RANDOM ASSIGNMENT

When we desire to form equivalent groups of subjects, then a table of random numbers is used to divide the available subjects into groups. The groups will be statistically equivalent and the researcher's bias will have no influence on which subject gets which group. The groups will be similar to all possible known and unknown variable that might influence the dependent variable.

EXERCISES

1. What is a sampling frame? Differentiate between probability and nonprobability sampling design.
2. What is random assignment? How is it different from random sampling?
3. Differentiate between stratified random sampling and quota sampling.
4. You have to study teachers' attitude towards corporal punishment. How would you choose a proportionate stratified random sample of 200 teachers from the following population?

Teachers	*Total Number*
Language	500
Science	230
Mathematics	200
Social Studies	110
Art and Craft	100

5. Differentiate between convenience sampling and snowball sampling techniques.

4

Tools of Research

4.1 QUESTIONNAIRE

It is a widely used and useful tool for collecting survey information. It can be administered without the presence of the researcher, provides both quantitative data and qualitative information, and is relatively easy to analyse.

Developing a good questionnaire requires expertise, time, reading, pilot work and refining of the questions. First of all the general purpose of the questionnaire is decided. The general purpose is reduced to specific purposes or aims. *For example*, the purpose of a questionnaire may be to obtain "a detailed description from secondary school science teachers about the difficulties encountered in science teaching". This is followed by identification of sub areas in which difficulties are faced and then preparing questions on these sub areas. These sub-areas may include: laboratory facilities, time allocation to theory and practical work, textbooks and supplementary reading materials, provision of in-service science education, and student motivation etc. After having identified the sub-areas, questions relevant to each sub-area as would elicit maximum usable information would be developed.

Usually there are three types of questions in questionnaires. These are structured, semi-structured and unstructured questions. Structured questions are close ended questions with a fixed alternative as an answer. *For example*, "Do you watch the Discovery Channel on T.V.?" The respondent has to answer in Yes or No. It is a close ended question with a fixed alternative. An open ended question would be "What major weakness have you observed in the homework notebooks of your students?" Here the respondent is free to write his answer.

When the study is to be conducted or a large sample, close ended and more structured questionnaire is suitable. It enables comparisons across samples and of groups within samples.

4.1.1 Framing of Questions

This involves wording of questions. Some guidelines for writing good questions are as follows:

- A question should be simple, short and direct. The language should be everyday language.
- A question should be understood by all respondents. Abbreviations, acronyms or slangs are not used.
- Questions should elicit unambiguous response. *For example*, "How often do you visit library?" Instead of the options usually, often, sometimes, words such as daily, twice a week and so on are used.
- Avoid two questions in one question. *For example*, "Do you read a lot and like meeting people?" The respondent may want to respond "Yes" to the first part and "No" to the second part of the question.
- Avoid questions which may embarrass the respondent. Such questions are usually of personal nature. *For example*, "Do you lie for face saving?"

- Avoid using prestige carrying, emotionally laden words in the questions. The respondent may get swayed which may affect his response.
- Provide adequate alternatives for response.
- Avoid leading questions, *for example*, is smoking bad? Do you smoke?

4.1.2 Order of Questions

The first question should be closely related to the topic under consideration as this would help in establishing the respondent's rapport with the questionnaire. Questions related to similar content should be grouped together.

4.1.3 Format of Questions

Besides closed and open ended questions, the other types of questions are as follows:

- Scaled questions, *for example*,

  "How would you rate reading skills of your students?"

  Poor –

  Adequate –

  More than Adequate –

  Insufficient Information –

- Check list questions, for example,

  "What type of teaching aids do you use in the classrooms?"

  Chalkboard –

  OHP –

  Computer Projector –

  Others (Please specify) –

- Ranking questions, *for example*:

  "What difficulties do your students feel in arithmetic calculations?"(Rank order)

  Addition –

  Subtraction –

  Multiplication –

  Division –

- Likert type, *for example*:

  "Do intelligent students soon get bored of repetitive work?"

  Agree Cannot say Disagree

4.1.3.1 Other considerations

- Printing of the questionnaire should be free from printer's devil.
- Directions or instructions for responding should be clear and without any ambiguity.
- Confidentiality of the information provided should be ensured.
- Purpose of seeking information should be clearly stated.
- A mailed questionnaire should be accompanied by a covering and request letter together with an adequately stamped and self addressed envelope.
- The word "Thanks" should be printed at the end of directions.

4.1.4 Follow up

The response rate of mailed questionnaire is poorer compared to group administration or one-to-one contact procedure. There is always the possibility of biased responses in mailed questionnaires. Usually, those who have strong feelings either positive or negative, toward the issue respond on the mailed questionnaire. To increase the response rate, the researcher will have to follow up the potential respondents. The usual intervals of follow up are 10 days after mailing, to be repeated after another 10 days and finally 6-7 weeks after mailing.

4.1.5 Validity of Questionnaires

Direct observation of the behaviour of the respondent to see whether it matches his responses to the questions, enables us to have validity evidence. Validity of a questionnaire is influenced by the interest of the respondent and the confidentiality or anonymity of his responses.

4.1.6 Advantages and Disadvantages of Questionnaire

As compared to interview it is less expensive and convenient especially when it is administered to groups in population.

It provides greater anonymity as compared to interview. The likelihood of obtaining true responses to sensitive questions increases when the respondent is asked not to write his name or discloses his identity.

On the disadvantages side, the questionnaire can only be administered to respondent who can read the language of the questions and write.

Response of the individual cannot be supplemented by other means especially in case of mailed questionnaires. Then the respondents have a tendency to answer in a socially desirable manner, rather than truthfully.

The answer to a question may be influenced by the answers to the preceding questions. The respondent may need certain clarification which is not possible because of non presence of the researcher. Finally, the response rate in case of mailed questionnaires may by very low in spite of the follow up. The researcher should consider himself lucky if the response rate is 50 per cent. This may include a large number of highly motivated respondents who have strong feelings for or against the issue.

4.2 INTERVIEW

Interview is a face-to-face interaction between the interviewer and the interviewee (respondent), with a purpose. It is a conversation with some purpose. It is also defined as an oral questionnaire. It is the oldest technique for getting information.

Interview may be classified in a number of ways, that is, the way it is conducted, its purpose and focus. Broadly it may be classified as structured, flexible, in depth or focus, face-to-face, telephonic or in the shape of video conferencing.

4.2.1 Structured Interview

In this interview, the interviewer asks a predetermined set of questions. Same order and wording as already determined, is followed. The interviewer follows the same procedure for every respondent. This provides information under similar conditions.

4.2.2 Flexible Interview

Here the interviewer has the freedom to change the order of the questions, the wording and the contents of the question depending upon the responses of the respondent. The interviewer has the freedom to seek clarifications on responses of the respondent. Thus, the interviewer can conduct an in depth interview.

Flexible interview is mostly used in qualitative research. In qualitative research the responses of the respondent are recorded in verbatim form. In quantitative research, the responses are categorised, codified and then quantified.

4.2.3 Guidelines for conduct of Interview

- The purpose and scheduling of the interview should be clear to the respondent.
- The place and the setting should be comfortable for the respondent.
- Interview should be conducted in a language in which the respondent is efficient or comfortable.
- Confidentiality of information should be assured to the respondent.
- Cooperation of the respondent should be obtained.
- The interview atmosphere should be business like, efficient and with a non threatening attitude of the interviewer towards the respondent.
- Data (response) recording should not interfere in the smooth and timely conduct of the interview.
- Conduct of a good interview requires advanced planning by the interviewer.
- Recording of responses should be objective, free from the biases of the interviewer.
- The interviewer should not put a word in the mouth of the respondent as this may lead to desired responses from the respondent.
- A good interviewer should note non verbal behaviours of the respondent as they provide clues to unconscious, hidden behaviours of the respondent.

4.2.4 Advantages and Disadvantages of Interview

The advantages of interview are:

- Non-response as with questionnaires is not a problem with interview.
- In depth probing is possible.
- The questions can be elaborated for a clearer meaning to the respondent.
- Can be used with persons having difficulties in writing.

The Disadvantages of interview are:

- The respondent may attempt to give inaccurate or wrong information in the absence of required information.
- It is time consuming and expensive.
- Predispositions and biases of the interviewer may affect the responses of the respondent.

4.3 OBSERVATION

The purpose of observation is to find out the extent to which a particular behaviour is present. The following are the major forms of observational research:

Structured or systematic observation

Participant observation

Non-Participant observation

Naturalistic observation

Contrived observation

- **Structured observation**

  In this kind of observation the observer decides in advance the behaviours to be observed, that is, what to look for, and the way the observed behaviour would be recorded. Each person who is under observation is observed for a pre-determined period of time and his behaviour is systematically recorded.

- **Participant observation**

  This method is primarily associated with qualitative research. The observer becomes a part of the group of whose behaviour is observed.

- **Non-participant observation**

  Here the observer observes but does not become a part of the setting or the group he is observing.

- **Naturalistic observation**

  Here the observer observes behaviour as it occurs in a natural setting. The observer does not participate in the group. Contrived observation is carried out under artificial situation or laboratory conditions. Observation of behaviour in situational tests is contrived observation.

An important consideration in observation is sampling of behaviour, that is, what to observe, when to observe and for how long to observe. The sampling strategy for observation of behaviours is as follows:

- Ad libitum sampling in which the observer records whatever is happening at the time.
- Focal sampling is sampling in which a particular individual is observed for a set period of time.
- Scan sampling is the procedure in which the entire group is scanned and behaviour of the individuals is recorded at that point of time.
- Behaviour sampling involves the entire group and the observer records as to who was involved in a particular kind of behaviour.

Central to any structured or systematic sampling is the use of observation schedule or coding scheme. This schedule specifies the categories of behaviours to be observed and how to allocate the observed behaviours to these categories. Flander's Interaction Analysis Categories is a classic example of the observation schedule for analysing classroom behaviours.

4.3.1 Guidelines for Effective Observation

- Select the aspects of behaviour to be observed.
- Define behaviour falling within a category.
- Define sampling of behaviours.
- Develop a system of counting of the observed behaviour.
- Ensure objective recording of behaviour.
- Train the observers.

4.3.2 Limitations of Observation

When participants know that they are under observation, their behaviour changes (may wish to create good impression or conceal their true or natural behaviour). The same situation may be reported differently by different observers.

4.4 PSYCHOLOGICAL TESTS

A test is a set of stimuli presented to a subject to elicit his responses to the stimuli. Numerical scores are assigned to the responses. These scores indicate the extent to which the subject has the characteristics being measured. Psychological tests are based on hypothetical constructs or abstractions which try to explain observable behaviours. *For example*, intelligence, aptitude, creativity, adjustment, motivation and anxiety are frequently used constructs in psychological tests. Psychological tests may give a measure of one single characteristic, trait or quality or they may be multi-dimensional or multi trait.

Hundreds of psychological tests to measure human characteristics have been developed over the years. They have been developed for individual or group administration, for different age groups, educational levels and for testing in different settings–academics, industry, clinical and non clinical settings. They assess different aspects such as intelligence, aptitude, adjustment, self concept, values and personality etc. In fact, psychological testing gained momentum on the beginning of the First World War.

The choice of a psychological test for use depends on a number of factors which are:

- The purpose of testing and the aspects of behaviour to be assessed.
- Validity, reliability and ease of administration including availability of parallel forms, norms, and evidence of cross cultural validity.
- Costs and time requirements for administration.

Qualities desired in a psychological test have been discussed in the Chapter 5.

Among the frequently and widely used tests for research purposes are as follows.

4.4.1 Personality Questionnaires and Inventories

- Cattell 16 Personality Factor Questionnaire
- Cattell High School Personality Questionnaire
- Eysenck Personality Questionnaire (Adult & Junior forms)
- NEO Personality Inventory (Revised)
- Rotter Locus of Control Scale

4.4.2 Tests for Assessment in Clinical Settings

- Minnesota Multiphasic Inventory-2
- Beck Depression Inventory
- Spielberger State-Trait Anxiety Inventory

4.4.3 Projective Techniques

In projective techniques ambiguous or relatively unstructured stimuli are presented to the subject who is asked to structure or give meaning to these. While doing so, he projects or reveals his unconscious motives, needs etc.

- Rorschach Ink Blots
- Murray Thematic Apperception Test
- Jung Word Association List
- Sentence Completion Test

4.4.4 Intelligence Tests

- Raven Progressive Matrices
- Weschler Intelligence Scales (For different age levels)
- Stanford Binet Intelligence Scale (2003)

4.4.5 Aptitude Tests

These tests give a measure of the likelihood of future success in some area.

- General Aptitude Test Battery
- Differential Aptitude Tests
- Multidimensional Aptitude Battery
- Bennett Mechanical Comprehension Test

The above examples are of foreign tests mostly standardised on U.S. population. Indian adaptations of these tests and those developed in India are available from commercial test suppliers (See Appendix IV).

Should a beginning researcher make use of a commercially available test or construct his own? The answer is use the test which "fits the purpose". Test construction is time demanding and a rigorous procedure.

4.4.6 Limitations of Psychological Tests

A major weakness of paper pencil tests especially those dealing with personality assessment is that the subject may respond in a socially desirable manner and not the way he actually feels or does. Another weakness in these test may be valid enough for group administration and prediction, but by and large they lack validity evidence for individual prediction.

Information about tests can be found in sources such as the Mental Measurements Yearbooks.

4.5 RATING SCALE

A rating scale is one of the most widely used measuring instruments. It presents a number of statements about a behaviour, activity or a phenomenon along with a scale of categories on which the rater gives his rating about the observed behaviour. *For example*, a student-teacher may be rated on teaching skill, by his supervisor as follows:

Skill	*Rating*				
• Blackboard writing	1 Very Poor	2	3	4	5 Very Good
• Speed of presentation	1 Very Slow	2	3	4	5 Very Fast

This type of scale is known as the graphic scale. Another type of scale is the category scale. *For example*:

- Skill of explaining with examples (check one)
  Good –
  Average –
  Poor –

The responses of the raters are usually categorized in 3 to 5 categories. Scales with more than 5 categories are not recommended because it becomes difficult for the rater to discriminate.

4.5.1 Limitations of Rating Scales

- The rater must be familiar with the characteristic of the ratee on which he is being rated. Otherwise, biased ratings may be obtained.
- Quite often the rater tends to be liberal in his ratings. This is called 'generosity effect' or he may be too harsh in his ratings which is called 'severity effect'. Then the preceding rating may affect the subsequent rating which is called the 'halo effect'. Suppose an individual has been rated high on 'honesty'. He may be rated high on the next item pertaining to his 'punctuality' not because of his punctuality but because of the carry over of the effect of preceding rating of high on honesty. Then, there may be an error on account of 'central tendency'. The raters' ratings are average for all the characteristics of the ratee.

Rating scales are widely used in standardized observation and interview procedures.

4.6 ATTITUDE SCALES

Attitudes are frequently studied in educational research. An attitude is a feeling, either positive or negative, towards some object, issue, individual, group or an organization.

For example, we may study attitudes towards 'coeducation', 'teachers' and 'compulsory military training' etc. Attitude assessment is based on the assumption that individuals can be placed along a continuum of favourableness-unfavourableness towards some object or issue.

Quite often the researcher has to construct his own scale for measuring attitudes. There are a number of different kinds of attitude scale which include Likert Scale, Thurstone Scale and Guttman scale. Here, the Likert technique has been taken up which is relatively an easier technique of scale development.

4.6.1 Construction of Likert Scale

- A large number of statements about the object are collected. Half the item express favourable attitude towards the object and the remaining half are unfavourable. There are no neutral items. The statements should constitute a representative sample of all the possible opinions or attitudes about the object.
- The statements along with five response categories on an agreement–disagreement or favourable-unfavourable continuum are presented to a group of subjects usually 100 or more. The statements are arranged in a random order so as to avoid any response set on part of the subjects.
- The subjects are asked to select the response category that best represents their reaction to the statement, that is, strongly agree (SA), agree(A), undecided(U), disagree(D), or strongly disagree(SD).
- The statement responses are then scored. The numeric values for strongly agree-strongly disagree are 5, 4, 3, 2,1 for favourable statements. *For example,*

Female foeticide should invite a minimum of 5 year imprisonment to the perpetuator.

(SA) (A) (UD) (D) (SD)

Endorsement of strongly agree (SA) would be scored 5. Strongly disagree will get a weight or score of 1.

Unfavourable statement is scored in the reverse order. *For example,* smoking should be allowed in public places.

(SA) (A) (UD) (D) (SD)

Here strongly agree response will get a weight of 1 and strongly disagree a weight of 5.

- The highest possible score on the scale would be 5xN where N is the number of statements in the scale; the lowest possible score would be 1×N.
- An item analysis for the scale is carried out to identify the best functioning items. Highest scoring 27 per cent and lowest scoring 27 per cent subjects are identified as the high group and the low group. The way each statement has been responded by these groups is subject to statistical analysis (*t*-test) to find whether the statement discriminate between the two groups. If it fails to discriminate, then it is dropped from the final scale.
- Validity and reliability indices of the scale are established.

4.7 ACHIEVEMENT TESTS

These tests are widely used in educational research and in schools. Achievement tests measure mastery and proficiency in different areas or school subjects. A standard set of questions is presented to the subjects. Responses are scored right/wrong, pass or fail. Achievement tests may be standardised or teacher made.

- **Standardized Tests:** These are published tests and prepared by experts and cover broad academic objectives. Their reliability, validity are established, directions for administration and scoring are prescribed. Norms for these tests are established on large samples. The mean score of a particular class level or age level in the sample becomes the norm for that level. A norm represents 'what is' and not 'what ought to be' which is a standard.

Standardized achievement tests are available as single tests or in the form of a battery of achievement tests measuring achievement in a number of areas.

Teacher or researcher made achievement tests are tailor made tests to serve local needs and for testing some particular aspects of classroom learning.

The above tests may further be classified as norm referenced and criterion referenced achievement tests. In the norm referenced tests, the individual's performance is compared to the performance of others on the test. Criterion referenced tests enable to describe what an individual can do or the level of mastery attained by him in some skill or content domain.

Standardized achievement tests are not much in vogue in India. Even the national level entrance tests are not standardised, in the strict sense of the term.

EXERCISES

1. What precautions would you take while framing questions for a questionnaire? Explain with examples.
2. What steps would you take for an interview to be objective? What are the advantages of interview as a tool for data collection?

3. What is the difference between an achievement test and a personality questionnaire? What are the relative advantages and limitations of personality questionnaires in personality assessment?
4. Prepare a four item Likert type rating scale for measuring attitudes toward "free higher education for all."
5. What are the limitations of questionnaires and rating scales as tools of data collection?

5

Reliability and Validity of Measuring Instruments

5.1 RELIABILITY

Reliability is the consistency with which an instrument measures whatever it measures.

Suppose we have a weighing scale. A standard weight of 5 kgs is placed on it and it gives a reading of 5 kgs. This process is carried out a number of times and every time, the scale gives a reading of 5 kgs. We say that the scale is consistent or accurate in its measurements. Had the scale given different readings we would have said that it lacks consistency or it is not dependable.

In education and social sciences we construct and use instruments, usually in the form of tests or questionnaires to measure constructs, or characteristics of an individual, in quantitative and qualitative studies. The reliability of the measuring instruments developed or used by the researcher is understood in three contexts: stability, equivalence and internal consistency.

5.1.1 Reliability as Stability

It is the consistency of a measure over a period of time. Suppose we have administered a biology achievement test to a group of students today and under similar conditions it is readministered to the same group say after a week. If the students obtain the same marks or ranks on the two occasions then we say that our test is reliable. Evidence for test retest reliability will be obtained by working out coefficient of stability through Pearson's correlation coefficient between the two sets of marks.

5.1.2 Reliability as Equivalence

It may not be possible to readminister the test under identical conditions. Further, there may be a carry over effect of the learning in the first administration of the test to the second administration which may affect the second performance. To overcome these difficulties, an alternate, equivalent or parallel form of the test is constructed with same contents and difficulty level of the items.

The same group is administered both the forms one after another without time gap. Pearson's product moment correlation coefficient is worked out for the two sets of marks to obtain coefficient of equivalence.

This approach is considered to be better than test retest method. But it is difficult to construct equivalent forms of a test.

5.1.3 Reliability as Internal Consistency

It refers to whether all the items in a test are measuring the same thing. This approach requires only one administration of the test. A test is administered to a group of subjects. The test is split into two equal halves, usually the odd items in the one half and even items in the other. The marks on the two halves are correlated through Pearson's product moment correlation coefficient method. This gives internal consistency for half the test. Reliability for the full test is worked out using Spearman Brown formula which is

$$r_t = \frac{2r_{oe}}{1+r_{oe}} \qquad ...(5.1)$$

r_t = reliability for the whole test

r_{oe} = correlation coefficient between two halves (odd-even split)

If the correlation coefficient between two halves is .70, the estimated reliability for the full test will be

$$r_t = \frac{2(.70)}{1+.70}$$

$$= 0.82$$

- **Kuder-Richardson Procedures:** For determining homogeneity or internal consistency reliability K-R formula 20 is widely used for tests where items are scored as true/false or right/wrong

$$r_t = \frac{K}{K-1}\left(\frac{s_x^{\,2} - \Sigma pq}{s_x^{\,2}}\right) \qquad ...(5.2)$$

where r_t = reliability of the whole test

K = number of items in the test

s_x^2 = variance of marks on the test (Square of SD)

p = proportion of correct answers on a single item

q = proportion of wrong answers on the same item,

$q = (1-p)$

The product pq is calculated for each item, and then products are added for all the items to get Σpq.

Another formula, KR-21 which is relatively simpler requires that all the items on the list are of equal difficulty, is

$$r_t = \frac{Ks_x^2 - M(K - M)}{(K - 1)s_x^2} \qquad \text{...(5.3)}$$

where r_t = reliability of the whole test

K = the number of items in the test

s_x^2 = the variance of the marks on the test

M = Mean of the marks

If a test is measuring a single trait and all the items are equivalent, the reliability estimate provide by K-R procedure will be similar to that provided by the split half. All forms except for the split half provide lower estimates of reliability.

- **Cronbach Coefficient Alpha:** When items are scored dichotomously, coefficient alpha gives same results as the KR-20. An advantage of coefficient alpha is that it can be used when items can be responded in more than two ways, *for example*, attitude scales.

The formula for coefficient alpha is

$$\alpha = \frac{K}{K - 1}\left(\frac{s_x^2 - \Sigma s_i^2}{s_x^2}\right) \qquad \text{...(5.4)}$$

Here K = the number of items in the test

Σs_i^2 = the sum of the variance of the item marks

s_x^2 = the variance of the marks (all the K items)

5.2 FACTORS AFFECTING TEST RELIABILITY

The interpretation of the reliability coefficients of measuring instruments in education and social sciences should be based on a number of considerations.

- The reliability of a test is influenced by its length or the number of items in it. A shorter test with a few items is likely to be less reliable than a longer test on the same content area. A short test of 4 to 5 items on the capitals of the states in India will not give an accurate information about students knowledge as compared with a 15 item test. However, the items in the test should not overlap, and belong to the domain of states in India.

- The reliability of a test is influenced by the heterogeneity of the group being measured. If the group being measured is more variable on the trait under consideration, the higher reliability estimate would be obtained. Lower reliability estimate would be obtained when the group is homogeneous, that is, there is little variation on the trait.
- The reliability of a test is influenced by the ability level of the group. When the test is difficult, it is beyond the ability level of the students and they may resort to guessing. If the test is easy, all the students have correct answers on most of the items. In both the situations, lower reliability estimates would be obtained.
- The reliability of a test is influenced by the technique employed for estimation. Estimates obtained through equivalent forms with time lapse are lower than those obtained through test - retest and split half procedure. This is because form-to-form as well as time-to-time fluctuations are present.
- The reliability of a test is influenced by the nature of the variable being measured. Academic achievement is relatively easier to measure. Therefore achievement tests have high reliability (.90 or more). Aptitude tests are designed to predict future behaviours which is a difficult task. Thus, lower estimates of reliabilities will suffice.

5.3 MINIMUM ACCEPTABLE RELIABILITY

As a rule of thumb a test has good reliability if it is equal or more than the reliabilities of competing tests. A biology achievement test with reliability coefficient of .80 is unsatisfactory if competing tests with reliabilities coefficients of .90 or more are available.

The requirement of the degree of reliability also depends upon the nature of decisions we are going to make from the test scores. For research and decisions for a group, modest reliability coefficients in the range .50 to .60 may be acceptable. If the decisions are to be made about individuals such as placement in a course or a job or in a special education group then instruments with highest reliability with a minimum of .90 should by used.

5.4 THEORY OF RELIABILITY

On a theoretical level, reliability is concerned with the effect of error on the consistency of measurements or scores. There are two kinds of errors of measurement: random errors and systematic errors. Random error is a chance error and may increase or decrease the score of an individual in an unpredictable manner. Systematic error increases or decreases the scores in a known way. Random errors are concerned with the reliability problems. Systematic errors are at the root of validity problems.

5.4.1 Causes of Random Errors

Fluctuations in the mood, motivation and mental condition of the test taker may result in inconsistency in his scores on repeated measurements.

Variation in conditions of administration and readministration of the measuring instrument affect its reliability. Testing conditions such as heat, humidity, light and distraction may affect the performance of the test taker. Inexperience of the test administrator, ambiguous instructions and errors in scoring may result in inconsistent scores.

The measuring instrument may itself be faulty and the source of error. A small sample of test items will give unstable scores than a long test. Guess work and luck exert more influence on a short test. Suppose we have constructed a mathematics achievement test in which the language of the items is difficult. The scores of individuals who are not sufficiently familiar with the language may find it difficult to comprehend what they are expected to do. In this instance we are not only measuring their mathematics achievement but language comprehension as well.

5.5 RELATIONSHIP BETWEEN RELIABILITY AND VALIDITY

Reliability is concerned with how consistently we are measuring whatever we are measuring. Validity is defined as the extent to which a measuring instrument measured what it claimed to measure. Now it is understood as appropriateness of the interpretation of the results obtained on the test. Validity is specific to the intended use. A test which is a valid measure of biology achievement is not a valid measure of mathematics achievement. The relationship between reliability and validity is as follows: A measuring instrument can be reliable without being valid. Reliability of a measuring instrument is necessary but not a sufficient condition for it to be valid. A highly reliable measuring instrument may be valid for some purpose but not for the intended purpose. We may obtain highly consistent measurements of the head circumference (highly reliable) but these measurements will not yield valid inference about intelligence because the relationship between head circumference and intelligence is not supported by evidence or theory of intelligence. Therefore, though our measurements of head circumference are very reliable but meaningless for measuring intelligence.

5.6 EQUATIONS FOR RELIABILITY

It is now an accepted fact that measurements of human qualities suffer from random errors.

Suppose we administer a test to a student. We obtain his score. This score is called the observed score. Had we tested this student on some other occasion with the same test, we would have not obtained the same observed score because of the effect of random errors of measurement. If the score were free of the error component then it would have been perfectly accurate score or the true score on the test. The true score is conceptualised as the hypothetical average score obtained from many repetitions of the test. In an equation form the observed score of the individual may be expressed as

$$X = T + E$$

Where X = Observed Score

T = The True Score

E = Error of measurement

In the above equation if the error score is positive the observed score will be inflated. If it is negative, then the observed score would be deflated. Usually, in research situations the researcher has one measurement of each individual in the group, on a variable. It has been shown mathematically that the variance of a large group of subjects is equal to the variance of their true scores plus the variance of their errors of measurement or

$$\sigma_x^2 = \sigma_t^2 + \sigma_e^2$$

Reliability may be defined theoretically as the ratio of the true score variance to the observed score variance in a set of scores. It is expressed as

$$r_{xx} = \frac{\sigma_t^2}{\sigma_x^2}$$

where r_{xx} = reliability of the test

σ_t^2 = variance of the true scores

σ_x^2 = variance of the observed scores

Mathematically, reliability is the proportion of the variance in the observed scores that is free of error. This is expressed as

$$r_{xx} = 1 - \frac{\sigma_e^2}{\sigma_x^2}$$

Thus, if the error variance is more, the reliability coefficient will be depressed.

5.7 STANDARD ERROR OF MEASUREMENT

The reliability coefficient tells us about the consistency of test scores. It does not tell us about the amount of error in an individual's test score. Suppose on a mathematics aptitude test the score of a student is 80. Repeated administration of the test will yield a number of scores of the student. Some will be above 80, others below it and a few may be 80. The mean of all these scores will be the best estimate of the true score of the student. Standard deviation of these scores would indicate the error of measurement. This standard deviation is called the Standard Error of Measurement. Since a test is not administered repeatedly to the same individual, standard error of measurement can be obtained from single administration of the test with the formula

$$S_M = s_x \sqrt{1 - r_{xx}} \qquad \text{...(5.5)}$$

where S_M = standard error of measurement

s_x = standard deviation of the test scores

r_{xx} = reliability coefficient

If the mathematics aptitude test has a reliability coefficient of .75 and standard deviation 10, then

$$S_M = 10\sqrt{1-.75}$$
$$= 10\sqrt{.25}$$
$$= 5$$

The score of the student is 80. If the test is readministered 100 times the likelihood is that 68 times his true score will lie between 75 and 85, and 95 times his true score will lie between $80 \pm 1.96(5) = 70.20$ and 89.80. These are 68 per cent and 95 per cent confidence intervals.

Whereas reliability coefficient is an indicator of consistency of a group of scores, standard error of measurement is an estimate of the consistency of an individual's performance on a test. As reliability of a test increases, standard error of measurement decreases.

5.8 VALIDITY

Validity is the most important quality desired in a measuring instrument. Validity is the extent to which a measuring instrument measures what it claims to measure. It is concerned with the question, "Does the instrument measure the trait, characteristic, quality or whatever for which it is intended?" The recent focus is on the interpretation and meaning of the scores obtained on the test. Tests yield scores. What interpretation do we make of these scores? *For example*, a science achievement test for eighth class students would allow us to make valid interpretations about eighth class students science achievement, but this test will not yield valid interpretations about the students ability of essay writing.

5.9 VALIDATION PROCESS

Basically there are two approaches for determining the validity of measuring instruments in education and social sciences. The first approach is through a logical analysis of content or a logical analysis of what would make up a characteristic, trait or a construct in educational setting. This is essentially based on judgement. The second approach makes use of some criterion which is some sort of standard or desired outcome. The criterion may by some immediate performance or future performance.

Instruments used in education and social sciences are usually designed for measuring hypothetical constructs such as intelligence, creativity, motivation, anxiety, and attitudes etc. These are abstract variables derived from observation or some theory. We do not have direct means of measuring these constructs, rather these are inferred from the observable behaviour of the individual. In physical sciences the researchers have the direct means of measuring characteristics such as length, weight and volume.

5.9.1 Evidence based on Test Content

This involves the test's content and its relationship to the construct it intends to measure. The test items or questions should give an adequate and balanced coverage to the domain of content. This type of evidence is especially important for achievement tests. The contents covered in the questions, the wording of the questions and the adequacy of items to measure the desired outcome are the essential considerations for content related evidence of test validity. *For example*, there are five units in science syllabus. The teacher prepares an achievement test with items based only on first three units. The test will lack content related evidence of validity. For adequate content coverage the teacher will have to prepare a blue print with relative weightage to each unit and further to each subunit. The items would be framed and included in proportion to the weightage accorded to different units in the total domain of five units.

5.9.2 Evidence based on Relations to a Criterion

Two types of criterion related validity evidence are used. These are: concurrent validity and predictive validity. The distinction is made on the basis of the time the criterion data will be collected.

5.9.3 Concurrent Validity

Concurrent validity evidence is based on the measures obtained on the test being correlated with the scores obtained on a criterion at the same time. Suppose we have constructed an objective biology achievement test for twelfth class students. We search and select an existing well known and validated biology achievement test. Both the tests are administered to a group of twelfth class students under similar conditions. A substantial positive correlation between the two sets of scores will indicate that the objective biology achievement test constructed by us is valid for measuring biology achievement of twelfth class students.

5.9.4 Predictive Validity

Here we seek evidence for the relationship between scores on the test and the criterion scores available at a future time. Suppose we have developed a teaching aptitude test. We select a group of prospective teachers on the basis of their scores on this test. On successful completion of the teacher education course, they are put on teaching jobs. Their performance as teachers will be correlated with their scores on the teaching aptitude test. If the correlation between the scores on the teaching aptitude test and the criterion (success in teaching) is substantial and positive, then we say that our teaching aptitude test has predictive validity.

5.9.5 Construct Validity

This type of validation is more comprehensive and subsumes the other types. This kind of evidence focuses on test scores as a measure of the psychological construct being measured. *For example*, intelligence, creativity and motivation are constructs. Evidence has to be provided that the scores on the test reflect the construct we are trying to measure. Construct related evidence is provided through the following:

- **Known-groups Techniques**

  Two extreme groups on the construct are measured with the test. The group high on the construct will give better performance on the test.

- **Related Measures Studies**

  Here two types of evidence based on relations to other variables: convergent and discriminant are used. Relationship between the test scores and scores obtained on similar test will provide convergent evidence. An intelligence test scores should substantially correlate with scores on other similar intelligence tests. Scores on the test and scores on tests measuring different constructs provide discriminant evidence.

- **Intervention Studies**

  Through experimental manipulation of the constructs being measured by the test we can obtain evidence of validity of the test. Suppose on the basis of an anxiety scale we have identified a high anxiety group of students. If in a stressful situation these individuals indicate higher levels of nervousness and bodily symptoms associated with anxiety, then we say that our anxiety scale is a valid measure of anxiety.

- **Internal Structure Studies**

  Analysis of the items of the test is another way of establishing validity of the test. If an individual answers similar items in the same way then we have evidence based on internal structure. For a single trait measurement scale, inter item correlations should be high.

- **Response Process**

  In this the test taker is asked to "think aloud" or articulate as he thinks through the answers to the item. On a biology achievement test, if the students are findings it difficult to comprehend certain words in the language of the test items, then this would point towards construct-irrelevant evidence. Test validation is not a one time affair. In the light of new evidence, the test items undergo a change or modification accordingly.

5.10 VALIDITY COEFFICIENT

The correlation coefficient between test scores and the criterion is called a validity coefficient (r_{xy}). The size of a validity coefficient is influenced by the strength of the relationship between test scores and criterion. The higher the validity coefficient, the stronger the evidence that the test is useful for the purpose for which it has been constructed.

High concurrent validity evidence is aimed at and important for classification, diagnosis and certification. A test used for predictive purposes, for example, selection purposes should have high predictive validity evidence. As a rule, the higher the validity coefficient, the better the evidence.

Whether the validity is high, average or low depends on the purpose of the test and the context in which it is being used. Also, validity of a test is evaluated relative to the validities of the competing tests.

5.11 COMPARISON BETWEEN VALIDITY AND RELIABILITY

Validity of a test is a more important consideration than it reliability. Evidence for validity is a more challenging task. It involves a great deal of accumulation of evidence to support the interpretations based on scores on the test. Validation process involves defining the trait the test measures, appropriateness of contents, and the adequacy of the criterion. All these involve judgements and collection of data and evidence from many sources.

Reliability is relatively easier to establish, no data other than obtained on the test is required for establishing reliability. For a measure to be valid it must be first reliable. Scores obtained on a test with zero reliability are entirely random and therefore do not correlate with any criterion. The possibility of correlation with any possible criterion increases as the reliability of the measuring instrument increases. However, measurements or scores obtained with the measuring instrument may be highly reliable without being valid. A foot ruler is not a valid instrument for measuring weight.

EXERCISES

1. Define Reliability. How is internal consistency reliability established?
2. Define Validity. What is criterion related evidence for validity? Explain with examples.
3. For a group of students their scores on odd items were correlated with the scores on the even items of

a test. The correlation coefficient was $r = .80$. What is the reliability coefficient for the whole test?

4. A teacher has administered a 60 item test to her class. The mean score is 40 with a standard deviation of 5. Estimate the reliability of the test.
5. Explain the meaning of standard error of measurement. A mathematics achievement with a reliability coefficient of .90 has been administered to class X students. The standard deviation of the scores obtained by these students is 6. Calculate the 95 percent confidence interval for the true score of a student whose obtained score is 75 on the test.
6. Explain how will you increase the reliability of a test being constructed by you?
7. Differentiate between random errors and systematic errors in measurement.

6

The Hypothesis

After a research problem has been formulated and objectives outlined, the next step is the construction of hypothesis(es). A hypothesis is a tentative solution to the problem under investigation. Hypothesis brings clarity, focus and direction to the research activity. It provides directions regarding what data to collect and what procedures to follow.

6.1 DEFINING HYPOTHESIS

Kerlinger (1986:17) defines hypothesis as "a conjectural statement of the relationship between two or more variables."

According to Bryman (2008:694), "A hypothesis is an informed speculation, which is set up to be tested, about the relationship between two or more variables".

We may say that a hypothesis is a hunch, an assertion or an assumption about a situation, a phenomenon or a relationship, whose truth or reality is yet to be verified.

Some studies do not generate hypothesis(es) especially when there is no sufficient accumulated background information. Survey studies that attempt to measure attitudes and opinions of groups, studies which describe characteristics of some phenomenon, often do not generate any hypothesis(es). Also, in qualitative research, hypotheses are not formulated in the beginning of the investigation. They are formulated when the researcher has gained some insight into or some understanding of the phenomenon.

A hypothesis is a speculation or guess about the solution of a problem whose validity is unknown.

6.2 PURPOSES OF THE HYPOTHESIS

Hypothesis serves a number of purposes of assisting the researcher in his investigation.

- The hypothesis provides direction to research. It tells the researcher what to do, what to look for, that is, what information needs to be collected. It tells about sampling procedure and the statistical techniques for data analysis.
- The hypothesis relates together information. It relates information on the problem so as to make a tentative statement about the expected relationships between the variables in the study. Information obtained from the related literature, theory and experience is related to make prediction or to suggest the best solution to the problem.
- The hypothesis provides a relational statement that is directly testable. Research questions are not tested directly. They are changed into statements of the hypotheses. *For example*, our research question is "Does immediate feedback result in more improvement in student learning as compared with the delayed feedback?" This research question in a hypothesis form will be "The performance scores of students who are provided immediate feedback will be higher than the performance scores of students who are provided delayed feedback". This

statement provides a better clarity and focus to the researcher as to what he is expected to do. He would proceed to setup two equated groups of students. After having operationally defined the performance scores, the immediate and delayed feedback, he conducts his investigation.

- The hypothesis provides a framework for reporting results and conclusion. Each hypothesis, on the basis of data obtained, is tested for its acceptance or rejection using the relevant statistical technique. On the basis of the results obtained and conclusions drawn, the hypothesis is verified. This stepwise procedure of hypothesis testing provides a consistent and elaborate framework for attaining the purpose of the investigation.

6.3 CHARACTERISTICS OF A USABLE HYPOTHESIS

- **A hypothesis states the expected relationship between the variables:** *For example*, we are studying the relationship between intelligence and academic achievement, "If children differ on intelligence, they will differ from one another on academic achievement." This statement appears to be a hypothesis, but there is no statement of an expected relationship. An expected relationship could be "Higher intelligence is a likely condition for higher academic achievement." This hypothesis can be stated as "There will be a positive relationship between intelligence and academic achievement." The hypothesis states an expected relationship between intelligence and academic achievement.
- **A hypothesis must be testable:** A usable hypothesis should be verifiable. Inferences or

conclusions drawn from the hypothesis should be either supported or not supported by the empirical observations made in the study. A testable hypothesis enables the researcher to determine by his observations whether the results that are deductively implied actually occur. Therefore, the quality of a good hypothesis is that it is capable of verification. *For example*, "On the death of a person his soul migrates into the body of a yet to be born child" cannot be verified because soul and its migration process cannot be measured or operationally defined.

While formulating hypothesis it should be ensured that the variables in it can be operationally defined. They should be defined in terms of identifiable and observable behaviours.

Value statements should be avoided while formulating hypothesis. "It is desirable to have midday meals in elementary schools" cannot be investigated. "Elementary school children getting midday meal will verbally express greater satisfaction with the school than those who do not get midday meal" as a hypothesis can be tested. Satisfaction can be measured but 'desirable' is a value judgement.

- A hypothesis should be consistent with the existing body of knowledge. The hypothesis formulated should agree with the knowledge which is already well established. This holds true for a beginning researcher. Even landmark and revolutionary studies are based on previous works. They build upon, improve upon and develop new insights on existing information.
- A hypothesis should be stated simply and concisely. A good hypothesis is presented in a simple and declarative form. If the researcher is studying more

than one relationship, he should state more than one hypothesis.

6.4 TYPES OF HYPOTHESIS

The Research Hypotheses

These hypotheses are also called substantive hypothesis. They are the hypotheses which have been developed on the basis of observation, the related literature, and on some theory. They are statements of the expected relationship or the expected difference between the variables in the study. *For example*, "There is a positive relationship between IQ and academic achievement of elementary school children" is a hypothesis of the expected relationship. "High IQ children will have higher academic achievement than low IQ children," is a hypothesis of expected difference.

Research hypothesis may be directional or non directional. The above two hypotheses are the examples of directional hypothesis.

A non directional hypothesis states that a relationship or difference exists, but the direction of the difference is not stated. *For example*, "There is a relationship between IQ and academic achievement of elementary school children", or "High IQ and low IQ children differ on academic achievement". These hypotheses do not state the direction of the relationship of difference.

The Null Hypothesis (H_0)

The null hypothesis is a hypothesis of no relationship or no difference between the variables in the population. It is not the reverse of the expected relationship. *For example*, "High IQ and the low IQ children do not differ on academic achievement," or "There is no relationship between IQ and academic achievement of elementary school children" are null hypotheses.

A null hypothesis enables the researcher to see whether the apparent relationship is genuine or is likely to be a function of chance alone. It says that the results obtained have occurred by chance. Statistical tests are used to test the probability that the null hypothesis is true. If the tests indicate that the observed relationship or difference has only a slight or low probability of occurring by chance, the null hypothesis becomes an unlikely explanation. It is rejected or refuted.

The Alternate Hypothesis

If in the above example we say, "High IQ children will give low academic achievement than the low IQ children", it will the case of an alternate hypothesis. In a way, an alternate hypothesis is opposite of the research hypothesis.

The retention of a null hypothesis is not a positive evidence that the null hypothesis is true. It simply indicates that the evidence is insufficient and that the null hypothesis, the research hypothesis and the alternate hypothesis are all possible.

A hypothesis is not proved to be true. It is not proved or disproved, it is only supported or not supported. A hypothesis is probabilistic in nature, or an explanation that is probably true, it is reasonable to accept the hypothesis. While accepting or rejecting a hypothesis, we conclude not in terms of certainty but in terms of probability or possibility.

EXERCISES

1. What is a Hypothesis? Why do we need it in research studies?

2. Through an example differentiate between research hypothesis and null hypothesis.
3. Explain the characteristics of a good hypothesis.
4. For the research hypothesis "women are better at multitasking than men", formulate null and alternate hypotheses.

7

Writing the Research Proposal

7.1 NEED OF THE RESEARCH PROPOSAL

A research proposal in an overall plan or scheme regarding how research willbe carried out. Specifically, it addresses the following questions:

- What is being proposed to do?
- What strategy is proposed for the conduct of research? How will it be done?
- Why is it being done?

Requirements for a research proposal may vary from university to university and from one subject area to another, the broad lines are more or less similar for the research proposal. The main function of the research proposal is to give the details of the operational plan for obtaining answers to research questions in an objective and accurate manner. After going through the research proposal, the researcher, his research supervisor and those associated with the review of the proposal get information about the intent, methodology and justification of the proposed study.

7.2 MAJOR SECTIONS OF THE RESEARCH PROPOSAL

The sections of the research proposal are in a sequence so that the continuity of thought of the reviewer or the reader is not broken. The length of the research proposal or synopsis of the study will vary according to the magnitude of the proposed research and the complexity of the methods. The main body of the research proposal can vary any where between 3 to 5 typed A-4 size pages for a master's level dissertation, and between 10-15 pages for a doctoral dissertation, though there are no hard and fast rules. The main consideration is that all the relevant sections give pertinent information without repetition and padding. The various sections of the research proposal are as follows:

- **Preliminary Section:** This section includes 'Cover Page' and 'Abstract'. Title of the problem, researcher's particulars and institutional affiliation are written on the cover page. If the research proposal is lengthy then an abstract in a page about the proposed research is given.
- **Main Section:**
  - Introduction
  - Definition of Terms
  - Objectives
  - Hypotheses
  - Significance of the Study
  - Research Design
  - Instruments
  - Sampling Design
  - Sample Size
  - Data Collection Procedure
  - Data Processing Techniques
  - Delimitations of the Study
  - Educational Implications

- Limitations of the Study
- Proposed Chapters of the Study Report

• **Supplementary Section:** Proposed Time-Frame for the Study
- Appendixes
- References

Introduction gives how the problem has been identified. What information is available through a review of previous studies? What are the gaps or missing links? What are the contradictions in the existing body of knowledge about the problem or phenomenon? Definition of terms outlines operational definition of the terms or variables involved in the study. *For example*, if our proposed study is "the relationship between anxiety and socioeconomic status" then we should define as to how we propose to measure anxiety and socioeconomic status. In the objectives of the study we specify the goals of the proposed study. *For example*, in the study of the relationship between anxiety and socioeconomic status, the objective could be, "To find out the extent of relationship between anxiety and socioeconomic status", or it could be, "To find out anxiety levels among high SES, average SES and low SES groups".

The hypotheses part in the proposal pertains to hypotheses we have formulated in the light of the objectives. *For example*, the hypothesis for the above objective could be, "There is a significant relationship between anxiety and SES". Significance of the study part tells as to what purpose the proposed study will serve. Would it verify the existing information in a changed context?

Research design pertains to the method that will be used to conduct the study. Would it be a survey study, an ex post facto study or a quasi experimental study?

Instruments part tells about the tools or instruments we propose to use for collection of information or data. Do we propose to construct our own instruments or use standardised and commercially available instruments?

Sampling design gives information as to the procedure of sampling we propose to use in our study. Would it be probability sampling or non probability sampling? Within these which specific technique will be used? Sample size gives information about what would be the overall sample size or subgroups sizes?

Data collection procedure gives information about how we propose to collect data. *For example*, would a mailed questionnaire be used or face-to-face interview? What are the steps and stages of data collection? Data processing techniques give information about our proposed method of data analysis. Would it be computer processed and use which statistical package, or would be it manually analysed? It gives information about statistical techniques-descriptive or inferential that will be employed for data analysis to obtain results.

Delimitations of study point to the boundaries of the proposed study with reference to specific issues, objectives, samples, tools and geographical limits.

Educational implications tell about the relevance of the proposed study for theory and practice of education. Limitations of the proposed study identify the factors beyond the control of the researcher, that is, lack of controls, experimental mortality or the problems of internal and external validity.

Proposed chapters of the report includes brief outline of the chaptertization of the report or dissertation. The scheme of chapterization may vary according to nature of the study whether it is quantitative or qualitative, and according to the requirements of the accepting institution or organisation. A brief outline of the chapters is as follows:

Introduction (Chapter 1)

Review of Literature (Chapter 2)

Method (Chapter 3)

Analysis and Interpretation of Data (Chapter 4)

Summary and Conclusions (Chapter 5)

EXERCISES

1. What information is included in the Introduction Part of the research proposal?
2. Give a broad outline of the various parts of a research proposal.
3. Your study is "A survey of mid-day meal scheme implementation in Chandigarh". Formulate four objectives of the study.
4. Differentiate between Delimitations and Limitations of the Study.

8

Research Methods

8.1 EXPERIMENTAL RESEARCH

An experiment is a research situation in which at least one independent variable is deliberately manipulated or varied to see the effect of this manipulation on the dependent variable. The independent variable is called the experimental variable.

8.1.1 Experimental Design

An experimental design is a plan for conducting an experiment. It gives details of the ways the variables have been positioned or built into the experiment. It includes the independent variable(s) both the experimental and the extraneous. How the extraneous variables have been controlled and taken care of is explained. The measurements of the effect of the experimental variable are taken, or the changes in the dependent variable on account of changes in the experimental variable are observed and recorded. Suppose a researcher wants to study the effect of method of instruction on solving the problems in the topic 'Fractions' of mathematics. Method of instruction is the experimental variable. Suppose it has two levels. The first is "interactive learning group" and the second is "Learning through lecture group". The participants in the experiment are fifth class pupils called the subjects. Two groups are formed and twenty subjects are randomly assigned to each group by the researcher. The subjects in the first group receive interactive instruction. The second group receives instructions as through lecture. The diagram of the experiment is given in Figure 8.1. The experiment layout in symbol form is below the box in

Groups	Instructions Type
$G_1(20)$	Interactive Learning
$G_2(20)$	Lecture

Fig. 8.1

$$R\ G_1 \text{------------} X_0 \text{------------} O_1$$
$$R\ G_2 \text{------------} X_g \text{------------} O_2$$

Fig. 8.1: Experimental layout

R indicates random assignment of the subjects in the two groups.

X indicates the application of the experimental variable. The subscripts "0" and "g" on X indicate the levels of the experimental variable. O_1 and O_2 are the observations of the performances of the two groups to solve fractions after they have been instructed.

The research design enables the researcher to have a synoptic view of as to how the independent and the dependent variables have been situated, what the levels of the independent variable(s) are, what variables need to be controlled, and what patterns of results are likely to emerge on account of the effects of the experimental variable.

8.1.2 Criteria of a Well Designed Experiment

- **Experimental Control:** A well designed experiment takes care of or control of all such conditions as may vitiate the relationship between the experimental variable and the dependent variable. Any change in the dependent variable should have been caused by the experimental variable.
- **Lack of Artificiality:** It should be possible to generalise findings from the experimental to non experimental situation or real life situations.
- **Basis of Comparison:** A well designed experiment makes use of a control group which does not receive the experimental treatment. This enables the researcher to assess any change from pretest to posttest condition on account of variables other than the experimental variable.
- **Uncontaminated Data:** A good experimental design enables error free measurement of the dependent variable or the changes in it.
- **Representativeness:** The subjects in the experiment should have been randomly selected from the population. There should be a random assignment of the subject in experimental and control groups. This facilitates the generalization of the results to the population from which the subjects were taken.
- **Parsimony:** All other things being equal, a simpler design is preferred to a complex one as this makes the task of interpretation of findings easier. However, the design chosen must fulfil the purposes of the experiment.

8.1.3 Experimental Validity

The criteria of a well designed experiment should enhance its experimental validity. Experimental validity is of four types: internal, external, construct validity and statistical conclusion validity.

Internal validity of an experiment refers to whether the manipulation or change in the experimental variable is the only cause of change in the dependent variable and no other extraneous variables have caused the change in the dependent variable. To increase the internal validity of the experiment, such extraneous variables as are likely to influence the relationship between the independent and the dependent variables are identified, controlled or eliminated by the experimenter from the experimental setting.

External validity refers to the extent to which the findings obtained from the experiment can be held to be true for the population from which the subjects were taken for the study. *For example*, would a study conducted on a sample of pupils taken from a village elementary school would be true for other rural elementary schools, and may be for urban elementary schools as well? Would the findings hold true for secondary school students? Thus, external validity deals with the extent of generalisability of findings from the experimental or laboratory situation to the real life situations.

Construct validity deals with the definition of the independent variable or the experimental variable. The experimental variable and its levels need to be defined so that others can replicate the study. Similarly, the measurement of the dependent variable needs to be operationalised so that other researchers know what to measure or the changes expected in the dependent variable. Statistical conclusion validity deals with the validity or accuracy of the conclusion arrived through statistical analysis of data. The researcher should be versed in the statistical methods he uses. He should be able to interpret his results in the context of the strengths and limitations of the statistical methods. Otherwise mistake may result in conclusion.

8.1.3.1 Threats to Experimental Validity

Campbell and Stanley (1963) have identified eight threats to internal validity of an experiment. Internal validity is essentially a matter of control of the experiment so that an uncontaminated relationship between the experimental treatment and the dependent variable is obtained.

- **History:** Any unanticipated event may occur while the experiment is in progress. This affects the subjects' performance on the dependent variable. *For example*, power failure when the experimental group is taking a test. Their performance on the test will get affected by this event.
- **Maturation:** Changes may occur in the subjects not because of the experimental treatment, but because of the long time duration of the experiment. Some biological or psychological processes like fatigue, stress, hunger and lack of motivation in the task may set in.
- **Pre-testing:** Exposure to pre-test may serve as learning experience for better performance on the post-test.
- **Instruments:** Inconsistencies in the administration of the measuring instruments, observers' differences etc. may cause change in scores on the post-test of the subjects.
- **Statistical Regression:** Subjects selected on the basis of extreme scores have a tendency to move towards an average performance on subsequent testing.

- **Selection:** The comparison groups may not have been formed on the basis of random assignment of subjects. As such the groups may differ on some important variable which has a bearing on the dependent variable. *For example*, better performance of the experimental group may not be due to the teaching method. From the outset, the experimental group was high achieving than the control group.
- **Experimental Mortality:** If subjects leave the experiment in between in an unrandom way then this would affect the expected results of the experiment. *For example*, if low scoring subjects drop out from the experimental group, the group's superior post-test performance may not be because of the experimental treatment, but because the low scoring subjects have dropped out.
- **Interaction between selection and maturation, selection and history, diffusion effect:** Differences due to interaction between variables such intelligence, motivation, sex and age may be there on the dependent variable. Interaction between subjects from the experimental and the control groups may affect the performance of the control group on post-test.

8.1.3.2 External Validity

It is of two types–population validity and ecological validity. Population validity is concerned with whether the findings of the experiment can be generalised. *For example*, the researcher has found that aloud reading is superior to silent reading in the learning of English for fourth class pupils. Is it also true for the population of pupils from which the samples for the experiment were taken? If the principle of randomization has been strictly followed while choosing the subjects, the findings of the experiment can be generalized without difficulty. While drawing the samples from the accessible population of fourth class pupils the researcher should ensure that the characteristics of the accessible population and the target population are similar.

Ecological validity is concerned with the generalisation of the experimental findings to other populations. *For example*, can we generalize the above findings to pupils of other grade levels?

Ensuring high internal and external validities is a balancing act. As one increases the other decreases. Too many controls in an experiment tend to reduce its external validity.

8.1.3.3 Types of Experimental Designs

There are a number of experimental designs which vary in complexity. Choice of a design depends on the purpose of the experiment, nature of the experimental variable(s), the nature of observations and data, facilities available for experiment, and the skills of the researcher.

8.1.3.3.1 Symbols and Conventions in Educational Experiments

O refers to the process of observation or measurement.

X refers to the exposure of a group to the experimental variable whose effects are measured

Mr refers to matched pairs and then random assignment of each subject to a different group

R represents random assignment of subjects

Xs and Os in a given row refer to the same group

Xs and Os vertical to one another are simultaneous

Left to right is the temporal sequence of the experiment.

Parallel rows not separated by broken lines represent groups equated by randomisation. Parallel groups separated by broken lines are not equated by randomization.

8.1.3.3.2 Pre-experimental Designs

These designs do not provide controls of extraneous variables and are of two types

- **One Group Pre-test Post-test Design:** In this design the experimenter measures the dependent variable before and after the application of the independent or experimental variable. It can be represented as follows:

$$O_1 \, X \, O_2$$

Suppose a physical education teacher wants to study the impact of 30 minutes of daily aerobics on the pulse rate of students. He takes a group of students and measures their pulse rate. The group is put through 30 minutes of aerobic exercises daily for three months after which their pulses are measured again. Any difference between the present and the past readings of pulse (O_2–O_1) is indicative of the impact of daily aerobic exercises.

This design suffers from a number of limitations. A number of extraneous conditions such as motivational level of students during exercise, their general health status, reactivity to the situation, maturational factors, errors in pulse measurement, what they do rest of the day etc. may contaminate results.

- **The Groups, Static Design:** Here two groups which are assumed to be equivalent are taken. Only one group is exposed or treated with the independent or the experimental variable. The other group serves as the control group. On the completion of the exposure i.e. the independent variable, both the groups are measured on the dependent variable. If the mean of the measurements of the experimental group significantly differ from the measurements on the control group, it implies that the independent or the experimental variable has an effect on the dependent variable.

Experimental	O_1	X	O_2
Control	O_3	X	O_4

The main limitation of this design is that the two groups have been assumed to be equivalent with respect to relevant extraneous variables, but no actual randomisation has been done while assigning subjects in the two groups.

8.1.3.3.3 "True" Experimental Designs

These designs try to control threats to their internal validity, that is, effects of history, maturation, mortality etc. These are of four types:

- **Two Groups, Randomized Subjects, Post-test Only.**

This design is relatively simple but powerful. The available subjects are randomly assigned to the two groups. Only one group is exposed to the experimental variable and the other serves as the control group. On the completion of the exposure, both the groups are measured on the dependent variable. The means of the two groups are compared using appropriate statistical technique.

Experimental	(R)O_1	X	O_2
Control	(R)O_3	X	O_4

An advantage of this design is the random assignment of subjects in the two groups. This ensures statistical equivalence of the groups on extraneous variables. Since no pretest has been used, the main effects of history, maturation and pretesting get controlled.

The major limitation of this design is that it restricts the external validity of the experiment.

- **Two Groups, Randomised Matched Subjects, Post-test Only Design**

Instead of the random assignment of the subjects in the two groups, the subjects are matched on one-to-one basics on the relevant variables. The matching variables must have a significant correlation with the dependent variable. Of the matched pair of subjects, one is assigned to the one group and the second to the other group, through flip of a coin. Which group would be the experimental is also decided through the flip of the coin. The experimental group is exposed to the treatment variable after, which both the groups are measured on the dependent variable.

Experimental	(Mr)O_1	X	O_2
Control	(Mr)O_3	X	O_4

The main advantage of this design is that besides random assignment of the subjects, one-to-one matching adds to the strength of this design. This limitation is that sometimes it is not possible to form matched pairs because of lack of subjects on the matching variable.

- **Randomised Groups, Pre-test Post-test Control Group Design**

Here the subjects are assigned to the two groups by random procedures. Both the groups are administered a pre-test as a measure of the dependent variable. The experimental group is exposed to the experimental treatment. This is followed by administration post-test to the groups. Differences between pre-test and post-test scores for the two groups are found. The difference between these differences is found and evaluated for statistical significance to see the effect of the experimental variable.

Experimental	(R)O_1(Pre-test)	X	O_2(Post-test)
Control	(R)O_3(Pre-test)	–	O_4(Post-test)

The major advantage of this design is that the pre-test provides additional information on the similarity of the two groups on the dependent variable. The limitation is that the pre-test may sensitise the experimental group and affect its post-test measurement on the dependent variable.

- **The Random Solomon Three Group Design**

Here three groups instead of two are taken with random assignment of the subjects. The first group is the experimental and the other two are control 1 and control 2 groups. This design helps in getting rid of the interaction between pre-test sensitisation and the experimental treatment. The effect of the pre-test and the experimental treatment is determined by comparing the means of the post-test scores of the three groups. If the mean post-test score of the first group is higher than for the second group, the experimenter cannot claim with certainty that this is due to experimental treatment. The difference may be due to pre-test sensitisation and treatment interaction. If the post-test mean score of the third group is higher than that of the second group, it may be concluded that the difference between the first and the second group post-test mean scores is due to the experimental variable (X).

Experimental	(R)O_1 (Pre-test)	X	O_2(Post-test)
Control 1	(R)O_3 (Pre-test)	–	O_4(Post-test)
Control 2	(R)O_5 ______	X	O_6(Post-test)

The advantage of the three group design is that the third group provides control over the interactive effect of pre-testing and the experimental treatment. The limitation is that the design does not have control over any possible contemporary effect that may occur between pre-test and post-test scores of the first and the second group.

- **The Randomized Solomon Four Group Design**

Here the subjects are randomly assigned to four groups with no pre-test for the third and the fourth group. Also, no experimental treatment is given to the second and the fourth group.

Experimental	(R)O_1 (Pre-test)	X	O_2(Post-test)
Control 1	(R)O_3 (Pre-test)	–	O_4(Post-test)
Control 2	(R)O_5 ______	X	O_6(Post-test)
Control 3	(R)O_7 ______	–	O_8(Post-test)

If the mean post-test score of the first group (experimental) is higher and significant than the mean post-test score of the second group, and the mean post-test score of the third group is higher and significant than for the fourth group, it is concluded that this is on account of the effect of the experimental treatment.

In fact this design consists of two experimental designs. One with pre-tests and one without pre-tests. This design provides control over any contemporary effects that may occur between pre-test and post-test.

The limitation of this design is that it is difficult to conduct because of time constraints, effort, and non-availability of a large number of matched subjects on relevant extraneous variables.

8.2 FACTORIAL DESIGNS

Factorial designs involve two or more independent variables, called the factors, in a single design. In a factorial design all levels of each independent variable are taken in combination with the levels of the other variables. A factorial design requires at least two independent variables and with at least two levels of the each variable. The simplest factorial design is called two by two (2×2) factorial design. The Solomon four group design is a 2×2 factorial design with two independent variables-the experimental variable and pretesting variable with two levels of each. A 3×5 factorial design will have three levels of one independent variable and 5 levels of the other independent variable, thereby forming 15 groups. As the number of the independent variables and their levels increases, the number of groups in the factorial design increases. A 2×2×2 factorial design would have 8 groups whereas a 2×2×3 factorial design would have 12 groups.

The advantages of factorial designs over simpler designs are that they allow simultaneous study of the effects of the independent variables on the dependent variable, rather than setting up a research design separately for each independent variable. The second advantage of factorial designs is that they allow the study of interaction or combined effects of the independent variables on the dependent variable. Interaction between the independent variables occurs when the effect of one independent variable changes over the levels of the other independent variable. The third advantage of factorial designs is that by including additional independent variables and their interactions, the random error variance gets reduced. This increases the probability of finding a significant experimental treatment effect.

Theoretically it may be possible to have any number of independent variables and their levels in a factorial design. However, a complex design may not be possible in terms of the availability of the subjects, and the interpretation of the complex interactions may become difficult for practical purposes. The simplest interaction is the first order interaction where two independent variables with two levels each are involved.

An illustration of two by three (2×3) factorial design is as follows.

A teacher is interested in finding out the effectiveness of two methods of teaching mathematics to fifth class pupils. The methods of teaching are 'the conventional method'(M_1) and 'the activity method' (M_2).There are sixty pupils in the class who have been identified as high achievers, average achievers, and low achievers on the basis of a mathematics achievement test. Let us say 14, 30 and 16 pupils have been identified as high achievers, average achievers and low achievers respectively. Half of each these three would be assigned to method M_1 and the remaining to method M_2 through random assignment. The three groups will be instructed by the method M_1 and method M_2 respectively. When the instructional phase is over, they will be post-tested on mathematics achievement (the dependent variable). The diagram of the design would be as follows:

		(Method M) M_1	M_2	
Achievement	A_1	High ach. Ss n = 7	High ach. Ss n = 7	↑
Level (A)	A_2	Av. ach. Ss n = 15	Av. ach. Ss n = 15	Post-Test
	A_3	Low ach. Ss n = 8	Low ach. Ss n = 8	↓

⟵ Instruction in Maths ⟶

where M_1 = Conventional method
M_2 = Activity method
A_1 = High achievement
A_2 = Average achievement
A_3 = Low achievement

8.3 REPEATED MEASURES DESIGNS

In repeated measures designs the same subject is measured more than once on the dependent variable. Sometimes, while working with educational variables it is difficult to anticipate as to how much time would be required for the experimental treatment to continue to show its effect on the dependent variable. Experimental design can be extended to get this information by taking additional observations, over an extended period of time, that is, through repeated measures designs. A diagram of the extended post-test only group design would be as follows:

$$(R)G_1 \ \mathbf{X} \ O_1\text{–}O_2\text{–}O_3$$
$$(R)G_2 - O_4\text{–}O_5\text{–}O_6$$

After the experimental treatment (X) has been given to G_1, observations are taken on both the groups. Afterwards, at a specified regular intervals, observations are taken on both the groups. The length of intervals between observations would depend on the variables under study.

A limitation of such designs is the carry over effect of multiple observations because groups are measured more than once. Earlier observation may affect subsequent observation. However, this effect depends on the variables involved. Also, due to extended time, these designs are susceptible to history and maturation effects as threats to internal validity.

EXERCISES

1. Give the criteria of a well designed experiment.
2. Explain the various threats to the internal validity of an experiment.
3. What are the advantages of a Factorial Design? Give a diagramatic representation of a two by two factorial design.
4. What is a first order interaction in a factorial design? Explain with an example.
5. Differentiate between the following:
   (*a*) Independent variable and dependent variable
   (*b*) Internal validity and external validity
   (*c*) Random selection and random assignment
   (*d*) One group pre-test post-test and pre-test post-test control group design.

9

Non Experimental Quantitative Research

Non experimental quantitative research is the most widely used type of educational research. It includes ex post facto research, correlation research and survey research.

9.1 EX POST FACTO RESEARCH

The literal meaning of this phrase is 'from what is done afterwards'. In the context of educational research it means 'after the fact' or 'retrospectively'. It refers to those studies which investigate possible cause-and-effect relationships by observing an existing condition and searching back in time for the possible causal factors. The search is for those factors which seem to be associated with certain occurrences, or conditions, or aspects of behaviour. Kerlinger (1970) defines ex post facto research as that in which the independent variable(s) have occurred, and the researcher starts with the observation of a dependent variable or variables. He studies the independent variable(s) retrospectively for their possible effect on, or relatively to the dependent variable(s).

Suppose a researcher wants to study the effect of socioeconomic status on academic achievement of eighth class pupils. It will not be possible for him to directly manipulate the SES of pupils. Instead, he will take eighth class pupils from schools where children from high SES, average SES and low SES are enrolled. He will take academic achievement scores of these pupils and study the differences among the three groups.

Two kinds of designs may be identified in ex post facto research. These are 'criterion group study' and the 'correlational study'. The former is sometimes given the name of 'causal comparative research' and the latter 'causal research'. In the criterion group or causal-comparative approach, the researcher attempts to find out the possible causes for a phenomenon being studied. He compares the subjects in which the variable is present with similar subjects in whom it is absent. *For example*, the researcher wants to identify the causes of teacher being effective, or not effective. He identifies one group (O_1) of effective teachers on the basis of their ratings by their pupils. Similarly, the other group (O_2) of not effective teachers is identified. Then the researcher may then examine some variable(s) X(s), such as qualifications, training, experience or personality characteristics which differentiate between the two groups. The basic design of this kind of study will be:

	O_1
X	
	O_2

A correlation or causal study is concerned with identifying the antecedents of a present condition. It involves collection of two sets of data, one of which will be retrospective, and the relationship between these would be determined. Any strong association or relationship between the two variables - the independent and the dependent variable, three interpretations for the relationship are possible. X has caused

O, O has caused X; some third unidentified and unmeasured variable has caused X and O. The basic design of such an experiment is as follows:

X	O

9.1.1 Characteristics of Ex post facto Research

- The researcher takes the effect (dependent variable) and examines the data retrospectively to establish causes or relationships and their meaning.
- In ex post facto design, O is observed. Then a retrospective search for X begins. An X is found that is a plausible explanation for O and agrees with the hypothesis. Due to lack of control of X and other possible Xs, the truth of the hypothesised relationship between X and O cannot be asserted with the same level of confidence as in an experimental study. In an experiment, the experimenter can exercise greater control or manipulation of the X variable.
- Ex post facto research is suitable in situations where the independent variables lie outside the control of the researcher. *For example*, independent variables such as sex, socio-economic status, intelligence and religious affiliation of the subjects cannot be manipulated by the researcher.

9.1.2 Advantages and limitations of Ex post facto Research

- It is particularly suitable when simple cause-and-effect relationships are to be studied.

- Certain experiments cannot be conducted on human beings. To study the effect of deprivation on academic achievement, deprivation cannot be introduced in children. In such a situation the already deprived children will be taken up.
- When too much of artificiality by an experimental study is expected, then ex post facto research is the alternative.
- Ex post facto research gives a sense of direction to research in new or unexplored area. It can provide fruitful sources of hypotheses that can be tested through experimental method.

Among the limitations are

- Lack of control, that is, researcher cannot manipulate the independent variable(s). Random assignment of subjects is not possible.
- It is not certain whether the causative factor has been included in the study or even identified.
- It may be that the causative variables are more than one.
- It may be difficult to identify which variable is the cause and which is the effect. *For example*, 'smoking causes cancer' is plausible because reverse relationship 'cancer causes smoking' is not true. However, 'excessive watching of TV causes obesity in children' may have a reverse relationship. 'It is possible that obese children watch TV more' because they dislike physical activity.
- The relationship between the two variables does not necessarily mean cause-effect relationship is established. At the most, an association be there.

9.1.3 Designing Ex post facto Research

There are two designs for ex post facto research which are as follows:

Independent Variable	Dependent Variable
X	O

The second design is as follows:

Independent Variable	Dependent Variable
X	O
	O_1

The basic designs of ex post facto research and experimental research are similar, but in the former the independent variable is beyond the control of the researcher because it has already occurred. In true experimental design, this independent variable is under control and therefore manipulable.

9.2 CORRELATION RESEARCH

Correlation research serves a number of purposes: it enables us to determine relationships between variables, helps in assessing consistency, and in prediction.

Correlation research methods are used to determine relationships and their patterns among variables in a single group of subjects. *For example,* is there a relationship between mathematics aptitude and achievement in physics? If the relationship exists then what is its direction and magnitude?

The application of correlation helps us in assessing consistency. *For example*, consistency of a test through test retest, equivalent form and split half methods. Two observers rank student-teachers on skill of explaining. How much consistency or agreement is there among their rankings of student-teachers?

If two variables are correlated, we can use one to predict the other. A student who has got high marks in the various school examinations and the final Board examination, is likely to get high marks in the college than a student who got low marks on predictor variables, provided other conditions are similar.

9.2.1 Designing Correlation Research Studies

The researcher specifies the problem by asking questions about the relations between the variables of his interest. He may select the variables on the basis of his observations, previous studies, or through a theory. The population of interest is identified. In simple studies, the researcher gathers data on two or more variables from one group of subjects. *For example*, the teacher may correlate maths achievement scores and science achievement scores of a group of pupils of a class. Sometimes, a correlational study may investigate relationship between scores on one measure for logically paired groups such as twins, siblings, fathers and sons. There have been many correlation studies on IQs of identical twins, fraternal twins and siblings reared together and apart.

9.2.2 Interpreting a Correlational Coefficient

- The magnitude of a correlation coefficient must be assessed in relation to other correlations for the same or similar variables. This is especially true for evaluating reliabilities of tests.

- While evaluating the size of the correlation coefficient, it is important to consider the sample size on which it has been calculated. Too much importance should not be attached to large correlations when the samples are small. The sample size should be at least 30.
- Statistical significance and practical significance of a correlation coefficient are two different things. A correlation coefficient of 0.08 would be statistically significant at the .01 level for a sample of 1000 subjects. What practical significance shall we attach to it? Information on X variable accounts for less than 1 per cent (.64 per cent) variance in the variable Y. Would it be worthwhile to collect data on the predictor variable X, to predict the other variable Y? A predictor with a high correlation that is difficult to obtain may be of less practical value than a cheap and easily available predictor with lower correlation.
- A correlation coefficient only gives the extent of relationship between two variables which depends on operational definitions of the predictor and predicted variables for a given sample of subjects. Its value can easily change if operational definitions or sample are changed.
- A correlation coefficient does not necessarily indicate a causative relationship between the two variables. *For example*, we have found a significant and positive correlation coefficient between self-esteem and academic achievement. The possible interpre-tations from this finding are self-esteem causes achievement; achievement causes self-esteem; social status causes both self-esteem and academic achievement.

9.2.3 Other Correlation Techniques

When we deal with more than two variables in a research study we need to have procedures that study relationships among several variables. Partial correlation technique is used to determine the extent of relationship between two variables when the effect of the third variable is removed. The correlation between two variables when their correlation with a third variable is removed is called first-order partial correlation. Because of interpretive difficulties, partial correlations involving elimination of more than one variable is rarely used. Suppose we wish to study the relationship between vocabulary and abstract ability among adolescent boys. Sixteen year old adolescents will be more developed on both the variables as compared with 14 year old adolescent boys. Vocabulary and abstract ability scores will correlate with each other because both are correlated with age. Partial correlation technique will be used to eliminate the effect of age.

9.2.3.1 Multiple Regression

This correlational procedure works out the relationships among several variables. It enables the researcher to find the best possible weighting of two or more independent variables to yield maximum correlation with a single dependent variable. Suppose intelligence, introversion and motivation scores are the predictor variables of academic achievement at the class XII level. For a large number of class XII students we have their intelligence, introversion and motivation scores and their final class XII examination marks. We determine correlation coefficients of each of the predictor variables with the criterion variable class XII examination marks. Suppose the correlations are as follows:

	Intelligence	Introversion	Motivation
Class XII marks	.40	.32	.29

All the three variables in a multiple regression analysis are used to determine the correlation of the best possible weighted combination of the three predictor variables with class XII marks. With the help of computer program a prediction equation is set up with the predictor variables weighted in appropriate way to yield the highest correlation with class XII marks and have the best prediction. The school can use the equation with similar groups of prospective class XII students whose intelligence, introversion and motivation scores are known, to predict their yet to be known class XII marks. The regression equation would be as follows:

$Y' = a + b_1X_1 + b_2X_2 + b_3X_3$ where Y' is the predicted class XII marks; a, b_1, b_2 and b_3 are constants provided by regression analysis, and X_1, X_2 and X_3 are the independent variables intelligence, introversion and motivation.

9.3 SURVEY RESEARCH

Survey research attempts to describe and interpret the present status, condition or 'what is' of persons, groups, institutions, objects, events, practices and beliefs. It describes the effects being felt and the trends that are emerging.

Surveys may be classified according to their focus and scope, and time frame for data collection.

A survey that covers the entire population of interest is called a census. *For example*, we have census every ten years which covers the population of the entire country. In educational research the word 'population' does not imply all the individuals of the country. The term population refers to the total group of individuals to whom the findings of the study apply. The researcher defines the population of his interest. *For example*, his population may be all the secondary school teachers in a district. Since it is difficult to study all the individuals of the defined population, a smaller portion called 'the sample' is taken from the population, for study. A survey based only a portion of the population is called a 'sample survey'. Further, survey may pertain to simple tabulation of 'tangibles', or it may attempt to measure 'intangibles'. An example of a survey of tangible may be average class enrollment in unaided schools. It is easy to identitfy unaided schools and obtain data regarding average number of children per class per school. In a survey of intangibles, the researcher collects data by indirectly measuring the variable in which he is interested. The public opinion surveys do not observe opinions directly, but the opinions are inferred from the responses of the subjects to questionnaires or interviews.

9.3.1 Longitudinal Designs

These surveys collect data over a period of time which may be short or long. The data are collected at specified point in time for two or more points in time.

Longitudinal designs may be 'trend' studies, 'cohort' studies and 'panel' studies. In a trend study a general population is studied over time. Random samples are taken at various point of time. Though different from one another, these samples represent the population. Trend studies are often used to study opinions and attitudes over an extended period of time. *For example*, we may conduct a trend study on 'attitude towards privatization of professional education.'

Panel study is a variation of the longitudinal study in which the same sample is measured two or more times. The individuals in the sample are randomly selected. An advantage of this approach is that it enables the researcher not only to measure the net change but also to identify the individuals in the sample who are changing. The difficulty with this kind of survey is that it difficult to keep in contact with the individual members in the panel especially when the population is very mobile.

In a cohort study the term 'cohort' refers to a group of people with some common characteristics. In a cohort study a specific population is tracked over a specified period of time, but selective sampling within the sample occurs. That is, some members of the cohort may not be included each time.

9.3.2 Cross-Sectional Designs

These designs involve collection of data at one point in time from a random sample representing some given population at that time.

Suppose a researcher in conducting a survey on height and weight measures of school going girls in the age group 12 to 16 years in a given geographical region. Random samples are selected that include girls of ages 12, 13, 14, 15 and 16 years. The heights and weights of girls in the samples are measured. The researcher gets data of girls' height and weight in the age group 12-16 years. If a longitudinal study were to be conducted then the same sample would have been repeatedly measured at the ages 12, 13, 14, 15 and 16 years

The limitation of the cross-sectional design is that change in an individual cannot be measured because he has been measured only once.

Selecting samples from two populations or more simultaneously and conducting the same study is called 'parallel sample' design. *For example*, in the above study of girls' height and weight, parallel samples of 12 to 16 year old boys may be taken. The results of boys and girls could be compared for the relative changes.

9.3.3 Methodology of Survey Research

Conducting a survey involves a series of detailed steps. Each step is carefully planned.

The first step is 'Planning' which includes the following activities: The research problem is carefully defined. The definition of the research problem should include the variables to be studied, their operational definition as to how they will measured. Identification and definition of the problem is facilitated through a carefully review of the literature. Developing of the design of survey begins simultaneously. Which survey design-longitudinal, or cross sectional will be employed? It is decided on the basis of resources, time frame and expertise of the researcher to conduct a longitudinal survey especially when he is working on his dissertation.

The second step is the development of the sampling design which is based on the target population, accessible population, sampling procedure, sampling technique along with the identification of the unit of the sample, and the sample size. The sample should represent the population.

The third step is the preparation for data collection. If the survey involves data collection through interview or questionnaire, then the instruments must be constructed or adapted, their reliabilities and validities established. While constructing instruments it is also decided how data will be tabulated and analysed. The procedures of data analysis, and relevant techniques should be identified. Such data should be generated through the survey as would help in answering the questions raised by the research problem. Survey studies using questionnaire or interview require background and demographic information such as sex, age, marital status, residential and occupational status etc. of the respondent for identifying him in terms of classifying variables for the analysis of data. Initial drafts of questionnaires should be tried out through pilot study to check for ambiguities, confusion and poorly drafted items. The pilot study can be done on five to ten individuals who are similar to those in the sample of the study, but are not a part of the sample. After the measuring instrument has been developed according to standard procedures, the fourth step is to train the observers or interviewers in the handling and administration of the instrument so that objective recordings are obtained.

The fifth step is to collect data through interviews, administration of questionnaires, tests etc. Quite often, when the questionnaire is mailed, there is a need to follow up the respondents maybe two or three times.

The sixth step is tabulation and coding of data which is essentially translation of data. Data may be in frequency or numeric form. Qualitative data may require description. Results and conclusion are then reported.

There may be a number of problems, both foreseen and unforeseen. *For example*, sampling procedure may break down, non response may bias the results, or a question may not be understood by a large number of respondents or that the researcher has constructed a questionnaire in a language with which the respondents lack familiarity.

Careful planning, and step-wise and systematic carrying out of the various phases will mitigate serious difficulties.

EXERCISES

1. Explain with an example the ex post facto research method.
2. What purpose does correlation research serve? How is a correlation coefficient interpreted?
3. Differentiate between longitudinal design and cross sectional design. What are the relative strengths and weaknesses of the two?

10

Qualitative Research Methods

10.1 HISTORICAL RESEARCH

It is concerned with 'What happened so far', that is, it is a systematic study of events that happened in the past. It tries to locate, evaluate and synthesise evidence from a number of sources about an event that occurred in the past, and then arrives at some conclusion.

Though historical research is qualitative, it may use quantitative approach for collection and analysis of data. It may use dates, figures, numbers and statistics as its data. However, in historical research, the task of understanding the context and the deeper causes of the occurrence is important.

Wiersma and Jurs (2009:254) define historical research as "a systematic process of searching for the facts, and then using the information to describe, analyze and interpret the past".

Historical research is not just collection of bits and pieces of information, or isolated facts about a past event. It is an act of reconstruction of a past event. In order to reconstruct the past, the researcher seeks information from a variety of sources such as observations of knowledgeable persons, documents, relics, remains and artifacts. Such information is difficult to obtain. Often there may be gaps and inconsistencies in the information collected.

Historical research serves the following purposes:

- It enables to understand 'why' and 'how' of an event or phenomenon that occurred in the past, and which may have implications for the present and future.
- It helps in making better policies and decisions.
- It distinguishes between myth and reality.

10.1.1 Doing Historical Research

For a beginning researcher the selection of a problem or topic of historical research could be a difficult task. A few suggestions for selection of a problem are:

- Defining and delimiting the problem so that the study is intensive rather than extensive, in-depth and penetrating rather than superficial and at surface level.
- Generating relevant research questions which need to be answered through research. Hypotheses may be developed, if needed.
- Availability of data from primary sources.
- Data collection should lead to its evaluation and interpretation in the context in which the event occurred.
- Resources available for the conduct of research.

10.1.2 Sources of Data

For historical research, data already exists which has to be located, identified, related and validated. There are two sources of data–'Primary Sources' and 'Secondary Sources'.

Primary sources are the life line of historical research. They are also known as original sources and are of two kinds. The first kind is the remains and ruins of a given period. *For example*, fossils, skeletons, buildings, tools, weapons, coins, pottery and art objects are the original sources for archaeological and historical research. Though not (active agents) for passing on information to subsequent eras, they provide sound evidence about the past. The second kind of primary sources has a direct relationship with the past event being reconstructed. This may include written or oral testimonies of actual participants in, or witnesses to an event. Documents in the form of manuscripts, records, notifications, files, letters, memoirs, biographies, films, paintings, maps, publications and inscriptions relating to the event or period, which transmit firsthand information are considered as a source of primary data.

Secondary sources are used when primary sources are not available or when supplementary information is needed. Secondary sources do not have a direct physical relationship to the event that is being studied. Secondary sources may include quoted materials, text-books, encyclopedias and replicas or reproductions of original objects.

The relevance of secondary sources should not be negated, but a limitation of secondary sources is that communication error creeps in as the information passes on from one person to another.

10.1.3 Evaluation of Historical Data

Also known as historical criticism, it is very important for validation of data. Historical criticism is undertaken as 'external criticism' and 'internal criticism'. External criticism deals with the establishing of genuineness of data. It examines whether a document or an object is genuine or fake. The authority of the written material is established. Authentication with respect to authorship may be based on such evidences as signatures, handwriting, style and spellings. Additional evidence may be obtained from the writing of other authors at that time. Now, chemical analysis techniques are being increasingly used for authentication.

Internal criticism pertains to whether the written content or data gives a true or faithful picture of the event. The contents are examined with reference to author's competence to record and report, his relationship with the event, his biases and prejudices etc. These factors have a bearing on the credibility of the observations recorded in the document.

The process of establishing reliability and validity of primary and secondary sources is known as historical evidence.

Historical studies in education provide insights into educational problems that have their roots in the past practices. The relationship between politics and education, caste and education, and between school and society as they exist today can be better understood in the context of what happened in the past. "Secularization" or "saffornization" of Indian education has its roots in the past.

10.2 CASE STUDY

A case study is an in-depth study of a single entity as an individual, group, institution, community, programme, process or a phenomenon. Case study provides an in-depth description of a specific unit that might have been selected for study because of its uniqueness, typicality or for some other reasons. The unit is defined within specific boundaries, referred to as "bounded system". In other words, case study attempts to understand the individual in the totality of his environment. Case study uses observations based on real life as its data. It permits an in-depth examination of factors that explain present status and that bring about change over time.

Case study reports are based on observations of the researcher who may be a participant or a non-participant observer. In participant observation, the researcher is a part of the group or phenomenon which he is observing. In non-participant observation, he is aloof. Recording of observation is a difficult task even for an experienced researcher. What to record, when to record, how much and in what form to record are some of the issues of concern.

Data collection for case study may include exploratory, descriptive and explanatory case studies. Descriptive case studies are narrative accounts of phenomena observed. Explanatory case studies are used for testing theories. Then case studies may be of various kinds such as ethnographic, psychological, sociological, evaluative, action research case study and educational case study.

10.2.1 Strengths and Weaknesses of Case Studies

Through a case study an in-depth and intensive study of a unit in its natural environment is possible. *For example*, it is possible for a research worker to study the behaviour of children during the school lunch break in real life situation. Case study enables the researcher to know the why of an observed behaviour. As observations are carried out over an extended period of time, some new facts or incidents may come to the knowledge of the researcher which might have not been possible otherwise. These critical incidents may have important implications for the observed behaviour.

Case studies are longitudinal in perspective and are down-to-earth. They enable the researcher to catch unique features of a situation that differentiate it from other similar situations.

On the weaknesses side, the observations of the researcher may be biased and loaded with personal prejudices. Their objectivity may be doubtful. The preconceptions of the researcher may influence which behaviours are observed and which are ignored, and the way they are interpreted. Another weakness of case study is that it is difficult to generalise the findings. The dynamics of one entity or individual may have no relationship to the dynamics of others. Therefore, case study is limited in producing valid generalisations. Case studies are more useful in producing, rather than testing of hypotheses.

Case studies of Jean Piaget which explained cognitive development in children, and those of Sigmund Freud on the unconscious are landmarks in education and psychology. These studies provided useful hypotheses which have been investigated from time to time through other methods.

10.3 CONTENT ANALYSIS

It is also known as document analysis. Content analysis is used for identifying specific characteristics of the written or verbal materials. The written material may be text-books, documents, newspapers and popular literature. Content-analysis can be used to analyse speeches, musical compositions and television programmes.

In education, content analysis is used for the following purposes:

- Content analysis may be used to analyse bias, prejudice and propaganda in text-books, especially history text-books.
- Content analysis may be conducted with reference to relative importance to different issues and topics such as gender equality, environmental concerns and equitable development.

- Difficulty level of materials in textbook can be studied through content analysis. *For example*, concepts and vocabulary levels in textbooks may be studied with reference to maturity levels of the intended users.
- Content analysis may be carried out for errors in written work of pupils. *For example*, nature and frequency of errors in spellings, syntax, or grammar.
- Content analysis of the prevailing practices may be carried out. *For example*, teacher-education curriculum as prescribed by different universities could be content analysed.

10.3.1 Steps in Content Analysis

- Specify the aspect or phenomenon to be investigated. *For example*, relative weightage to different aspects of pollution in class IX science text-book prescribed by the CBSE.
- Formulating exhaustive and mutually exhaustive coding categories so that verbal, symbolic or numeric contents can be coded.
- Analysing the data which may involve frequency count, percentages or more descriptive accounts.

10.3.2 Advantages of Content analysis

It does not suffer from the presence of someone or observer what is being observed is not being influenced by the presence of the observer.

Studies based on content analysis are easy to replicate. Finally, there is no need of human subjects as a sample.

10.4 ACTION RESEARCH

Action research has its roots in the works of Kurt Lewin (1890-1947) in the 1940s. He suggested that action research is a spiral of planning, acting, observing and reflecting.

Action research is usually undertaken by a practitioner for solution to his professional problems, at a local level. It may be undertaken in situations such as classrooms, schools, clinics, hospitals and offices. Action research is conducted to resolve specific problems which a practitioner faces. The purpose of action research is not to suggest any theory or generalisations for wider application. Some salient characteristics of action research are as follows:

- Both quantitative and qualitative approaches may be used by action research as it does not regard superiority of the one over the other. However, qualitative approach is more often used.
- It tries to formulate solutions to local levels problems, in the local context.
- It makes a limited review of literature.
- It makes use of purposeful, need based samples.
- Subjective opinions and judgements of the researcher and those involved are given due regard.
- Its procedures are less rigorous but focus on experienced reality of everyday.
- Anaylsis of data looks for practical and not statistical significance of data.
- Research is conducted by the one who has to use it, that is, the practitioner.
- Makes use of locally developed or convenient tools for data collection.
- It occurs in natural contexts, but embraces complexity.

10.4.1 Areas of Educational Action Research

Burnaford, Fischer and Hobson (2001) have identified four categories for action research. These are:

- Problems arising from a desire to improve student learning. *For example*, improvement in physical environment of the classroom, improving interpersonal interactions among students, or develop students' capacity to reflect.

- Problems arising from a desire to improve curriculum. How to best construct the curriculum, how to integrate subjects, and how to make use of technology in learning.
- Problems arising from a desire to adopt instructional strategies. *For example*, fostering active learning, guiding students' self evaluation, or implementing a specific instructional approach.
- Problems arising out of desire for one's own professional development. In the classroom context, action research may focus on the student, the teacher, the curriculum, the instructional practices or the intersection of these areas, according to Ary et al. (2006:545).

10.4.2 Action Plan in Action Research

The most important step is the development of an action plan which is based on the interpretation of the results of action research based study. Action plan provides actions to be taken on priority basis; objectives and goals are specified, sequence of activities is outlined, resources required are worked out, specifies who will carry out what tasks, and the time frame needed to complete the action.

EXERCISES

1. What are the sources of data in historical research? What is historical criticism?
2. How is a case study different from a survey study? What are the relative strength and weaknesses of case study?
3. How is educational action research different from other forms of educational research? Explain.

11

The Research Report

A complete, stepwise and a detailed account of the research activity is called a research report. It may take the form of a thesis or dissertation. A shorter version may be in the form of a journal article or a conference paper.

11.1 GENERAL FORMAT OF THE REPORT

Most universities and accepting authorities have style manuals prescribed by them. These style manuals give the form for writing the report. A general outline and the sequence of the various sections and subsections is as follows:

(A) **Preliminary Section:** It includes the title page, abstract, acceptance page, acknowledgement, table of contents, and list of figures. All these are paginated with lower case Roman numerals ii, iii, iv, and so on.

(B) **The Text:** It is the main body of the report and includes introduction, review of literature, research design, analysis and interpretation of data, summary and conclusions, as chapters.

(C) **Supplementary Section:** It consists of bibliography, appendices and other pertinent materials which are not very important but relevant.

The outline of the text part of the report is as follows:

CHAPTER I: INTRODUCTION

1.1 Statement of the problem
1.2 Significance of the study
1.3 Objectives of the study
1.4 Hypotheses formulated
1.5 Assumptions
1.6 Definition of terms
1.7 Delimitations of the study

CHAPTER II: REVIEW OF LITERATURE

This section will include the analysis of the studies reviewed.

CHAPTER III: RESEARCH DESIGN

3.1 Method used
3.2 Instruments used
3.3 Sampling technique
3.4 Procedure

CHAPTER IV: ANALYSIS AND INTERPRETATION OF THE DATA

This section includes text, tables of data and results, figures. Each table is followed by interpretation of results and discussion.

CHAPTER V: SUMMARY AND CONCLUSIONS

5.1 Statement of the problem

5.2 Procedure
5.3 Findings and conclusions
5.4 Implications
5.5 Limitations
5.6 Suggestions for further research

There may be some variations in the above format. *For example*, review of literature may be taken up in the first chapter if it is limited and not very extensive. Some researchers prefer to place hypotheses after the review, and significance of the study at the end of chapter 1.

11.2 SUGGESTIONS FOR WRITING AND TYPING THE REPORT

Though not exhaustive, these suggestions are useful for a beginning researcher.

- Good quality paper of size A-4 and weight 75 gsm should be used. The left, top, right and bottom margins on the page should be 4cms, 3 cms, 2 cms and 2.5 cms respectively.
- All the material in the text should be typed in Times New Roman font size 14 and double spaced.
- Chapters should be superscripted with centre headings as CHAPTER 1, CHAPTER II, CHAPTER III, and soon. The chapter number should be in capital Roman numerals.
- Titles of the chapters should be typed as INTRODUCTION, REVIEW OF LITERATURE, and so on. These should be centred on the page below the chapter number and placed one double space below.
- Arabic numerals such as 1, 2, 3, and so on are used for pagination beginning with the first page of

chapter I. The page number of the first page of every chapter is not typed. The page numbers are placed at the top right hand corner of the page. Each chapter begins with a new page. Pagination is continued till the last page of the report.

- Short quotations of 3 to 4 lines are a part of the running text and placed within double quotation marks. A quotation within a short quotation is enclosed in a single quotation mark. A long quotation of 5 or more lines is single spaced and indented 3 spaces from the left hand margin.
- Table headings should be placed three spaces above the tables. Headings should be self explanatory and match the contents of the tables.
- Figures are numbered below the figure and consecutively throughout the report.
- The title of the study should be brief and limited to 15-20 words. The title should be in capitals and with no punctuation marks. *For example*, STUDY HABITS OF FIRST GENERATION LEARNERS
- Tables should not be split on two pages.

11.2.1 Writing of References

Picking up the ideas and writings of others and using them as researcher's own is called plagiarism. If we have quoted or cited some author in our work then it must be acknowledged in the citation as well as in the references. Referred sources of borrowed information are indexed as follows. Broadly, the titles of the books or the names of the journals from which information has been cited, are underlined or italicised.

- **Book of a single author:** Glasser, W. (1965). *Reality therapy: A new approach to psychiatry.* New York: Harper and Row.
- **Subsequent edition of a book:** Koul, L. (1997). *Methodology of educational research.* (3rd ed.). New Delhi: Vikas.
- **When the author is also the editor of the book:** Sinha, B.L. (Ed) (2002). *Statistics in psychology and education.* New Delhi: Anmol.
- **When the author is an organization:** *American Psychological Association.* (2001). Publication manual (5th ed.). Washington, DC: Author.
- **When no author is given:** *Hutchinson Dictionary of Ideas.* (1994). Oxford:Helicon.
- **Chapter from an edited book:** Sikes, P. (2004). Methodology, procedures and ethical concerns. In C. Opie (Ed.), *Doing educational research* (pp. 15-33). London: Sage.
- **More than one article of a single author, in a year:**
- Singh, M. (2003 a) ...
- Singh, M. (2003 b) ...
- **Article in a Journal:** Cronbach, L.J. (1951). Coefficient alpha and the internal structure of tests. *Psychometrika,* 16, 297-334.
- **Newspaper Article:** Giddens, A. (2009, March 26). End of the end of history: Climate change challenge will reshape the way we live. *The Times of India,* p. 8.
- **Electronic or Online Source:** 'Learning Hierarchies' by R.M. Gagne, Educational Psychologist, 6, pp 1-9 Retrived 20 May 2009 from http://www.ibstpi. org/Products/pdf/chapter-2, pdf.

- **Personal communication, e-mail, interview:** .... (B.P. Singh, personal communication July 2, 2011) (Personal communication etc. is not listed in the references)

11.2.2 Citing the Works of Others

The borrowed works or sentences of others are cited in the text as follows:

Thapan (2006) writes "there were some pupils who were disinterested in school work and in school goals in general." (p. 237).

Its source will be referred as:

Thapan, M. (2006). *Life at school: An ethnographic study.* (2nd ed.). New Delhi: Oxford University Press.

- Multiple authors

When there are three to five authors of an article then the names of all the authors are cited for the first time. Subsequent citations will include the name of the first author, followed by et al. which means 'and others'. *For example,* Ary et al. (2006).

When there are six or more authors for a work, then et al. is written after the name of the first author.

- When the same idea is expressed by two or more authors: the names would be cited in the same order as they have been listed in the references, with semi-colon inserted between the names. *For example,* (Smith, 1980; Thorpe, 1980).

11.2.3 Abstract

The accepting authorities require a separate abstract of the dissertation. It includes statement of the problem, concise description of methodology, major findings, conclusion, and implications. In a dissertation, abstract is placed after the title page. The abstract should consist of 600 or less words.

11.2.4 Supplementary Section

It includes references and appendices. Reference list, in an alphabetic order, must include all the sources that have been mentioned in the text. Bibliography, besides mentioned sources, also includes such sources which might have been used but not mentioned in the text. *For example*, the researcher might have consulted some dictionary or thesaurus to check spellings and meanings of certain words.

Appendices constitute relevant materials that are not so important to find place in the text. Such materials could be the copies of the test, instructions to the subjects, and scoring procedure. Appendices may include tables that are very long.

11.3 Qualitative Research Report

It includes the following components, with some variation of these:

1. Abstract
2. Introduction
3. Research Design
4. Method
5. Findings
6. Interpretation and Implications
7. References
8. Appendix

- Abstract is a very brief summary of the major aspects of the qualitative study and includes: problem, design, method, and outcomes.

- Introduction includes problem's background and purpose of the study. Review of literature which is relevant, is presented and discussed. This section may include an interesting story or quote to create interest in the reader.
- Research design explains the approach used and the reason for its choice to investigate the problem. Steps undertaken to ensure credibility, confirmability and transferability, such as triangulation, audit trail etc. are explained. How biases were controlled, and limitations of the study are also explained.
- Method section includes description of the site of the study, participants and the way they were selected. Data collection methods describe how the data were collected – interview, observation, document analysis, and why these were chosen. Data analysis procedures describe the approach undertaken for analysis of data.
- Findings section would include major findings relevant to the focus of the study. Since findings are based on voluminous data, it is decided what not to include in the report. This section also includes interpretation of the data.
- Interpretations and Implications section includes interpretation of what the researcher has found. What are the major conclusions and implications of the study? Directions for future research are suggested.
- Reference Section includes alphabetic listing of all the works which have been cited in the report.
- Appendix includes interview schedules, observation schedules and other documents that will help the reader understand the report.

EXERCISES

1. Write the following sources for a bibliography, according to American Psychological Association publication style.
   (*a*) Fourth edition of the book 'Writing the Modern Research Paper' by R. Dees and published in 2003 by Longman from Boston in USA.
   (*b*) Article by P.A. Graham and titled 'Historians as Policy Makers', published by the Journal Educational Researcher in its Vol. 9 of 1980, at pages 21 to 24.
2. On a class V mathematics achievement test, for a sample of 40 boys and 30 girls means are 50 and 52 with standard deviations of 4 and 5 respectively. Depict the data in tabular form with a suitable table title.
3. An investigation is to be conducted to compare study habits of class VII students from science and arts streams. Prepare a research proposal for the same.
4. Describe the qualities of a good quantitative research report.

12

Measurement and Data Description

A beginning researcher must have working knowledge of some basic statistical procedures in order to carry out quantitative research. This knowledge helps in the analysis and interpretation of data which is then communicated to others. Though computer softwares such as Excel and SPSS are available to process data and give results, interpretation of results is done by the researcher. This would become difficult in the absence of working knowledge of statistics. Knowledge of statistics is also essential for making educational decisions based on evidence.

12.1 Scales of Measurement

One of the basic requirements in the conduct of a quantitative study is the task of measurement. Measurement is a process through which our observations are changed into numbers, according to some rules. First of all the variables to be observed are identified. Rules are used to determine the way the observations would be measured and expressed numerically.

The most widely used scales of measurement in education and social sciences are nominal, ordinal, interval and ratio scales, which have been proposed by S.S. Stevens.

12.1.1 Nominal Scale

This is a scale which provides the lowest or the crudest measurement of the change in the variable being measured. It involves placing observations, objects or individuals in categories that are qualitatively rather than quantitatively different. The observations may be categorised on the basis of gender (male, female), academic stream (arts, science, commerce) and residence (urban, rural). We may assign numerical labels 1,2,3 and so on to these categories, but it does not mean that one category is "more" or "less" than the other.

The identifying numbers in a nominal scale cannot be arithmetically manipulated through addition, multiplication, subtraction or division. However, we can count the observations or objects in the categories and express them as a proportion or percent of the total observations or objects. *For example*, we have categorized 10 students as 6 girls and 4 boys. This implies that of the total, 60 per cent are girls and the remaining 40 per cent are boys.

12.1.2 Ordinal Scale

The next higher level of measurement is through the ordinal scale. It classifies observations or objects on the basis of the extent or magnitude of quality possessed by them on which they are being measured. *For example*, students are ranked from first to last on the basis of their performance on a test. They are ranked from tallest to the shortest on the variable of height. However the rank 1,2,3,4 and so on does not necessarily meant that the difference between 1 and 2 is equal to the difference between 2 and 3, or that the rank 2 is two times the rank 4. All can be said is that 1>2>3>4. Ordinal scale provides more information than the nominal scale. It gives information about "more than" or "less than" when one thing is compare to another on some characteristics.

12.1.3 Interval Scale

This scale is more precise as it orders objects according to the amount of the characteristic they possess, and also it has equal intervals between the units of measure. However, there is no true zero on an interval scale. With an interval scale, both the rank order and the distance between ranks (numbers) are meaningful. *For example*, we may say that difference between 30 and 40 is the same as the difference between 60 and 70. Since interval scale does not have a true zero, therefore it is arbitrarily set on the scale. On the celsius scale of temperature, zero is arbitrarily set at the temperature at which water freezes at sea level. Therefore, a zero point on the scale does not indicate an absence of the variable being measured. Further, if there are two measurements, say 30 and 60 or an interval scale, we cannot say that 60 is two times 30.

Psychological and educational tests such as intelligence, personality and achievement give measures on the interval scale. Therefore, a score of zero on an intelligence test does not mean that a person has zero intelligence. Similarly, we cannot say that an IQ of 120 is twice the IQ of 60. Arithmetic operations of addition and subtraction on scores obtained on an interval scale are justified, but not the operations of multiplication and division.

12.1.4 Ratio Scale

A ratio scale is the highest level of measurement scale. It has a true zero point, as well as equal intervals. Ratios can be formed for any two value obtained through this scale. While using a yardstick we can say that 24 inches is four times six inches. This is possible because the origin on the scale is an absolute zero corresponding to no length at all.

A few variables of interest in education are measured on ratio scale, *for example*, motor performance such as long jumps or physiological measures of heartbeat and pulse rate. We can say that a long jump of 10 feet is twice the long jump of 5 feet, or a pulse rate of 180 beats is three times the pulse rate of 60 beats. However, we cannot say that a performance of 80 marks is twice the performance of 40 marks on an achievement test because achievement test scores are interval data.

12.2 ORGANIZING RESEARCH DATA

After the data have been obtained they are arranged in some order without which if is difficult to describe them. Data may be organised as a frequency distribution or presented in a graphic form Frequency Distribution.

A systematic arrangement of individual scores or measures from the highest at the top of the lowest at the bottom is called a frequency distribution.

The steps for preparing a frequency distribution are as follows:

- List the scores in a column from the highest at the top and the lowest at the bottom.
- Include all possible intermediate scores or measures even if they have not been obtained.
- Create a second column under which the frequency of each scores is recorded as a tally mark.

Table 12.1 shows scores of 50 class IV pupils on an arithmetic achievement test. Part A shows the unorganised scores and Part B shows the scores in a frequency distribution form.

Table 12.1: Scores of 50 class IV Pupils on arithmetic achievement test

Part A. Unorganised Scores

25	28	30	31	20	22	33	30	29	28
28	23	28	30	29	26	30	28	22	27
21	24	26	26	27	28	31	29	26	25
23	24	28	28	27	24	23	22	35	26
24	27	26	29	28	28	24	27	25	22

Part B. Frequency Distribution

Scores (X)	*Tallies*	*f*	*f(X)*
35	/	1	35
34		0	0
33	/	1	33
32		0	0
31	//	2	62
30	////	4	120
29	////	4	116
28	~~////~~ ~~////~~	10	280
27	~~////~~	5	135
26	~~////~~ /	6	156
25	///	3	75
24	~~////~~	5	120
23	///	3	69
22	////	4	88
21	/	1	21
20	/	1	20
		N=50	$\Sigma fX=1330$

The frequency distribution in the Part B of Table 12.1 reveals:

- The score 28 has the highest frequency 10.
- Twenty nine frequencies are within the range 26 to 30.
- More frequencies are on the lower side than on the upper side of the frequency distribution.

12.3 GRAPHIC PRESENTATION OF DATA

Data can be presented in graphic form. The most widely used graphs are the frequency polygon and the histogram. The steps in their construction are:

- Scores are laid out on the horizontal dimension called abscissa. The order of the scores is from the lowest to the highest from the left to right direction. Some space is left at both the ends, for additional score.
- Frequencies of the scores are laid out on the vertical axis called ordinate.
- A dot is placed above the centre of each score and at the level of the frequency of that score.
- Adjacent scores are connected. The end points are connected with the base at the points representing 1 score less than the lowest score and 1 more than the highest score as shown in figure12.1

For the histogram, a horizontal line is drawn through each dot and equal to the width of the score. Perpendicular are dropped from the ends on to the base.

The scores of 15 students on a class test are given a frequency distribution form in Table 12.2. These have been presented as frequency polygon and histogram in figures 12.1 and 12.2 respectively.

Table 12.2: Score on a class test

Scores(X)	*f*
25	1
24	2
23	6
22	3
21	2
20	1
	N=15

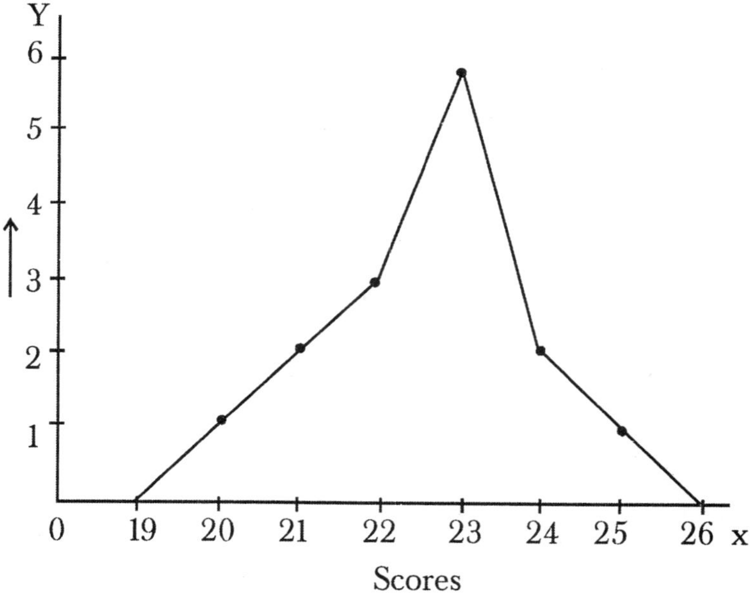

Fig. 12.1: Frequency Polygon of data in Table 12.2

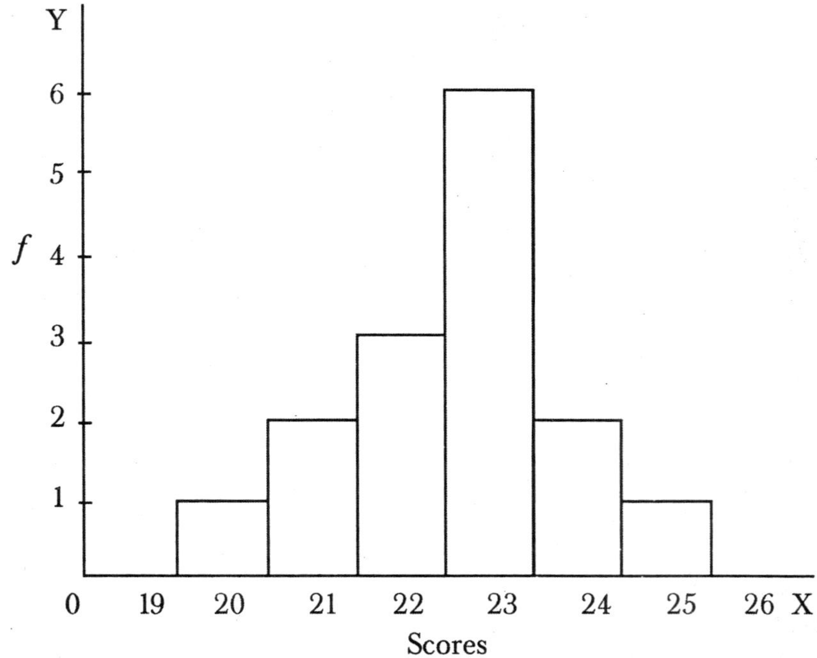

Fig. 12.2: Histogram of data in Table 12.2

12.4 MEASURES OF CENTRAL TENDENCY

Suppose we have scores of 50 individuals on a test. If we find a single score or index that represents all the scores then this score will be a useful indicator for comparison with such indicators of other groups. In statistics, three measures mean, median and mode are available for this purpose. These are known as measures of central tendency.

12.4.1 The Mean

It is the most widely used measure of central tendency. Also called arithmetic average, it is the sum of all the scores in a distribution divided by the number of scores or cases. *For example*, we have the following scores:

18 10 15 25 20

The mean of these scores would be

$$\overline{X} = \frac{18 + 10 + 15 + 25 + 20}{5} = \frac{88}{5} = 17.6$$

The general formula for calculating mean is

$$\overline{X} = \frac{\Sigma X}{N} \qquad ...(12.1)$$

here $\overline{X}$ = The mean
Σ = The sum of
X = raw score
N = number of scores or cases

For calculating mean, it is not necessary to order the scores from the lowest to the highest. When the scores are in a large number, it is convenient to start with a frequency distribution as given in the Table 12.1. Each score is multiplied by its frequency. For scores in the Table 12.1 (Part A) this is shown under column 4 of the Part B of the table. Adding all the values under the column 4, we get = 1330. The mean would be

$$\overline{X} = \frac{\Sigma fX}{N} = \frac{1330}{50} = 26.60$$

Table 12.4: Calculation of mean by short method

Class Interval (1)	*f* (2)	*X* (3)	*X-am* (4)	*(X–am)/ i = x'* (5)	*fx'* (6)
35-37	1	36	9	3	3
32-34	1	33	6	2	2
29-31	10	30	3	1	10
26-28	21	27	0	0	0
23-25	11	24	–3	–1	–11
20-22	6	21	–6	–2	–12
	$N = 50$				$\Sigma fx' = -8$

Steps

- Determine the mid point X of each class interval in the column 1.

  The mid points are given the column 3.

- Assume a mean preferably the mid point of the interval which has the highest frequency. The highest frequency in column 2 is 21 and its corresponding mid value is 27(col. 3). Therefore, 27 is the assumed mean.
- Calculate the deviations of the mid values from the assumed mean. These are given under column 4.
- Divide the deviations by the size of the class interval (i) which is 3 for the frequency distribution. The score 3 represents the three scores of each interval, *for example* 20, 21, and 22 of the class interval 20-22 and son on.
- Multiply each x' value (in col. 5) with its corresponding f value (col. 2). The cross products fx' are reported in column 6.
- Using the following formula solve the mean value of the frequency distribution in the Table 12.4.

Mean $= \text{assumed mean} + (\Sigma fx'/N)i$ ...(12.2)

$= 27+(-8/50)3$

$= 27-.48= 26.52$

Here, assumed mean = 27

$i= 3$

12.4.2 Mean for a Grouped Frequency Distribution

When the data are in the shape of a grouped frequency distribution then the mean may be calculated by either long method or short (assumed mean) method. The scores in the Table 12.1 are expressed in a group frequency distribution in the Table 12.4 and the mean has been calculated by the long method.

Table 12.4: Calculation of mean by long method

Class Interval	*f*	*X*	*fX*
35-37	1	36	36
32-34	1	33	33
29-31	10	30	300
26-28	21	27	567
23-25	11	24	264
20-22	6	21	126
	$N = 50$		$1326 = \Sigma fX$

$$\overline{X} = \frac{\Sigma fX}{N} = \frac{1326}{50} = 26.52$$

12.4.2.1 Calculation of mean by short (assumed mean) method

This method is preferred when the data are large, multiplication work is tedious, and calculator or software is not available.

12.4.2.2 Qualities of Mean

- It is the most precise measure of central tendency because it is on interval or ratio statistics whereas the median is an ordinal statistic and mode a nominal statistic.
- The sum of the deviations of the scores from their mean value is equal to zero.
- Mean is needed when standard deviation of the scores is to be calculated.

12.4.3 Median of a Frequency Distribution

Median is that point in the distribution above and below which half of the scores or frequencies lie or fall. It is $\frac{(n+1)}{2}th$ score in the frequency distribution. Suppose we have the following scores:

20 30 25 22 32

For calculation of median of these scores they will be ordered from the lowest to the highest as

20 22 25 30 32

The median would be $\frac{(n+1)}{2}th$ score $= \left(\frac{5+1}{2}\right) = 3rd$ score which is 25. Two scores 20 and 22 fall below it and two scores 30 and 32 lie above it.

It we have a distribution as 20 22 25 28 30 35, then the median would be $\frac{(n+1)}{2}th$ score $= \left(\frac{6+1}{2}\right) = 3.5\,th$ score which is $\left(\frac{25+28}{2}\right) = 26.5$. Three scores in the distribution lie below it and three scores lie above it.

12.4.3.1 Median for a Grouped Frequency Distribution

Let us take the distribution in the Table 12.3 and calculate median for it.

Table 12.5: Calculation of median for grouped data

Class Interval	*f*	*cf*
35-37	1	50
32-34	1	49

29-31	10	48
26-28	21	38
23-25	11	17
20-22	6	6
	N = 50	

Steps

- The total frequencies are 50 half of which is 25.
- In the column 3 of the Table 12.5, cumulative frequency for each class interval is worked out beginning from the bottom end of the distribution. Frequency 6 has been added to the next frequency 11 to get a cumulative frequency of 17 which has been further added to 21 get *cf* = 38 and so on.
- The score for cumulative frequency 25 (half of total 50 *fs*) lies somewhere within the class interval 26-28. The lower limit of this interval is 25.5, frequencies within this interval (*fw*) are 21, and the total frequencies below this interval (*fb*) are 17.
- The formula for calculating median for grouped data is

$$\text{Median} = \text{Lower limit} + \left(\frac{N/2 - fb}{fw}\right)i \qquad ...(12.3)$$

where lower limit

$= 25.5$

$fb = 17$

$fw = 21$

Substituting these values in the above formula we get

$$\text{Median} = 25.50 + \left(\frac{25-17}{21}\right)3$$

$$= 25.50 + 1.14$$

$= 26.64$

Therefore, the median of the grouped frequency distribution is the score of 26.64, above and below which half the scores lie.

Qualities of Median

- Median is calculated where there are extreme scores in a frequency distribution which would unnecessarily affect the mean. *For example*, we have a frequency distribution of daily income (in ₹) of 7 persons as follows:

110 120 150 200 225 300 5000

Here, the mean daily income of this distribution should be ₹ 872.14, and the median income ₹ 200 daily. Since there is an extreme value of 5000 which unnecessarily affects the central tendency it would be appropriate to compute median in such a situation.

- Median is needed when we have to calculate quartile deviation of a distribution.
- When the exact mid point, that is 50% point of the distribution is wanted.

12.4.4 Mode

It is the crudest measure of central tendency and in a distribution it is the score which occurs most frequently. *For example*, in the distribution 10 12 13 13 15 16 18, the mode is 13. If there are no repeated scores in a distribution, for example, 13 15 16 17 then the mode is the highest score, that is, 17.

12.4.4.1 Mode for Grouped Data

The formula for calculating mode of a grouped frequency distribution is

$$\text{Mode} = 3 \text{ median} - 2 \text{ mean} \quad ...(12.4)$$

For the distribution in Table 12.3 the mode is

$$\begin{aligned} \text{Mode} &= 3 \text{ median} - 2 \text{ mean} \\ &= 3(26.64) - 2\,(26.52) \\ &= 79.92 - 53.04 \\ &= 26.88 \end{aligned}$$

Qualities of Mode

It is calculated when

- a quick and an approximate measure of central tendency is wanted.
- the typical value of a distribution is wanted. *For example*, we wish to know the average shoe size of men and women. The most selling shoe size would be the modal value.

12.5 MEASURES OF VARIABILITY

The means values of two or more distribution may be the same, but the variability of their scores may be different. The scores of one distribution may cluster around the central value. The scores of the other may be more scattered or dispersed. Suppose we have the following distributions:

5	11	11	12	14	19
6	10	12	14	14	16

The mean value for both the distributions is 12, but the scattering of the scores around their mean values differ. The scores in the first distribution are more heterogeneous than those in the second distribution. We need indices that can describe distributions in terms of variation, spread or heterogeneity of scores in them.

12.5.1 Range

It is the simplest index of variability. Suppose we have a frequency distribution as follows:

4 6 9 10 14

The lower limit of this distribution is 3.5 for 4 and the upper limit is 14.5 for 14. The difference between the upper and the lower limit is 14.5–3.5 = 11 which is the range of this distribution. In a generalised form, the formula is

$$R = (X_h - X_L) + 1 \qquad ...(12.5)$$

where

R = range
X_h = highest score
X_L = lowest score

Qualities of Range

The range is an unreliable index of variability because it is based on only two values, the highest and the lowest. Therefore, it is not a stable index of variability. It is used for inspectional purposes only, or it may be used along with other indices of variability.

12.5.2 Variance and Standard Deviation

Variance and standard deviation are the most frequently used indices of variability of data obtained on interval and ratio scales. They are based on 'deviation scores' which show the difference between a raw score and the mean of the distribution of the scores. The formula for a deviation score is

$$x = X - \overline{X}$$

where x = deviation of a score
X = raw score
$\overline{X}$ = mean of the scores

Scores falling below the mean will have negative deviation scores and those above will have positive deviation scores. The sum of the deviation scores will be zero ($\Sigma x = 0$). To get out of this situation the deviation scores are squared, summed up and then divided by the total number of the scores. The obtained value is called the variance which in mathematical form is

$$\sigma^2 = \Sigma x^2 / N \qquad ...(12.6)$$

Since calculating variance through this method may involve working with squares of the mixed-number deviation scores which is tedious, the following formula is labour saving and applies directly to the raw scores

$$\sigma^2 = \frac{\Sigma X^2 - (\Sigma X)^2 / N}{N} \qquad ...(12.7)$$

where

σ^2 = Variance

ΣX^2 = sum of the squares of all the scores

$(\Sigma X)^2$ = the square of the sum of the scores

N = no. of cases

12.5.3 Calculation of standard deviation by short method

This method involves extension of one step in the steps followed for the calculation of mean by short method. Let us calculate standard deviation for the frequency distribution in Table 12.3.

After the calculation of fx' (column 6), we undertake one step more which is $(fx')(x')$ or fx'^2 (col. 7). This follows determination of $\Sigma fx'^2$. The values under col. 7 would be 9 4 10 0 11 and 24 whose sum is $\Sigma fx'^2 = 58$.

The following formula is used to determine SD.

$$SD(s) = \left(\sqrt{\Sigma fx'^2 / N - c^2}\right) i \qquad ...(12.8)$$

where

$$\Sigma fx'^2 / N = \frac{58}{50} = 1.16$$

$$c^2 = (\Sigma fx'/ N)^2 = (-8/50)^2 = .025$$

$$i = 3$$

Substituting these values in the above formula, we get

$$SD(s) = \left(\sqrt{1.16 - .025}\right)3$$

$$= \left(\sqrt{1.135}\right)3$$

$$= 3.195$$

The variance for the frequency distribution would be the square of its SD, that is, 10.208.

12.6 MEASURES OF RELATIVE POSITION

Measures of relative position tell us about an individual's relative position in a group. They also enable us to compare his relative position on two or more measures. Measures of relative position indicate where a score falls in relation to all other scores in a group.

12.6.1 z-Score

It is the most widely used measure of relative position. It is the positive or negative difference between a given score and the mean of the group measured in standard deviation units. The formula for finding z score is

$$z = X - \frac{X - \overline{X}}{\sigma} = \frac{x}{\sigma} \qquad ...(12.9)$$

where X = raw score

$\overline{X}$ = mean of the distribution

σ = standard deviation of the distribution

x = deviation score $\left(X - \overline{X}\right)$

Suppose a student has obtained a score of 80 in mathematics. The mean and the standard deviation of his class are 75 and 3 respectively. On science his score is 83, the mean and standard deviation of the class are 78 and 4 respectively. In which subject his performance is better? Using the above formula his z score in mathematics and science would be

Mathematics

$$z_1 = \frac{X - \overline{X}}{\sigma}$$

$$= \frac{80 - 75}{3} = 1.66$$

Science $$z_2 = \frac{80 - 78}{4} = 1.25$$

For a z distribution, by definition the mean and standard deviation are always 0 and 1 respectively. Therefore, the above standard score can be compared directly. The raw score of 80 in mathematics indicates better relative performance than the raw score of 83 in science. Apparently, the performance in science (83 marks) appears to be better than the mathematics performance with 80 marks.

12.6.2 T-Scores

The z scores may be obtained in negative numbers or decimals. This may cause difficulty in interpretation for a layman. To overcome this difficulty, the z scores are converted to *T* scores by multiplying the *z* scores by 10 and adding 50. The obtained score will be obtained as a positive whole number. The formula for *T* score is

$$T = 10\left(\frac{X - \overline{X}}{\sigma}\right) + 50 \qquad ...(12.10)$$

Suppose for a class IX student the score on a maths test is 48 whereas themean and standard deviation of his class are 60 and 5 respectively. His T score will be

$$T = 10\left(\frac{48 - 60}{5}\right) + 50$$

$$= 10 \;\; + 50$$

$$= 26$$

12.6.3 Percentile Rank

In a frequency distribution percentile rank is that score below which a certain percentage of scores fall. Suppose in a given frequency distribution the percentile rank for a score of 60 is 70. This means that 70 per cent of scores in the distribution fall below 60. The median of a frequency distribution is the 50th percentile rank below which 50 per cent of the scores fall. The formula for the percentile rank is

$$PR = 100 - \left(\frac{100RK - 50}{N}\right) \qquad ...(12.11)$$

where PR = percentile rank

RK = rank of the score from the top

N = Total no. of scores

Suppose in a class of 140 students, the rank of a student is 40th from the top. His percentile rank is

$$PR = 100 - \left[\frac{100(40) - 50}{140}\right] = 71.79$$

This means that in the distribution 71.79 per cent of the students have scores below him.

The major advantage of the percentile rank is that it has universal meaning. A percentile rank of 90 is high in any distribution whereas 30 is low. The major difficulty with this scale is as with other ordinal statistics. Percentile ranks cannot be added, subtracted, multiplied or divided.

12.6.4 Stanine Scores

These scores are also known as standard nine. They avoid negative numbers and decimals. The Stanine scale has a mean of 5 and standard deviation 2. Thus, its formula is

$$\text{Stanine} = 5+2z \qquad \text{...(12.12)}$$

z-scores above +1.75 are assigned the Stanine score of 9. z-scores below −1.75 are assigned the Stanine score of 1. z-scores between −.25 and +.25 get the Stanine score of 5 which is the average score.

The major limitation of Stanine scores is that they are not useful for comparing extreme scores above +1.75 and −1.75 z scores because the scores above +1.75 and below −1.75 are clubbed together as 9 and 1 respectively.

12.7 THE NORMAL CURVE

Also known as the normal probability curve, it is a bell shaped curve of the distribution of measures of scores.

Suppose we have a large number of measurements of height of individuals. We plot the frequency distribution of these heights. The form of the graph will be a bell shaped curve. Maximum frequencies will fall in the central part and around the highest point of the curve. As we move away from the central part, the number of frequencies would decrease on both the sides, that is, a few measures will be at the lower and the upper end of the curve. If a perpendicular is dropped from the highest point of the curve, it will divide the curve in two symmetrical halves which have similar shape and equal area. This bell shaped curve is known as the normal curve.

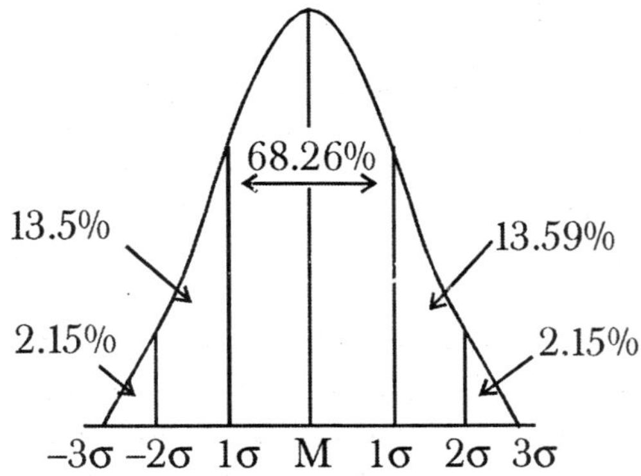

Fig. 12.3: The Normal Curve

12.7.1 Elementary Principles of Probability

For an understanding of the normal probability curve, it will be useful to study the elementary principles of probability. Probability of a given event is defined as the expected frequency of occurrence of this event among the events of the same kind. Mathematically, it is stated as a ratio. Suppose we have an unbiased coin and we toss it. The probability of this coin falling heads is 1/2. In the case of a dice, the probability of showing a two-spot or a three spot is 1/6. These ratios are called probability ratios, that is, desired outcome divided by the total possible outcomes. The dice has faces or sides and the appearance of any side has probability of 1/6. The limits of the probability ratio are 0 (impossibility of occurrence) and 1.00 (certainty of occurrence).

Suppose we toss a coin. It must fall either heads (*H*) or tails (*T*) 100 % of the time. As there are only two possible outcomes when the coin is tossed, that is, a head or a tail is equally probable. As a ratio, the probability of *H* is 1/2 and of *T* 1/2. Therefore, $(H+T) = 1/2+1/2=1.00$.

If we toss two unbiased coins '*A*' and '*B*' at the same time, there are four possible combinations that the coins may take:

(A)	(B)	(A)	(B)	(A)	(B)	(A)	(B)
H	H	H	T	T	H	T	T
(1)		(2)		(3)		(4)	

Both the coins A and B may fall H; A may fall H and (B) T; (B) may fall H and (A) T; or both of them may fall T. Expressed as a ratio the probability of combination(1), that is two heads is 1/4 and the probability of two tails is 1/4. Probability of an HT combination is 1/4 and of TH combination is 1/4. Since it does not matter which coin falls H or which falls T, these two ratios are added to obtain the probability as 1/2 of the HT combination.

Let us increase the number of coins to 3. There will be 8 combinations of we toss the three coins A, B and C simultaneously,

HHH	HHT	HTH	THH	HTT	THT	TTH	TTT
(1)	(2)	(3)	(4)	(5)	(6)	(7)	(8)

As ratios, the probability of three heads is 1/8 (combination 1); of two heads and one tail 3/8 (combinations 2, 3, and 4); one head and two tails 3/8 (combination 5, 6, and 7); and of three tails 1/8 (combination 8). The sum of these probability ratios is $1/8 + 3/8 + 3/8 + 1/8 = 1.00$.

By the above method we can determine the probability of different combinations of heads and tails for any number of coins. These various combinations may be obtained more directly. If there are n independent factors (coins), the probability of the presence or absence of each being the same, the compound probabilities of various combinations will be expressed by the expansion of the binomial $(p + q)^n$. Here, p

is the probability that a given event will happen, q is the probability that the event will not happen. If H and T are substituted for p and q respectively, we have for two coins $(H + T)^2$. Expanding it, we get

$$(H + T)^2 = H^2 + 2HT + T^2$$

This may be written as

$1H^2$	1 chance in 4 of getting 2 heads
$2HT$	2 chances in 4 of getting 1 head and 1 tail
$1T^2$	1 chance in 4 of getting 2 tails
Total 4	

The probability ratio for the above is 1/4, 1/2, 1/4 respectively.

The binomial expansion may be applied in situations where large number of independent factors is operating.

In the above examples, the probability of occurrence of H or non occurrence of H, that is, occurrence of T of a given factor is the same. However, there may be situations when p being not equal to q, the distributions obtained from the expansion of $(p+q)^n$ are skewed or not normal. *For example*, a situation in which the probability of an event's happening is 1/4, and its not happening 3/4.

12.7.2 Properties of the Normal Probability Curve

- For a normal probability curve, its mean, median and mode fall at the mid point of the distribution and are numerically equal. Because the curve is bilaterally symmetrical, all the measures of central tendency coincide at the centre of the distribution.
- The ends of the curve do not meet the base line.
- The equation of the normal probability curve is

$$y = \frac{N}{\sigma\sqrt{2\pi}} e^{-x^2} / 2\sigma^2$$

where

$x =$ Scores (expressed as deviations from the mean and laid along the base of the curve).

$y =$ The height of the curve above the base (X-axis), that is, the frequency of a given value.

The other terms in the equation are constants

$N =$ the number of cases or measures

$\sigma =$ standard deviation of the distribution

$\pi = 3.1416$

$e = 2.7183$

When N and σ are given or known, it is possible to calculate from the above formula, the value of y for a given value of x; the number of cases above and below a given point in the distribution; and the number of cases or their percentage between two points. However, these calculations are not needed as tables are available from which the information may be readily obtained (Appendix I: Table A).

12.7.3 Reading the Table of Areas under the Normal Curve.

Table A, column 1 gives distances in tenths of σ measured off on the base line and the mean of the normal curve. When X–M is divided by σ, the deviation X–M $= x$ is expressed in sigma units. Such scores (x/σ) are called sigma or z scores. Distances from means in hundredths of σ are given by the headings of the columns. To find the number of cases in the normal distribution between the mean and the ordinate erected at a distance of say 2σ from the mean, go down the column 1 until 2 is reached and under the next column under .00 take the entry opposite 2.00, which is .4772. This figure means that .4772 cases out of 1, or 47.72% of the entire area of the curve, lies between mean and $+2\sigma$. In other words, 47.72% of the cases fall within the area bounded by the base line of the curve, the ordinates erected at the mean and at a distance of 2.00 from the mean and the curve itself. If we wish to find the number of cases or percentage of distribution between mean and 2.02σ, then we shall pick up the value .4783 below the 2nd column and opposite to 2.02σ. This means that in the normal distribution 47.83% of the cases lie between mean and 2.02σ.

The above are examples for the upper or positive side of the normal curve. Because the curve is bilaterally symmetrical, the entries in the Table A apply to σ distances measured in the negative direction. The percentage of cases between mean and -2.00 σ is 47.72%.

For a normal curve 68.26% cases lie between mean and ± 1σ, 95.44% cases lie between mean and ±2σ, and 99.73% cases between mean and ±3σ.

12.8 CORRELATION

Suppose a class of 10 students has been taught simple interest in arithmetic. This is followed by a test on simple interest and the scores of the 10 students are reported in the column 2 of the Table 12.6. The same group of students now learns compound interest, followed by a test. The scores are reported in the column 3 of the Table 12.6. The z scores of the students on the tests 1 and 2 are shown in the columns 4 and 5 respectively. We have already studied that a z score = $(X - M)/\sigma$. This is a way of indicating the relative positions of scores.

Table 12.6: Raw scores and z scores on Tests 1 and 2.

(1) Student	*(2)* Scores (Test 1)	*(3)* Scores (Test 2)	*(4)* z Scores (Test 3)	*(5)* z Scores (Test 4)	*(6)* (z_x) (z_x)
A	40	43	+1.09	+1.33	+1.45

B	36	34	+0.61	+0.13	+0.08
C	45	44	+1.69	+1.46	+2.47
D	28	32	–0.36	–0.13	+.0.05
E	18	22	–1.57	–1.46	+2.29
F	25	28	–.73	–0.67	+0.49
G	32	37	+0.12	+0.53	+0.06
H	38	40	+0.85	+0.93	+0.79
I	27	26	–0.48	–0.93	+0.45
J	21	24	–1.21	–1.20	+1.45

Looking at the Table 12.6 we find that those who have obtained positive *z*-scores on test 1 also obtain positive scores on test 2. Those with negative *z*-scores on test 1 also get negative scores on test 2. The relative ranks of the scores obtained by students on two occasions are almost similar with a slight change of 1 rank in case of B, F, G and I. If we plot raw scores on test 1 along X-axis and Y-scores on test-2 along the Y-axis, we would plot a figure as follows.

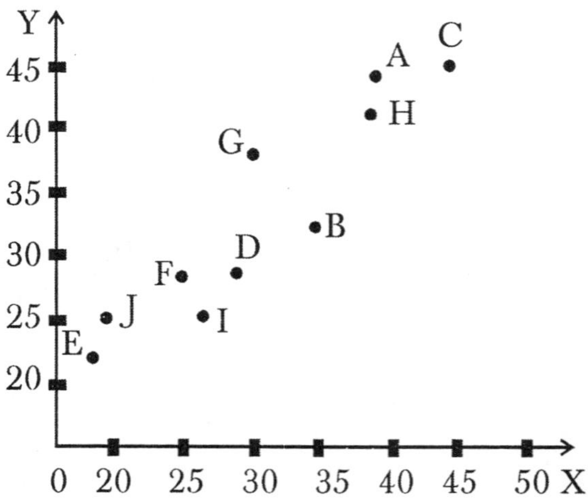

Fig. 12.4: Position of each student on both tests

The figure is known as the scatter-plot. A scatter-plot with dots going from lower left to upper right indicates as positive correlation. As scores on variable X go up so do the scores on the variable Y. A scatter-plot with dots going from upper left to lower right indicates a negative correlation. As one variable goes up, the other variable goes down. Further, the scatter-plot of scores also reveals the strength of relationship between the variables. If the dots in the scatter plot form a narrow band, so that when a straight line is drawn through the band, the dots will be closer to the line. This indicates a strong linear relationship between the two variables.

A correlation indicates the relationship between paired scores. The correlation indicates whether this relationship between paired scores is positive or negative and how strong this relationship is. The pairs may be two scores for the same individual such as his scores on two tests, or test and retest scores, or height and weight measures. Two individuals might have been paired on some measure such as science achievement scores.

12.8.1 Pearson Product Moment Correlation Coefficient

Pearson product moment correlation coefficient indicates both the direction and strength of the relationship between two variables without preparing a scatter plot. Pearson r is the mean of $z_x z_y$ product and its Formula is

$$r = \left(\frac{\Sigma z_x z_y}{N}\right) \quad \text{...(12.13)}$$

where

r = Pearson product moment correlation coefficient

$\Sigma z_x z_y$ = sum of the z-score products

N = number of paired scores

For the scores in the Table 12.6, $\Sigma z_x z_y = 9.58$. Therefore, r = 9.58/10=.96. The *z*-scores on the two tests are positively related. This relationship is very strong but not perfect.

A correlation coefficient can take any value between +1 and −1, that is, it can never take values greater than +1 or less than −1. It can take the value 0 which means there is no relationship between the two variables; +1 indicates a perfectly positive relationship between the two variables, and −1 indicates a perfectly negative relationship. Usually, a correlation coefficient very rarely takes the values +1 or −1.

A positive correlation between two variables indicates that the changes in both the variables are in the same direction, either positive or negative. A negative correlation coefficient between two variables indicates that as the one variable increases, the other decreases.

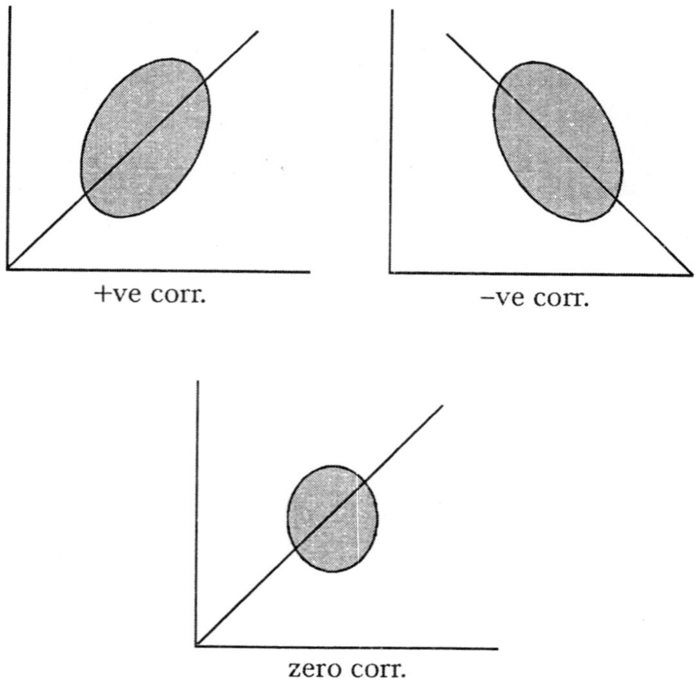

Fig. 12.4

Pearson Product Moment Correlation Coefficient can be calculated directly from the raw scores without first transforming the raw scores into *z* scores. Calculation of correlation from z scores is cumbersome and time consuming. The formula for calculating Pearson r directly from the raw scores on the two variables is as follows:

$$r = \frac{N\Sigma XY - (\Sigma X)(\Sigma Y)}{\sqrt{\left(N\Sigma X^2 - (\Sigma X)^2\right)\left(N\Sigma Y^2 - (\Sigma Y)^2\right)}} \quad ...(12.14)$$

where $r =$ Pearson r

$\Sigma X =$ sum of scores in X distribution

$\Sigma Y =$ sum of scores in Y distribution

$\Sigma X^2 =$ sum of the squared scores in X distribution

$\Sigma Y^2 =$ sum of the squared scores in Y distribution

$\Sigma XY =$ sum of the products of paired X and Y scores

$N =$ number of pairs of X and Y scores

Calculation of Pearson r for raw scores in Table 12.6 has been shown in Table 12.7

Table 12.7: Pearson *r* for raw scores in Table 12.6

(1) *Student*	*(2)* *X*	*(3)* X^2	*(4)* *Y*	*(5)* Y^2	*(6)* *XY*
A	40	1600	43	1849	1720
B	36	1296	34	1156	1224
C	45	2025	44	1936	1980
D	28	784	32	1024	896

E	18	324	22	484	396
F	25	625	28	784	700
G	32	1024	37	1369	1184
H	38	1444	40	1600	1520
I	27	729	26	676	702
J	21	441	24	576	504
	$\Sigma X=310$	$\Sigma X^2=10292$	$\Sigma Y=330$	$\Sigma Y^2=$ 11454	$\Sigma XY=$ 10826

In the Table 12.2 the column 2 shows the raw scores of the students on Test 1. Column 3 shows these raw scores squared (X^2). Column 4 shows the raw scores on Test 2. Column 5 shows these raw scores squared (Y^2). Column 6 shows cross product XY for each student, that is, his X score multiplied by his Y score.

Using the Formula (12.14), we get

$$r = \frac{10(10826) - 310(330)}{\sqrt{\left[10(10292) - (310)^2\right]\left[10(11454) - (330)^2\right]}}$$

$$= \frac{(10826 - (102300)}{\sqrt{(6820)(5640)}} = \frac{5960}{(82.58)(75.10)} = .96$$

12.8.2 Assumptions underlying Pearson *r*

Pearson *r* can be calculated when the data has been obtained either on an interval or ratio scale. The relationship between the two variables X and Y should be linear (straight line). A practical way to determine whether the relationship between the two variables is linear or curvilinear is to examine a scatter-plot of the data. If the relationship is curvilinear then correlation ratio is applied. Figures 12.5 and 12.6 depict linear and curvilinear relationship respectively between variables X and Y.

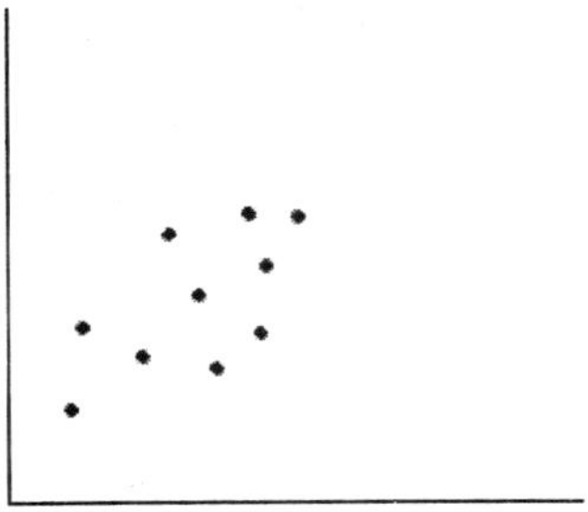

Fig. 12.5: Linear Relationship

Fig. 12.6: Curvilinear Relationship

12.8.3 Interpreting Pearson *r*

- Correlation does not necessarily mean causation.

When two variables X and Y are correlated, it does not necessarily mean that one is the cause of the other. At the most there may be an association between the two variables. It may indicate that relative positions in one variable are associated with relative positions in the other variable.

We may find that a correlation between two variables is there not because of some intrinsic relationship between them but because both related to a third variable. For example, there may be a high positive correlation between parents average salary per annum and average expenditure on children's education per annum, during the last ten years. This does not mean that with increase in salary, they spend more on children's education. A correlation between these two is because both of these are highly correlated with a third variable, general inflation.

- The size of the correlation coefficient is dependent on the variability of the two distributions being correlated. When the scores on the two variables are restricted in their spread, somewhat lower correlation coefficient would be obtained than when the scores are more spread out. The correlation coefficient between height and weight of a heterogeneous population will be higher than when the population is homogeneous with respect to its height and its weight.
- Correlation coefficient should not be interpreted in terms of percentage of perfect correlation. A correlation coefficient of .60 does not indicate 60 per cent of a perfect relationship. This interpretation is erroneous because an *r* of .60 does not express a relationship that is twice as large as an *r* of .30.

The degree to which one variable can be predicted from the other is through the calculation of the coefficient of determination. Coefficient of determination is the square of the correlation coefficient. It gives the percentage of variance in one variable that is associated with the variance in the other. *For example*, if the correlation between intelligence and achievement is +.60, 36 per cent of variance in achievement is associated with variance in intelligence test scores.

- Correlation coefficient should not be interpreted in an absolute sense. It should be interpreted in the context of the nature of the two variables being correlated. A predictive validity of .60 for an aptitude test would be something wonderful than a concurrent validity of .70 with some criterion.

EXERCISES

1. Calculate mean, median, and mode of the following distribution:

CI	70-79	60-69	50-59	40-49	30-39	20-29	10-19
f	1	5	9	11	7	3	2

(**Ans.** M = 45.29, *Mdn* = 45.86, Mo = 47.00)

2. Calculate SD for the following distribution, using assumed mean method.

CI	44-47	40-43	36-39	32-35	28-31	24-27	20-23	16-19	12-15	8-11
f	1	2	25	57	7	11	3	1	2	1

(**Ans.** SD=7.22)

3. Calculate Pearson r for the following paired X and Y scores and interpret your result.

X	30	42	35	25	32
Y	35	36	38	30	20

(**Ans.** $r = .146$)

4. For a given frequency distribution when is it appropriate to use mean, median, and mode?
5. From the Table of Normal Probability Curve determine the following:
   (*a*) Percentage of scores between 1.22 and 1.45z
   (*b*) Percentage of cases between $-1z$ and 1.79z
   (*c*) Percentage of cases below 2.24z
   (*d*) Out of 500, number of cases above 1.75z

   (**Ans.** (*a*) 3.77%, (*b*) 12.20%, (*c*) 1.25%, (*d*) 20.25 cases).
6. For a group of students, the means and standard deviations of their performances in science and maths are as follows:

   Science M = 60, SD = 15

Maths M = 75, SD = 12

A student has obtained 45 marks in science and 48 marks in maths. In which subject he performs better?

(**Ans.** Science)

7. In a group of 120 students, a student ranks 8th on a maths test. On a biology test alsohis rank is 8th but out of a group of 110 students. What are his percentile ranks on the two subjects?

   (**Ans.** Maths 93.75 percentile, Bio. 93.18 percentile)

13

Inferential Statistics

13.1 WHAT IS INFERENTIAL STATISTICS?

It is the science of making reasonable decisions from a limited amount of information about a population and which has been obtained from a sample drawn from the population. The statistical procedures performed before making the decisions are called tests of significance. A basic tool of these tests is the null hypothesis.

13.2 THE NULL HYPOTHESIS

Suppose we have a class of 60 students which has been split into two groups through random assignment. The first group is taught a concept in science by method A and the same concept is taught by method B to the second group. The environments of the two groups differ only in the way (method) they are taught the science concept. At the end of the experiment we administer a test based on the concept taught. We find that the mean of the group taught by the method A is higher than those taught by method B. How shall we interpret this difference? This difference may have been caused because of superiority of the method A over the method B, or that the difference could have occurred due to chance (sampling error). We cannot positively prove that the superiority of the method A caused the difference. However, we can estimate the likelihood of chance alone being responsible for the observed difference and then determine which explanation to accept as a result of this estimate.

The chance explanation is known as the null hypothesis, which is a statement that there is no actual relationship between the variables and that any observed relationship is only a function of chance. In the above example, the null hypothesis will be that there is no relationship between teaching method and the concept learning. This statement of relationship can be stated in another way that the mean for the group taught by the method A is equal to the mean of the group taught by method B. In formula form the statement would be

$$H_0 : \mu_A = \mu_B$$

where

H_0 = null hypothesis

μ_A = mean of the group taught by method A

μ_B = mean of the group taught by method B

In interpreting the observed difference between the groups, we shall have to choose between the chance explanation (null hypothesis) and the explanation that there is a relationship between variables (research hypothesis) - without knowing the ultimate truth but in terms of probability.

13.3 TYPE I AND TYPE II ERRORS

A null hypothesis is either retained or rejected. Either decision may be right or wrong. If the null hypothesis is true, the decision to retain it is correct and of rejectingit is wrong. The rejection of a true null hypothesis is labeled as a Type I error. If the null hypothesis is false, retaining it is erroneous and rejecting it is a correct decision. The retention of a false null hypothesis is called as Type II error. The four possibilities are summarised in the Table 13.1.

Table 13.1: Type I and Type II Errors

Decision	H_0 is true	H_0 is false
Rejecting H_0	Type I error	Correct
Retaining H_0	Correct	Type II error

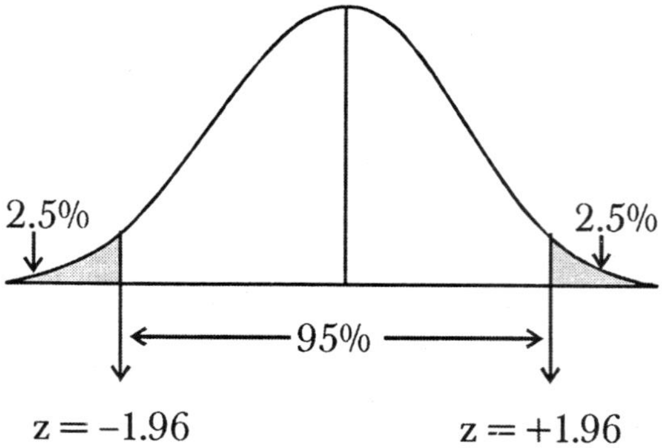

Fig. 13.1 (a): Critical region for a nondirectional two tailed test

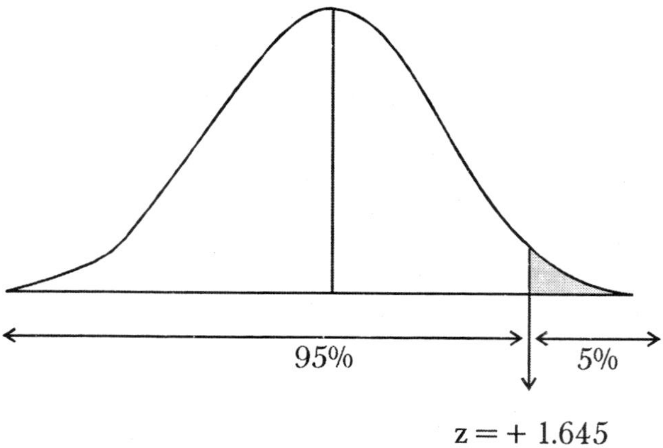

Fig. 13.1 (b): Critical region for a directional test (one tailed)

13.3.1 Type I Error

It is symbolised by the Greek small letter α. The researcher concludes that the treatment or the independent variable has an effect on the dependent variable, which in fact is not there. *For example*, the researcher may conclude that there is a relationship between teaching method and mastery of the science concept. That is, the method A is superior to the method B However, subsequent studies do not find evidence regarding the superiority of the method A.

13.3.2 Type II Error

It is symbolised by the Greek small letter β. Here, the researcher concludes that the treatment or the independent variable has no effect on the dependent variable, but on the contrary the effect is there. *For example*, the researcher may conclude that there is an insufficient evidence for concluding that the method A is better than the method B. Subsequent studies provide evidence of the superiority of the one method over the other in the mastery of the science concept.

13.3.3 Comparison between Type I and Type II Errors

Type I errors lead to changes that are not needed. Type II errors lead to maintain the existing state of affairs, though a change is needed.

The consequences of Type I error are considered to be more serious than the consequences of a Type II error. This kind of test is called non directional (two-tailed) test because we are interested in differences in either direction. In the figure 13.1(a) the region of rejection is equally divided between the two tails of the distribution. If a sample mean is observed to be sufficiently greater or sufficiently less than the hypothesised value, the null hypothesis will be rejected.

The direction of the difference is not important. If on the basis of evidence, we choose to state the direction of possible differences, then we would perform a directional test for which the critical region is located in only one of the two tails of the distribution (Fig. 13.1(b)). For the .05 level of significance, this critical region is the point equal to z=1.645. For the non directional (two-tailed) test the critical region is the point equal to z=1.96.

13.4 LEVELS OF SIGNIFICANCE

In scientific research all conclusions are statements that have a high probability of being correct. They are not the statements of absolute truth. What should be the probability level before it is declared that a relationship exists between the independent and the dependent variables? In other words, how strong the evidence must be before a null hypothesis is rejected? The predetermined level at which the null hypothesis is rejected is called the level of significance. In education and behavioural sciences the commonly used levels of significance are the .05 and the .01 levels.

The .05 level implies that the probability of getting the obtained difference by chance is less than 5 times out of hundred (p<.05). The .01 level implies that the probability of getting the obtained difference by chance is less than 1 in 100, and therefore the obtained difference is a true difference. This leads to the rejection of the null hypothesis. If the probability is greater than the predetermined level, the obtained difference is described as nonsignificant, and the null hypothesis is retained.

13.5 DIRECTIONAL AND NONDIRECTIONAL TESTS

While testing a null hypothesis, we are not usually concerned with the direction of the differences. We are interested in knowing the departure of the sample statistics from their population parameters. While comparing method A and the method B for mastering of the science concept, our purpose is to find whether treatment A is better than the treatment B or treatment B is better than the treatment A.

13.6 SIGNIFICANCE OF DIFFERENCE BETWEEN MEANS

13.6.1 Large and Independent or Uncorrelated Means

When samples have been drawn randomly from two different normally distributed populations, the samples means would also be normally distributed and independent or uncorrelated. The difference between means of the samples drawn from the two populations will also be normally distributed with a mean of zero and standard deviation also called the standard error of the difference between means equal to 1. The standard error of the difference between means is denoted by σ_{dm} and its formula is

$$\sigma_{dm} = \sqrt{\sigma^2 m_1 + \sigma^2 m_2} \quad \text{...(13.1)}$$

where

σ_{dm} = Standard error of the difference between means

$\sigma m_1 = \frac{\sigma_1}{\sqrt{n_1}}$ = Standard error of the mean of sample 1

$\sigma m_2 = \frac{\sigma_2}{\sqrt{n_2}}$ Standard error of the mean of sample 2

n_1 = number of cases in the sample 1

n_2 = number of cases in the sample 2

The means and standard deviations of two independent and large samples on a maths test are as follows:

We have to determine whether the two groups differ on maths achievement.

Measures	Group 1	Group 2
n	100	80
Mean	25	29
σ	5	4

We have to find out whether the difference between means 25 and 29 is significant. Using the formula 13.1 we find

$$\sigma_{dm} = \sqrt{\frac{(5)^2}{100} + \frac{(4)^2}{80}}$$

$$= \sqrt{.45} = .67$$

The null hypothesis would be set-up as 'there is no statistically significant difference in maths achievement scores of the two groups, except for sampling errors'. The deviation of the sampled difference in terms of standard measure would be

$$z = \frac{|M_1 - M_2|}{\sigma_{dm}} \qquad ...(13.2)$$

$$= \frac{|4|}{.67} = 5.97$$

13.6.2 When the Groups are Large and Correlated

When the subjects in the two groups being compared have been matched pair-wise on some variable relevant to the relationship between the independent and the dependent variables, or when the same group is tested twice, then the formula for the standard error of the difference between means is

$$\sigma_{dm} = \sqrt{\sigma_{m1}^2 + \sigma_{m2}^2 - 2r_{12}\sigma_{m1}\sigma_{m2}} \qquad ...(13.3)$$

where

r_{12} = the correlation between the two group on the matched variable, or the correlation between the scores of the single group, on two occasions.

13.6.3 The t Test for Independent Samples

The t-test is usually employed for small samples (N < 30) but it can be used for larger samples as well. The standard error of the difference between the means of two samples is given by the formula

$$\sigma_{dm} = \sqrt{\left(\frac{\Sigma x_1^2 + \Sigma x_2^2}{n_1 + n_2 - 2}\right)\left(\frac{1}{n_1} + \frac{1}{n_2}\right)} \quad ...(13.4)$$

where

σ_{dm} = standard error of the difference between means

n_1 = no. of cases in group1

n_2 = no of cases in group2

Σx_1^2 = sum of the squared deviation scores in group1, from their mean value

Σx_2^2 = sum of the squared deviation scores in group2, from their mean value

This is followed by dividing the observed difference between means by the difference expected by chance alone or σ_{dm}. The formula would be

$$t = \frac{|M_1 - M_2|}{\sigma_{dm}} \quad ...(13.5)$$

13.6.4 The t Distributions

It was Gossett (pen name Student) who showed that the normal curve was appropriate for assessing observation/

chance expectation ratios only when the population standard deviation $s = \sqrt{\Sigma x^2 / (N-1)}$. When s is used instead of σ, each statistical test has a unique probability distribution based on the number of subjects and the number of population estimates used, its degree of freedom.

13.6.5 Degrees of Freedom (d.f.)

The number of degrees of freedom (d.f.) is the number of observations free to vary around a constant parameter. Suppose a student is asked to name any four numbers that come to his mind. The student is free to name any four numbers he chooses to name. Therefore, he has 4 degrees of freedom. Suppose, the student is asked to name any four numbers but the mean of these four numbers should be 24. The student is free to name any three numbers but the last number should be such that it makes the total of the four numbers equal to 96 so as to get a mean of 24. If the first three numbers are 20,25 and 35 then the fourth number must be 16 so as to have a mean of 24. The student has four numbers to name and one restriction. Therefore, degrees of freedom allowed to him are 4–1=3, that is, $df = (n-1)$.

When unknown population standard deviation is estimated from the sample standard deviation $s = \sqrt{\Sigma x^2 / (N-1)}$, one df is lost. This is because the sample statistics (s) is derived from the deviations around the sample mean. The sum of these deviations must be zero. Thus, one degree of freedom is lost.

The solution of the following problem will clarify the application of the t-test.

- **Problem:** The following are the scores of two groups of students, on reasoning ability. Is the difference between the mean performances of the two groups significant at the .05 level?

Group 1			*Group 2*		
X_1	x_1	x_1^2	X_2	x_2	x_2^2
05	–2	4	10	–3	9
08	+1	1	12	–1	1
07	0	0	14	+1	1
10	+3	9	13	0	0
05	–2	4	16	+3	9
$\Sigma X_1 = 35$		$18 = \Sigma x_1^2$	$\Sigma X_2 = 65$		$20 = \Sigma x_2^2$
$M_1 = 7$			$M_2 = 13$		
$n_1 = 5$			$n_1 = 5$		

Substituting the above values in formula 13.4, we get

$$\sigma_{dm} = \sqrt{\left(\frac{18+20}{5+5-2}\right)\left(\frac{1}{5}+\frac{1}{5}\right)} = 1.14$$

Using the formula 13.5, we get

$$t = \frac{|7-13|}{1.14}$$

$$= 5.26$$

Now, we use the Appendix 1 (Table B). The first column in this table is labelled as *df.* Go downwards to 10 *df* and move right along the row to stop below the column .05. The *t* value is 2.33. The obtained t value of 5.26 exceeds this table value of 2.33 at the .05 level, for 10 *df.* The null hypothesis of no significant difference between the two groups on reasoning ability is rejected at the .05 level, for 10 *df.* The probability of obtaining the difference of 6 marks between the two groups by chance is less than .05($p < .05$). The difference between the two groups is a true difference.

13.6.4.1 The t Test for Non-Independent Samples

When the two groups have been matched pair-wise on some variable relevant to the relationship between the independent and the dependent variable, or when we have pre-test and post-tests scores of the same group, then the following formula is used to find out the *t*-value.

$$t = \frac{\overline{D}}{\sqrt{\dfrac{\Sigma D^2 - \dfrac{(\Sigma D)^2}{n}}{n(n-1)}}} \qquad \text{...(13.6)}$$

where

$t = t$ ratio

$\overline{D}$ = Mean of the difference

ΣD^2 = Difference scores squared and then summed

$(\Sigma D)^2$ = Difference scores summed and then squared

n = Number of pairs

Let us solve the following problem to understand the application of the formula 13.6.

- **Problem:** The attitude scores of a group of students towards smoking before and after a lecture on 'ill effects of smoking' are given below. Is the difference in scores significant at the (*a*) .05 level, (*b*) .01 level?

Before	15	12	18	16	12	14	10
After	12	8	12	10	12	9	12

The differences (D) between before and after scores of the 7 students are

D	3	4	6	6	0	5	–2
D^2	9	16	36	36	0	25	4

$$SD = 22; SD^2 = 126$$

$$\overline{D} = \frac{22}{7} = 3.14; (\Sigma D)^2 = 484$$

Applying the formula 13.6, we get

$$t = \frac{3.14}{\sqrt{\dfrac{126 - \dfrac{484}{7}}{7(7-1)}}}$$

$$= \frac{3.14}{\sqrt{1.35}}$$

$$= 2.706$$

From the appendix 1 (Table B), we find that for 6 *df* the table value of *t* for p=.05 is 2.45. The obtained t value of 2.70 exceeds this table value. Therefore, the null hypothesis of no significant change in attitude towards smoking is rejected at the .05 level of significance for 6 df. The Table value of t for the .01 level and 6 *df* = 3.50. The obtained value 2.706 fails to reach this value. As such the probability of the null hypothesis being true is greater than .01 (p>.01). Therefore, the null hypothesis of no significant difference between the two sets of attitude scores is retained at the .01 level for 6 *df*.

For large samples, the t values for the .05 and the .01 levels are 1.96 and 2.58 respectively. When the obtained t value is equal to or greater than these values, the null hypothesis is rejected.

A t-value which exceeds a lower level value, automatically exceeds a higher level value. There is no need to test a null hypothesis at the .05 level if the observed difference has been found to be significant at the .01 level.

Assumptions underlying the t-Test.

(a) The samples should have been taken from normally distributed populations.

(b) The samples should have been randomly selected.

(c) The data should have been obtained on interval or ratio scale.

13.7 ANALYSIS OF VARIANCE (ANOVA)

When more than two groups are to be compared, ANOVA instead of t test may be used because the *t* test can compare two groups at a time and groups comparison may become cumbersome if the number of groups is large. The rational of ANOVA is that variance of all the subjects in an experiment can be divided into two sources: Variance among groups and variance within groups.Variance among groups is taken as numerator in the F ratio following the analysis. Within groups variance is taken as error term in the denominator of the F ratio. When the numerator value is greater than the denominator value, the table for significance of F values (Table C) is consulted to determine whether the F ratio is large enough to reject the null hypothesis of no difference among the groups at the predetermined level.

Assumption underlying one-way ANOVA.

(a) The individuals in the various sub-groups should have been selected through random sampling and from normally distributed populations.

(b) The samples should be independent.

(c) The variances of the subgroups should be homogeneous.

(d) The data should have been obtained on interval or ratio scale.

Computing F ratio (One-way ANOVA)

Suppose we have three groups of students with random assignment. Their scores on an anxiety scale are as follows. We have to find out whether the groups differ on anxiety at the .05 level of significance.

Group A	Group B	Group C
10	7	12
12	12	14
15	18	22
8	20	6
5	16	11
	18	7
	10	9

Steps

1. The means of the three groups and the grand mean are:

   $M_A = 10,\ M_B = 14.43,\ M_C = 11.57,\ M_g = 12.10$

2. The sum of all the scores $\Sigma X_t = 232$
3. The sum of the squared deviation of each individual score from the grand mean is

$$SS_t = \Sigma X^2_i - \frac{(\Sigma X_t)^2}{N}$$

where

SS_t = Sum of squares total

ΣX^2_i = each score squared, then summed

$(\Sigma X_t)^2$ = all the scores summed, then squared

$$\therefore \qquad SS_t = 3366 - \frac{(232)^2}{19}$$

$$= 533.16$$

4. The sum of squares of the group means from the grand mean is

$$SS_A = \frac{(\Sigma X_1)^2}{n_1} + \frac{(\Sigma X_2)^2}{n_2} + \frac{(\Sigma X_3)^2}{n_3} - \frac{(\Sigma X)^2}{N}$$

$$= \frac{(50)^2}{5} + \frac{(101)^2}{7} + \frac{(81)^2}{7} - \frac{(232)^2}{19}$$

$$= 2894.55\text{-}2832.84$$

$$= 61.71$$

5. The sum of squares within the groups is

$$SS_w = SS_t - SS_A$$

$$= 533.16\text{-}61.71$$

$$= 471.45$$

6. Mean square among the means (MS_A)

$$= \frac{SS_A}{df_1} = \frac{61.71}{2} = 30.86$$

7. Mean squares within the groups (MS_W)

$$= \frac{SS_W}{df_2} = \frac{471.45}{16} = 29.46$$

8. The F ratio

$$= \frac{MS_A}{MS_W}$$

$$= \frac{30.86}{29.46}$$

$$= 1.047$$

The Table 13.2 summarises the results of the calculations:

Table 13.2: Summary of ANOVA of the Three Groups

(1) Source of Variance	*(2) SS*	*(3) df*	*(4) MS*	*(5) F value*
Among groups	61.71	2	30.86	1.047
Within groups	471.45	16	29.46	
Total	533.16	18		

From the Table of F values (Table C) we find that the table value of F (for $df_1 = 2$ and $df_2 = 16$) is 3.63 at the .05 level of significance. The calculated F ratio (1.047) fails to reach the F table value of 3.63 at the .05 level. Consequently, the null hypothesis of no significant difference among the groups on anxiety is retained.

GROUP COMPARISONS FOLLOWING THE F-TEST

Suppose we have found a significant F value. This implies that for the groups being compared, at least two groups significantly differ from each other. If we carry out several t-test it is more likely that some of these tests will give significant results just due to pure chance. Each test has a certain significant level indicated the probability of making type 1 error. If we carry out a number of t-test with an associated alpha then alpha becomes compounded. The probability of making a type error increases according to the formula:

$$P_{\text{Type 1 error}} = 1-(1-\alpha)^c$$

Where α = Significance level

c = Number of tests

If our alpha level is 0.05 and the number of comparisons to be made or tests be carried out is 4 then

$$P = 1-(1-.05)^4$$
$$= 1-(.95)^4$$
$$= 1-.814 = .186$$

The value .186 is high as compared to .05.

Multiple comparison can be made through Scheffe's tests.

Example: Memory retention scores of four groups of students are as follows. Do the groups differ in memory retention at the 0.05 level to significance? If yes, compare group means for differences.

A	*B*	*C*	*D*
6	8	10	7
5	7	11	6
8	9	9	8
6	5	9	5
5	6	6	6

Solution:

1. Sum of all individual scores $\Sigma X_t = 142$.
2. Group-wise total scores are 30,35,45 and 32 and means are 6,7,9 and respectively.
3. $SS_t = \Sigma X_i^2 - \dfrac{(\Sigma X_t)^2}{N}$

$$= \left(6^2+5^2+8^2+.....+8^2+5^2+6^2\right)-\frac{(142)^2}{20}$$
$$= 1055-1008.20 = 46.80$$

4. $SS_A = \dfrac{30^2}{5}+\dfrac{35^2}{5}+\dfrac{45^2}{5}+\dfrac{32^2}{5}-\dfrac{(142)^2}{20}$

$$= 1034.80-1008.20 = 26.60$$

5. $SS_W = SS_t - SS_A$
$$= 46.80 - 26.60 = 20.20$$

Table 13.2.1: Summary of ANOVA

Source	*SS*	*df*	*MS*	*F*
Among	26.60	3	8.87	7.04
Within	20.20	16	1.26	

6. The obtained F value 7.04 exceeds the critical F value 3.24 for df 3,16 at the .05 level. Therefore, the null hypothesis of no significance difference is rejected.
7. Posts hoc Test: Scheffe's test will be used the formula for which is

   Critical Difference

$$= \sqrt{(C-1)F_{.05}(3,16)} \times \sqrt{MS_W\left(\frac{1}{n_1}+\frac{1}{n_2}\right)}$$

CD for comparison of group A and B

$$= \sqrt{(4-1)(3.24)} \times \sqrt{1.26\left(\frac{1}{5}+\frac{1}{5}\right)}$$
$$= (3.117)(.709) = 2.21$$

As the size of all the groups is the same n = 5, therefore same value of CD = 2.21 for the remaining comparisons A and C, A and D, B and C, and C and D will be obtained.

Table 13.2.2: Post hoc comparisons using Scheffe's Test

Comparison	*Difference between Means*	*CD value at .05 value*
A and B	1	2.21
A and C	3	2.21

A and D	0.4	2.21
B and C	2	2.21
B and D	0.6	2.21
C and D	2.6	2.21

Mean difference between group A and group C is higher than the critical difference value at the .05 level. This difference is significant. Similarly mean difference between group C and group D is significant at the .05 level. All other differences are not significant.

In the above example since there are four groups the number of comparisons will be $K(K-1)/2 = 4 \times 3/2 = 6$.

13.8 MULTIFACTOR ANOVA

Suppose an independent variable X has an influence on the dependent variable Y. However, under varying conditions, X may not affect Y, in a consistent or same manner. *For example*, 'self-study' works well with high achieving students but not with low achieving students. That is, the method of study does not have the same effect on students performance when achievement is taken into consideration. We say that there is an interaction between the independent variable *X* (method of study) and the independent variable achievement (*Z*) on the dependent variable *Y*, which is classroom performance.

The layout of an experiment investigating the combined effects of two or more independent variables on the dependent variable is called a factorial design and the data are analysed through multifactor analysis of variance.

Suppose we have two groups of students high achieving and low achieving groups. Each group is further subdivided into two subgroups through random assignment of subjects. One subgroup of the each group studies through 'self-study'.

The other subgroup of the each group studies through 'assisted-study'. The total sample consists of (N= 20) subjects with 5 each in the 4 subgroups in the table as follows. The subject matter of the study is the unit on 'Our Environment' in the science textbook After the groups have studied the unit for one week, they are administered a class test on Our Environment.

The application of the multifactor (2 × 2) analysis of variance will reveal the following:

(1) Whether high achieving and low achieving groups differ on performance, irrespective of the method of study.

(2) Whether self-study group and the assisted study group, irrespective of achievement, differ on performance and

(3) Whether there is an interaction effect between the method of study and achievement level, on performance, that is, method of study has different effects at different levels of achievement.

The effects studied by the first and the second analysis are called the main effects and the third one is called the interaction effect.

Table 13.3: Performance Scores of High and Low Achieving Groups after Self-Study and Assisted Study

	High		*Low*	
	20		13	
	15	Group 1	10	Group 3
SS	18	M_1=17	12	M_3=11
	16		10	
	16		10	
	$\Sigma X_1 = 85$		$\Sigma X_3 = 55$	$\Sigma X_{r1} = 140; M_{r1} = 14$

Method of Study				
	20		18	
	16	Group 2	20	Group 4
AS	19	M_2=18	17	M_4=17
	17		15	
	18		15	
	$\Sigma X_2 = 90$		$\Sigma X_4 = 85$	$\Sigma X_{r_2} = 175$; $M_{r2} = 17.5$
	$\Sigma X_{c1} = 175$		$\Sigma X_{c_2} = 140$	
	$M_{c1} = 17.5$		$M_{c2} = 14.0$	

Steps:

1. Sum of Squares Total

$$(SS_t) = \Sigma X_i^2 - \frac{(\Sigma X_t)^2}{N}$$

$$= (20)^2 + (15)^2 + \cdots + (15)^2 + (15)^2 - \frac{(315)^2}{20}$$

$$= 5187 - 4961.25 = 225.75$$

2. Sum of Squares Between

$$(SS_t) = \frac{(\Sigma X_1)^2}{n_1} + \frac{(\Sigma X_2)^2}{n_2} + \cdots - \frac{(\Sigma X)^2}{N}$$

$$= \frac{(85)^2}{5} + \frac{(90)^2}{5} - \frac{(315)^2}{20}$$

$$= 5115 - 4961.25 = 153.75$$

3. Sum of Squares within

$$(SS_w) = SS_t - SS_w$$

$$= 225.75 - 153.75 = 72$$

4. Sum of Squares between Rows

$$(SS_{br}) = \frac{(140)^2}{10} + \frac{(175)^2}{10} - 4961.5$$
$$= 60.75$$

5. Sum of Squares between Columns

$$(SS_{bc}) = \frac{(175)^2}{10} + \frac{(140)^2}{10} - 4961.5$$
$$= 60.75$$

6. Sum of Squares Interaction $C \times R =$

$$SS_{int} = SS_b - (SS_{br} + SS_c)$$
$$= 153.75 - (60.75+60.75)$$
$$= 32.25$$

7. *df* for each source:

   df for between rows sum of squares $(R - 1) = 1$

   df for between columns sum of squares $(C - 1) = 1$

   df for interaction $(R - 1)(C - 1) = 1$

   df for between groups sum of squares $(G - 1) = 3$

   df for within groups sum of squares $(N - G) = 16$

   df for the total sum of squares $(N - 1) = 19$

where

R = the number of rows

C = the number of columns

G = the number of groups

N = the number of subjects in all the groups

The results obtained are presented in the table 13.

Table 13.4: Summary of 2 × 2 Multifactor ANOVA

Source of Variance	*SS*	*df*	*MS*	*F*	*Significance Level*
Between rows (method of study)	60.75	1	60.75	13.5	.01
Between columns (achievement level)	60.75	1	60.75	13.5	.01
Rows by columns (interaction)	32.25	1	32.25	7.17	.05
Between groups	153.75	3	51.25		
Within groups	72.00	16	4.5		
Total	225.75	19			

Entering the table of F values (Table C), we find that F ratios of 4.54 and 8.53 are needed to be significant at the .05 and .01 levels respectively, for *df*= 1,16.

For the between rows (method of study), our obtained F ratio 13.50 is greater than the table value of 8.53, we reject the null hypothesis of no significant difference in performance of self-study and assisted study groups. The mean performance score of subjects in the group 1 and 3 is Mr_1 = 14. That of the groups 2 and 4, it is Mr_2 = 17.5 It is concluded that better performance can be expected of students who are put through assisted than the students who self-study.

The F ratio between the column means is significant at the .01 level. It may be inferred that irrespective of the method of study, better performance can be expected of high achieving students than the low achieving students.

The third F ratio 7.17 shows the interaction effect of achievement level and method of study on performance.

Among the high achieving groups 1 and 2, the mean difference in performance is 1 point (17-18). For the low achieving groups 3 and 4, this difference is 6 points (11-17). Since the F ratio 7.17 is significant at the .05 level, we conclude that assisted-study is superior for low achieving students than for the high achieving students.

The significant interaction between the method of study and achievement is shown in the Fig. 13.2.

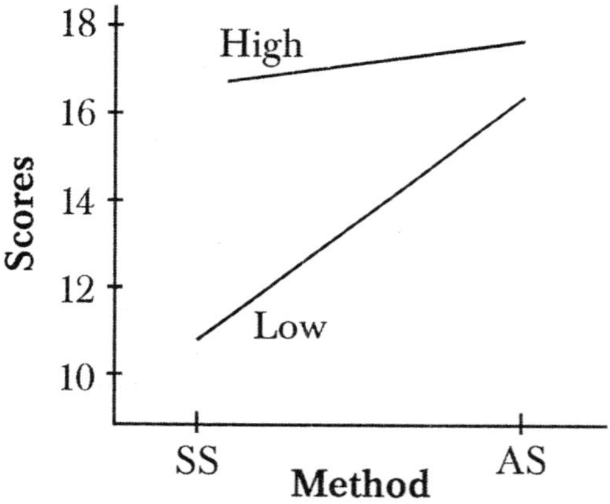

Fig. 13.2: Interaction between method and achievement

Multifactor analysis of variance can be extended to more than two independent variables and their more than two levels. *For example*, if we have to study the main effects on three independent variables with two levels of each, on a dependent variable, then we shall make use of a $2 \times 2 \times 2$ factorial design and 3 way analysis of variance. Not only would we be able to study simultaneously the effects of the different levels of each independent variable but also their combined effects by taking two variables at a time and then all the three variables together, thereby studying the double interactions $a \times b$, $b \times c$, $c \times a$ and the triple interaction $a \times b \times c$. Usually, more than four independent variables are rarely used in factorial designs because calculations become cumbersome. Also, it becomes difficult to explain significant interactions.

13.9 THE CHI-SQUARE TEST OF SIGNIFICANCE

For data obtained on nominal scale, the most widely use test of significance is the chi-square test. It compares the observed and the expected frequencies of an event. Observed frequencies are the actual frequencies which have been observed. Expected frequencies are theoretical frequencies that would be observed when the null hypothesis is true. The chi-square formula is as follows:

$$\chi^2 = \Sigma\frac{(fo - fe)^2}{fe} \qquad ...(13.7)$$

where

fo = Frequency of occurrence of the observed event

fe = Expected frequency of occurrence on some hypothesis

The close the observed and the expected frequencies, the smaller the value of chi square and therefore closer the agreement between the observed data and the hypothesis being tested. If the value of chi-square is larger, the greater the probability of a real difference between the observed and the expected results. The significance of chi-square is tested from the table of χ^2 (Table D) by comparing the obtained and the table value for a given probability level and the *df*

13.9.1 One-Variable Chi-Square Test

Suppose 50 male teachers have been asked to express their attitude towards compulsory military training. Thirty teachers respond favourably, 12 respond unfavourably and

8 are neutral. We have to find whether or not the difference in responses is a true difference or just a chance difference.

Table 13.5 Response Count of Male Teacher Towards Compulsory Military Training

	Favourable	*Unfavourable*	*Neutral*	
fo	30	12	8	50
fe	16.67	16.67	16.66	50
$fo - fe$	13.33	4.67	8.66	
$(fo - fe)^2$	177.69	21.81	74.99	
$\frac{(fo - fe)^2}{fe}$	10.569	1.308	4.50	

$$\chi^2 = \Sigma\frac{(fo - fe)^2}{fe} = 16.47$$

The observed responses (fo) and the expected responses (fe) are given in the rows 1 and 2 respectively of the table 13.5. Below the table are given the differences $(fo - fe)$. Each difference is squared and then divided by its fe to give $\chi^2 = 16.47$. Of the observed frequencies, there is only one row and three columns. The *df* are (C – 1) = (3 – 1) = 2.

Entering the table D of Chi Square (Appendix 1) we find that the table value for the null hypothesis to be true is 9.210 ($df = 2$, $p = .01$). But our obtained value is 16.47, which far exceeds the table value. The null hypothesis of no significant difference in the attitudes of male teachers toward compulsory military training is rejected at the .01 level of significance.

13.9.2 The Two-Variable Chi-Square Test of Independence

This method uses more than one variable with different levels of each variable. The purpose is to see whether or not the two variables are independent of each other. *For example,* in the previous problem, we include female teachers also. Thus for teachers we have two levels – male and female, and for attitude three levels favourable, unfavourable and neutral. For a sample of 40 female teachers, 60 per cent favour compulsory military training, 35 per cent are against it and 5 per cent neutral. Their frequency counts are shown in the table.

Table 13.6: Response Counts of Male and Female Teachers

	Favourable	*Unfavourable*	*Neutral*	*Total*
Male	30(30)	12(14.44)	8(5.56)	50
Female	24(24)	14(11.56)	2(4.44)	40
Total	54	26	10	90

We can calculate expected frequencies for the observed frequencies in the above table. Multiply each total sum for a row with the total column sum for the observed frequencies and divide this product with the grand sum of frequencies (N = 90). *For example,* the expected frequency for the first entry 30 in row 1 will be (54 × 50)/90 = 30, which has been shown in parenthesis beside *fo* = 30. The other expected frequencies have been similarly worked out and reported in parenthesis beside each *fo*.

Applying the formula (13.7) we get

$$\chi^2 = \frac{(30-30)^2}{30} + \frac{(12-14.44)^2}{14.44} + \frac{(8-5.56)^2}{5.56}$$

$$+ \frac{(24-24)^2}{5.56} + \frac{(2-4.44)^2}{4.4}$$

$$= 0 + .412 + 1.070 + 0 + .515 + 1.353$$

$$= 3.350, df = (r-1)(c-1) = (2-1)(3-1) = 2$$

The table value of χ^2 for significance level .05 is 5.991. The obtained value of 3.350 falls short of the table value. Null hypothesis of no difference in the attitudes of the male and female teachers is retained.

13.9.3 The Chi-Square test when entries are Small

The chi-square is not stable when any of the observed or experimental frequencies is less than 5, and especially when the table is (2×2) fold ($df = 1$). Chi Square is subject to considerable error for which correction for continuity (Yates' correction) is applied. The correction value .5 is subtracted from $(f_0 - f_e)$ that is,

$$\chi^2 = \Sigma \frac{(fo - fe - .5)^2}{fe} \qquad ...(13.8)$$

13.9.4 Assumptions of Chi-Square

For making valid interpretations from the results obtained through chi-square, the following assumptions should be fulfilled.

- The observations are measured as frequencies
- Each observation can appear in one and only one of the categories in the table, that is, categories must be mutually exclusive.

13.10 THE SIGNIFICANCE OF DIFFERENCE BETWEEN TWO *rs*

Suppose the correlation coefficient between science and maths achievement for class X students is .60. For another section of the same class, this correlation coefficient is .75.

There are 50 and 40 students respectively in these sections. We have to find out whether or not these correlations differ significantly from each other.

For determining the standard error of the difference between the two correlation coefficients, we need to convert each r into Fisher's *z* function, the formula for which is

$$\sigma d_Z = \sigma_{Z1-Z2} = \sqrt{\frac{1}{(N_1-3)}+\frac{1}{(N_2-3)}} \qquad ...(13.9)$$

Applying this formula to the data in the above problem we get

$$\sigma d_Z = \sigma_{Z1-Z2} = \sqrt{\frac{1}{(50-3)}+\frac{1}{(40-3)}}$$

$$= .932$$

From the table of conversion of a Pearson r into a corresponding Fisher's *z* coefficient (Table E) we find that the corresponding Fisher's z correlation coefficient values for Pearson rs of .60 and .75 are .69 and .97 respectively. Dividing .97-.69=.28 by .932 we get a *z* value of .30, which is well below the *z* value of 1.96 for significance at the .05 level. Consequently, the null hypothesis of no significant difference in correlation coefficients between science and maths achievement for the two sections is retained, at the .05 level.

EXERCISES

1. For samples of boys and girls, the data are as follows. Is the difference between the two sample means significant at the .05 level?

	Boys	Girls	
N	60	50	
M	30	32	
SD	5	6	(**Ans.**1.87, NS)

2. The scores of two groups of students on maths are as follows. Do the groups differ on maths achievement?

Group I	10	15	6	8	10	11	
Group II	12	13	10	5	4	9	10

(**Ans.** .56, NS)

3. For a group of students the scores on a test under non stress and stress conditions are as follows. Is the difference in test performance under the two conditions significant at the .05 level, and .01 level?

Non Stress Condition	10	12	14	15	14
Stress Condition	11	11	10	10	8

(**Ans.** $t = 2.31$, $p < .05$, $p > .01$)

4. Calculate F ratio for the data given in exercise 2.

(**Ans.** F=.31)

5. Forty-five B.Ed. students have been classified as good, average and poor on skill in teaching as follows. Does this distribution differ significantly from equal probability hypothesis?

Good	Average	Poor
10	30	5

(**Ans.** = 23.34, $p < .01$)

6. Correlation coefficients(r) between social studies and language achievement for two groups of students are as follows. Do the groups differ on correlation coefficients between social studies and language?

	Group I	Group II
N	200	250
r	.40	.50

(**Ans.** $z = 1.37$ $p > .05$)

14

Additional Statistical Methods

14.1 THE MEAN OF COMBINED SAMPLES

Suppose we have three samples of class X boys whose mean heights and sample sizes are as follows. We have to find combined or weighted mean of all the three samples.

Sample	Mean	N
I	663	20
II	653	40
III	673	90

The formula for the combined or weighted mean is

$$M_{comb} = \frac{M_1N_1 + M_1M_2 + \cdots + M_nN_n}{N_1 + N_2 + \cdots + N_n} \qquad ...(14.1)$$

Applying the above formula for the three samples, we get

$$M_{comb} = \frac{66 \times 20 + 65 \times 40 + 67 \times 90}{20 + 40 + 90}$$
$$= 66.33 \text{ inches}$$

14.2 AVERAGE OR MEAN DEVIATION

The average deviation of the ungrouped scores given in a series is determined by the following formula.

$$AD = \Sigma \frac{|x|}{N} \qquad \text{...(14.2)}$$

where Σ = the sum of

x = X − M, that is, deviation of each score from the group mean

$| \; |$ = ignoring the signs

N = number of scores

Suppose we have the following scores:

5, 8, 10, 11, 16

The mean of the above scores is 10. The deviations of the scores from their mean score are

−5, −2, 0, +1, +6

Applying the formula (14.2), we get

$$AD = \Sigma \frac{|x|}{N}$$

$$= \frac{14}{5} = 2.80$$

When the scores are in the form of a grouped frequency distribution, the formula for *AD* is

$$AD = \Sigma \frac{|fx|}{N} \qquad \text{...(14.2.1)}$$

Suppose we have the following grouped frequency distribution:

(1) *Scores*	*(2)* *f*	*(3)* *X*	*(4)* $\lvert x \rvert$	*(5)* *fx*
38-43	3	40.5	7.85	23.55
32-37	5	34.5	1.85	9.25

26-31	3	28.5	4.15	12.45
20-25	2	22.5	10.15	20.30
	N = 13			65.55 = $\Sigma|fx|$

The mid points or typical scores representing each interval are given in column 3. The mean of the frequency distribution is $M = \frac{|fx|}{N} = 32.65$.

The deviations of X scores from their mean scores are given in column 4.

Each deviation has been multiplied with its frequency in column 5 and the sum of all these is = 65.55.

Applying the formula (14.2.1) we get

$$AD = \frac{65.55}{13} = 5.04$$

The criticism of *AD* is that we arbitrarily ignore the deviations signs.

14.3 THE QUARTILE DEVIATION

The quartile deviation (Q) is one-half the scale distance between the 75th and 25th percentiles in a frequency distribution. The 75th percentile (Q_3) is the third quartile below which 75 per cent of the cases lie or fall. The 25th percentile (Q_1) is the first quartile on the score scale below which 25 per cent of the scores in the frequency distribution lie or fall. The quartile deviation of a frequency distribution is given by the formula

$$Q = \frac{Q_3 - Q_1}{2} \qquad ...(14.3)$$

For working out Q we shall have to obtain Q_3 and Q_1 values of the frequency distribution. Q_3 and Q_1 are worked out the same way as median is worked out which is the 50th percentile. The formulas for Q_1 and Q_3 are

$$Q_1 = l + \left(\frac{N/4 - cf_1}{fq}\right)i \qquad ...(14.3.1)$$

$$Q_3 = l + \left(\frac{3N/4 - cf_1}{fq}\right)i \qquad ...(14.3.2).$$

where l = lower limit of the interval in which the quartile falls

i = length or size of the interval

$cumf_1$ = cumulative frequency upto the interval which contains the quartile

fq = frequency of the interval containing quartile.

Suppose we have the following distribution whose Q is to be calculated:

Scores	*f*
70-79	5
60-69	6
50-59	8
40-49	10
30-39	4
30-29	3
	N = 36

Calculation of 25th percentile (Q_1):

25 % of N = 36 is = 9

l (Lower limit of the in which Q_1 lies) = 39.5

$cumf_1$ (Cumulative frequencies up to the interval in which Q_1 lies) =7

fq (Frequency of the interval in which Q_1 lies) = 10

(Length or size of the class interval) = 10

Applying the formula (14.3.1), we get

Calculation of 75th percentile (Q_3): 75% of N=36 is = 27

l (Lower limit of the interval in which lies) = 59.5

cf_1 (Cumulative frequencies up to the interval in which 3 lies) = 25

fq (Frequency of the interval in which lies) = 6

i (Length or size of the class interval) = 10

Applying the formula (14.3.2) we get

$$Q_3 = 59.5 + \left(\frac{27-25}{6}\right)10$$

$$= 62.83$$

Applying the formula (14.3) we get

$$Q = \frac{Q_3 - Q_1}{2}$$

$$= \frac{62.83 - 41.50}{2}$$

$$= 10.67$$

14.4 THE STANDARD DEVIATION OF COMBINED DISTRIBUTIONS

When two or more distributions of scores are combined into one lot, it is possible to calculate the standard deviation of the total distribution from the standard deviations of the individual distributions.

Suppose we have data for two groups of students as follows:

	Mean	SD	N
Group I	60	10	40
Group II	65	12	60

First, we shall find out the combined mean for the two groups which is

$$M_{comb} = \frac{60 \times 40 + 65 \times 60}{100} = 63$$

The formula for finding combined standard deviation is

$$SD_{comb} = \sqrt{\frac{N_1\left(s_1^2 + d_1^2\right) + N_2\left(s_2^2 + d_2^2\right)}{N_1 + N_2}} \quad ..(14.4)$$

where = standard deviation of the first group

= standard deviation of the second group

$$d_1 = \left(M_1 - M_{comb}\right)$$

$$d_2 = \left(M_2 - M_{comb}\right)$$

Applying the formula (14.4), we get

$$SD_{comb} = \sqrt{\frac{40(100-9)+60(144-4)}{100}}$$

$$= \sqrt{\frac{40(91)+60(140)}{100}}$$

$$= 10.96$$

14.5 COEFFICIENT OF VARIATION

Coefficient of variation is used to compare variability when means of groups being compared are unequal, or where the units of measurement of the groups being compared are different. Also known as the coefficient of relative variability, the coefficient of variation is

$$V = \frac{100s}{M} \qquad ...(14.5)$$

V gives the percentage which standard deviation is of the mean. Thus, it is a ratio which is independent of the units of measurement. It is appropriate to use V when the scale of measurement is ratio. A ratio scale has equal units and there is a true zero as reference points. *For example*, physical scales for measurement of height, weight and time.

Suppose we have a group of 10 year old boys whose height and weight measures are as follows and we have to find on which measure they are relatively more variable.

	Mean	SD
Height	48"	3"
Weight	45 Kg	3 Kg

Relative variability for the two measures as per formula (14.5)

$$V_{Ht} = \frac{100 \times 3}{48} = 6.25$$

$$V_{Wt} = \frac{100 \times 3}{45} = 6.67$$

The boys are slightly more variable on weight as compared to height.

Let us take another situation. Suppose we have the mean scores for two groups on a reasoning test, as follows:

Group	Mean	SD
I	50	6
II	100	11

The V values for the two groups are 12 and 11 respectively. These are almost similar, but in terms of the second group is almost the twice of the first group.

14.6 MEASURING DIVERGENCE FROM NORMALITY

For a normal curve its mean, median and mode coincide. There is a perfect balance between the left and the right halves of the figure of the normal curve.

A distribution of scores is "skewed" when the mean and median fall at different points in the distribution. A distribution is skewed negatively or to the left when a large number of scores lie at the right end of the curve and fewer are spread out gradually toward the lower end (Fig. 14.1).

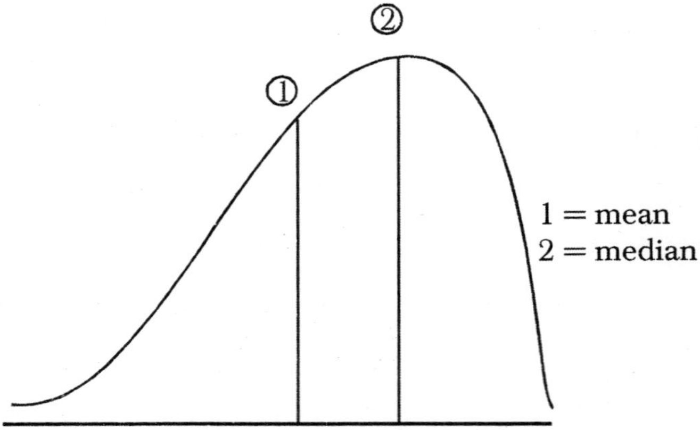

Fig. 14.1: Negative Skewness

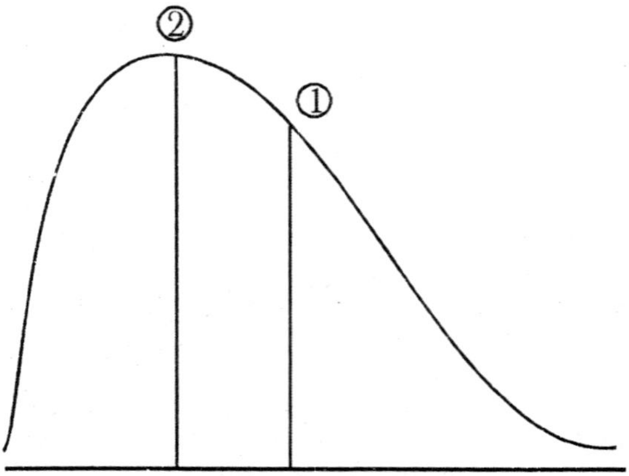

Fig. 14.2: Positive Skewness

A positively skewed distribution has scores massed at the left end of the curve and spread out gradually toward the right or upper end of the curve. For a skewed distribution, the mean is pulled more towards the skewed end than the median. The larger the gap between the mean and median, the greater the skewness.

Skewness of a distribution is calculated by the formula

$$SK = 3\frac{(mean - median)}{\sigma} \qquad ...(14.6)$$

Another formula for determining skewness is in terms of percentiles

$$SK = 3\left(\frac{P_{90} + P_{10}}{2}\right) - P_{50} \qquad ...(14.6.1)$$

Different results would be obtained through the application of formulas (14.6) and (14.6.1). However, both would agree with reference to the direction of skewness.

- **Kurtosis:** Kurtosis refers to the "flatness" or "peakedness" of a distribution as compared to a normal distribution. If a frequency distribution is more peaked than the normal, it is said to be leptokurtic. If it is flatter than the normal, it is platykurtic. A normal curve is a mesokurtic curve. A formula for measuring Kurtosis is

$$K_u = \frac{Q}{(P_{90} - P_{10})} \qquad ...(14.7)$$

For a normal distribution, *Ku* = .263. If *Ku* is larger than .263, it implies the distribution is platykurtic; if less than .263, it is leptokurtic.

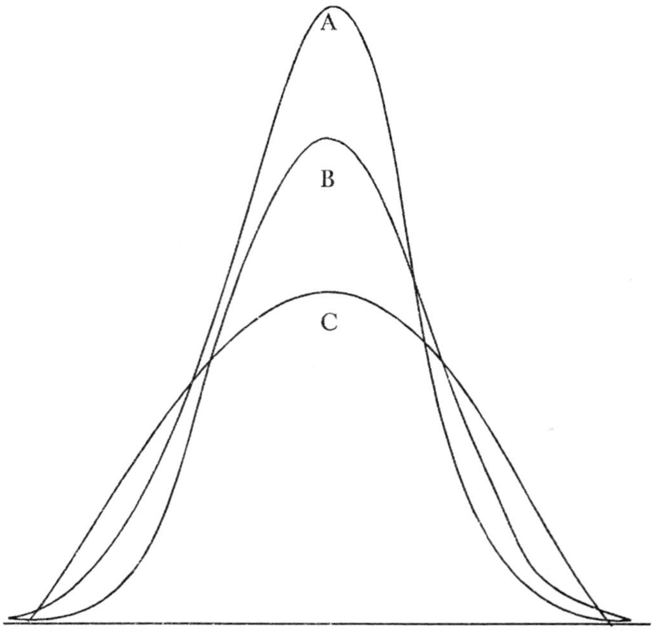

Fig. 14.3: (A) Leptokurtic, (B) Mesokurtic, (C) Platykurtic

14.7 SIGNIFICANCE OF MEAN

Usually it is not possible to measure all the members of a population. Since the samples will differ from one another, the means and standard deviations of such samples will differ from the population values or parameters. Some samples would have larger means and standard deviations, others would have smaller means and standard deviations than the population mean and standard deviation. Usually, we have a sample from the population. We wish to determine how well we can infer or estimate the population mean from the sample mean. After having calculated a statistic from the sample, *for example*, mean we ask "How good is this sample mean as an estimate of the population mean?"

We have already studied that for a given random sample, the representativeness of its mean depends on the number of cases sampled and the variability of these cases around their mean value on a measure. In a formula form, it becomes

standard error of mean $SE_m = \frac{\sigma}{\sqrt{N}}$ ...(14.8)

where σ = the standard deviation of the population mean (which is unknown)

N = number of cases in the sample.

Since the value of a sample statistic is lower than its population parameter, we apply correction to the sample standard deviation, when the number of cases in the sample is less than 30 ($N < 30$), as a matter of convention. The standard deviation of a sample ($N < 30$) is calculated by the formula

$$S = \sqrt{\frac{\Sigma x^2}{N-1}} \text{ instead of the formula } S = \sqrt{\frac{\Sigma x^2}{N}}$$

Standard Error of Mean (SE_m) may be taken as the standard deviation of a distribution of sample means. It measures the degree to which the mean (M) is affected by (1) errors of sampling, and (2) errors of measurement (error variance).

Suppose we have a population of 4000 class V students from which a sample of 400 students has been administered a maths achievement test. The mean score of the sample is 30 with a standard deviation of 5. We have to find out how good an estimate of the population mean the sample mean is. Applying the formula (14.8), we get

$$SE_m = \frac{5}{\sqrt{400}} = .25$$

The $SEm = .25$ can be thought of as the standard deviation of a distribution of sample means around the population mean (which we do not know). The sampling distribution of the sample means would be a normal curve, with population mean at the centre and standard deviation = .25. For a normal curve 68.26% cases lie between $\pm$ 1*SEm*, 95% lie between $\pm$2*SEm* (1.96 *SEm* to be more precise) and 99.73% between $\pm$ 3*SEm* (precisely 2.58 *SEm*).

Another approach for estimating M_{pop} is through setting-up of confidence intervals within which to expect population mean to lie. For a sampling distribution of means, $M_{pop} \pm 1.96SE_m$ provides the limits within which to expect 95% of the sample means to lie. $M_{pop} \pm 2.58SE_m$ provides the limits within which 99.73% of the sample means are expected to lie. We do not know the M_{pop}. We can infer about it as any one of a range of values of which M = 30 (the above example) is one of the values. Suppose we take $\pm$ $1.96SE_m$ as our working range. If our M = 30 falls at the upper limit of the sampling distribution, then $M_{pop} = M - 1.96SE_m$. If M=30 falls at the lower limit of the sampling distribution, then $M_{pop} = M - 1.96SE_m$. In a normal distribution, $\pm 1.96SE_m$ includes 95% of the cases and the limits $\pm$ $1.96SE_m$ may be said to define the 95% confidence interval. Therefore, we may say that 95 times out of 100, the M_{pop} will be within the confidence interval $M \pm 1.96SE_m = 30 \pm 1.96SE_m = 30 \pm 1.96(.25) =$ 29.51 to 30.49; and 99 times out of 100 the M_{pop} will lie between $M \pm 2.58SE_m = 30 \pm 2.58(.25)$ = 29.235 to 30.65. In other words, there are only 5 chances out of 100 for the M_{pop} to lie outside 29.51 to 30.49 and 1 chance out of 100 for the M_{pop} to lie below 29.35 and above 30.65.

- **Problem:** For a sample of 10 class V students, the scores on a reasoning test are as follows. Determine the .95 and .99 confidence intervals for the population mean

X = 10 12 8 12 7 10 11 13 14 13

- **Solution:** The mean of the above distribution is M

$$= \frac{\Sigma X}{N} = \frac{110}{10} = 11$$

The deviations of individual scores from the mean value are

$x = -1 \quad +1 \quad -3 \quad +1 \quad -4 \quad -1 \quad 0 \quad +2 \quad +3 \quad +2$

$x^2 = 1 \quad 1 \quad 9 \quad 1 \quad 16 \quad 1 \quad 0 \quad 4 \quad 9 \quad 4$

$$SD = \sqrt{\frac{\Sigma x^2}{N-1}} = \sqrt{\frac{46}{9}} = 2.26$$

$$SE_m = \frac{\sigma}{\sqrt{N}} = \frac{2.26}{\sqrt{10}} = .72$$

Since we have to use small sampling statistics and $df = (N-1) = 9$ the t values at the .05 and .01 levels, for $9df$ are 2.26 and 3.25 respectively (Table B).

.95 confidence interval for $M_{pop} = M \pm 2.226 SE_m$

$$= 11 \pm 2.26\ (.72)$$
$$= 9.37 \text{ to } 12.63$$

.99 confidence interval for $M_{pop} = M \pm 3.25 SE_m$

$$= 11 \pm 3.25\ (72)$$
$$= 8.66 \text{ to } 13.34$$

The probability p is .95 that the population mean is neither less than 9.37 nor more than 12.63. If a large number of similar samples are taken, we should be right 95% of the time and wrong 5%, for the M_{pop} to be within this range.

The probability p is .99 that the population mean will not be less than 8.66 or exceed 13.34.

14.8 FURTHER METHODS OF CORRELATION

14.8.1 Correlation from Ranks

There are situations when we do not have scores but the differences among individuals have been expressed in terms of ranks on some attribute. *For example,* 7 students have been ranked on their handwriting by two teachers as follows. In such a situation we calculate correlation coefficient ρ(rho) by the Spearman's Rank Difference Method, the formula for which is

$$\rho = 1 - \frac{6\Sigma D^2}{N\left(N^2 - 1\right)} \qquad ...(14.9)$$

where ρ = rank difference correlation coefficient

ΣD^2 = sum of the squares of differences in ranks

N = number of pairs

(1) *Students*	*(2)* *Teacher* *X*	*(3)* *Teacher* *Y*	*(4)* *D*	*(5)* *D²*
A	3	1	2	4
B	2	4	–2	4
C	7	7	0	0
D	1	2	–1	1
E	6	5	+1	1
F	5	3	+2	4
G	4	6	–2	4
				$\Sigma D^2 = 18$

Applying the formula 14.9, we get

$$\rho = 1 - \frac{6\Sigma D^2}{N\left(N^2 - 1\right)}$$

$$= 1 - \frac{6(18)}{7(48)}$$

$$= 1 - .32 = .68$$

14.8.1.1 Correlation Coefficient for Tied Ranks

Suppose we have scores on science and maths for a group of 10 students. We have to find correlation coefficient between the two performance using rank difference method.

(1) Science	*(2)* Maths	*(3)* R_1	*(4)* R_2	*(5)* $R_1 - R_2 = D$	*(6)* D^2
20	24	2	1	1.00	1.00
15	12	8.5	9	-0.50	0.25
18	14	3.5	6.5	-3.00	9.00
15	14	8.5	6.5	2.00	4.00
16	15	6	4.5	1.50	2.25
18	18	3.5	3	0.50	0.25
17	15	5	4.5	0.50	0.25
15	12	8.5	9	-0.50	0.25
22	20	1	2	-1.00	1.00
15	12	8.5	9	-0.50	0.25
					$\Sigma D^2 = 18.5$

In the column 1, the highest score in science is 22 which is ranked 1, followed by 20 which gets the rank 2. Both the ranks are written under column 3 in the same rows as of the scores 22 and 20. The next highest score 18 occurs twice, therefore the ranks 3 and 4 are equally divided as 3.5 between the scores 18. The next scores of 17 and 16 get the ranks 5 and 6 respectively. The next score of 15 occurs four times. Therefore, ranks 7, 8, 9 and 10 are equally divided as (7+8+9+10)/4=8.5 among the four scores each of value 15.

Ranks are assigned to the maths scores (column 2) and are shown under column 4. The differences between the ranks of the paired scores (column 1 and 2) are shown under column 5 which have been squared under column 6 to obtain $\Sigma D^2 = 18.50$.

Applying the formula (14.9) we get

$$\rho = 1 - \frac{6(18.50)}{10(100-1)}$$

$$= 1 - .11 = .89$$

Whenever N is less than 25, it is better to rank order the scores and calculate Spearman rho instead of r which is cumbersome.

14.8.2 Biserial *r* and Point-Biserial *r*

There are situations when a group is measured on one variable but simply classified into two categories. *For example*, a group of students has been measured on an academic achievement test. On the second variable level of motivation, it has been split into two categories 'high motivation' and 'low motivation' group. When the split has been imposed artificially on a normally distributed variable, then the biserial r is calculated. When one of the variables has been split into a genuine dichotomy, for example, male-female, adult-child, urban-rural and living-dead, then point biserial is calculated.

Biserial and point biserial correlation coefficients are helpful in item analysis during test construction. The formula for the biserial correlation coefficient is

$$r_{bis} = \frac{M_p - M_q}{\sigma} \times \frac{pq}{u} \qquad ...(14.10)$$

where M_p = mean of the Ist group on the dichotomised variable

M_q = mean of the 2nd group on the dichotomised variable

s = standard deviation of all the scores

p = proportion of individuals in the Ist group

q = $(1-p)$ or proportion of individuals in the 2nd group

u = height of the normal curve ordinate dividing p and q.

Another formula for calculating biserial r is

$$r_{bis} = \frac{M_p - M_t}{\sigma} \times \frac{p}{u} \qquad ...(14.10.1)$$

where M_t = mean of the entire group

Suppose we have achievement scores of a group of students who have been classified as 'high motivation group' and 'low motivation group'. We have to find out correlation coefficient between their achievement and motivation.

Scores	*High Motivation Group*	*Low Motivation Group*	*Total*
70-79	5	1	6
60-69	6	2	8
50-59	5	6	11
40-49	4	8	12
30-39	1	4	5
20-29	1	9	10
	$N_1 = 22$	$N_2 = 30$	$N_1 = 52$

Steps:

1. Calculate mean and standard deviation for the total distribution which are and respectively.
2. Calculate the means of the two groups which $M_p = 57.68$ and $M_q = 41.50$ respectively.
3. There are 22 cases or 42.31% of the total sample in the high motivation group and 30 cases or 57.69% of the total sample in the low motivation group. Assuming a normal distribution of motivation on what a split has been imposed at the point 7.69% above the mean, this can be figured as follows:

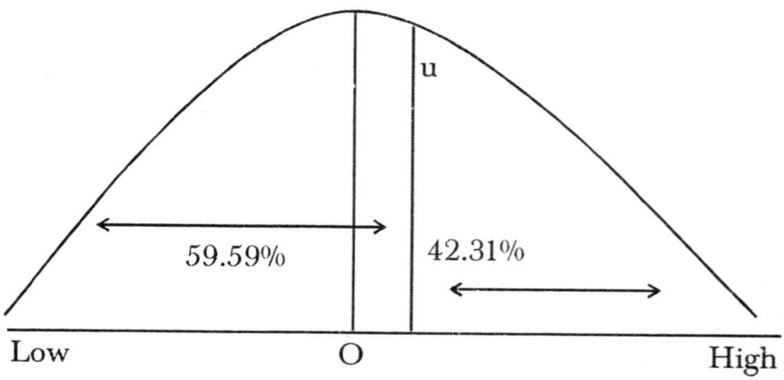

Fig. 14.4: Height of the Ordinate

The height of the ordinate of the normal curve (u) at the division point of the low and high groups may be found from the table of ordinates for given areas measured from the mean of a normal distribution (Table F). The table value of the division point 7.69% or .076 from the mean value O is u=.392.

Substituting the above values in the formula (14.10) we get

$$r_{bis} = \frac{57.68 - 41.50}{16.10} \times \frac{(.42)(.57)}{.392}$$

$$= .61$$

Alternatively, if we use the formula (14.10.1) we get

$$r_{bis} = \frac{57.68 - 41.50}{16.10} \times \frac{(.42)}{.392}$$

$$= .62$$

Formula (14.10.1) is relatively easier to apply than the formula (14.10).

14.8.2.1 The Point-Biserial r

This method is suitable when the variable which has been classified into two categories whose scores are not normally distributed. *For example*, in tests when items or answers are scored as right-wrong and true-false, or when the categorisation is a true subdivision of the variable, for example, male-female, urban-rural, living-dead and vegetarians-nonvegetarians.

The formula for the point biserial is

$$r_{pbis} = \left(\frac{M_p - M_q}{\sigma}\right)\sqrt{pq} \qquad \text{...(14.11)}$$

An alternative formula is

$$r_{pbis} = \left(\frac{M_p - M_t}{\sigma}\right)\sqrt{p/q} \qquad \text{...(14.11.1)}$$

Comparison between Biserial *r* and Point-Biserial *r*

Of the two, point-biserial *r* is more dependable statistics as it makes no assumption of the normally of distribution of scores on the dichotomised variable. But the point-biserial *r* value is always lower than the biserial *r* value, for the same data. However, when the dichotomised variable is normally distributed, it is better to calculate *r*.

For item analysis in test construction, both formulas can be used, but point-biserial is preferred.

14.8.3 Partial Correlation

There are situations when the correlation between two variables is because of the influence of a third or more variables. *For example*, the relationship between academic achievement and academic aptitude may be influenced by a third variable study hours per week. If academic achievement is represented by 1, academic aptitude by 2 and study hours by 3, then $r_{12.3}$ represents the first order partial correlation coefficient in which the influence of the 3rd variable (study hours) has been held constant or ruled out. The formula for this first order partial correlation coefficient is

$$r_{12.3} = \frac{r_{12} - r_{13}r_{23}}{\sqrt{\left(1 - r_{13}^2\right)\left(1 - r_{23}^2\right)}} \qquad \text{... (14.12)}$$

The general formula for a partial r of any order is

$$r_{12.3...n} = \frac{r_{12.34...(n-1)} - r_{1n3.4...(n-1)}r_{2n.34...(n-1)}}{\sqrt{\left(1 - r_{1n34...(n-1)}^2\right)\left(1 - r_{2n.34...(n-1)}^2\right)}} \qquad \text{...(14.13)}$$

Suppose we have scores for a group of individuals (N = 6) on three variables X, Y and Z as follows. We have to determine correlation coefficient between X and Z by holding Y constant.

X	*Y*	*Z*
10	11	9
12	13	14

X	*Y*	*Z*
8	7	8
11	9	10
13	10	10
10	11	9

Pearson *rs* for the three variables are XY = .578, YZ = .747 and XZ = .653. The correlation coefficient between X and Z while holding Y constant is

$$r_{XZ \cdot Y} = \frac{r_{XZ} - (r_{XY})(r_{YZ})}{\sqrt{(1 - r_{XY}^2)(1 - r_{YZ}^2)}}$$

$$= \frac{.653 - (.578)(.747)}{\sqrt{(1 - .578^2)(1 - .747^2)}} = .41$$

Therefore, the partial correlation coefficient between XZ = .41 with the influence of Y ruled out. Otherwise the correlation coefficient between X and Z under the influence of the variable Y was .653.

14.8.4 Multiple Correlation

In its simplest form, the multiple correlation is the relationship between one variable and a combination of two other variables. Suppose we have data for three variables as follows:

Variable 1: marks in the class X examination

Variable 2: scores on an adjustment inventory

Variable 3: score on a need for achievement inventory

$$r_{12} = .52, \; r_{13} = .65, \; r_{23} = .45$$

We wish to compute the multiple correlation coefficient between marks in the Class X examination and the combined effect of the variables 2 and 3. The formula is:

$$R_{1.23} = \sqrt{\frac{r_{12}^2 + r_{13}^2 - (2r_{12}r_{13}r_{23})}{1 - r_{23}^2}} \quad \text{... (14.14)}$$

$$= \sqrt{\frac{.52^2 + .65^2 - (2)(.52)(.65)(.45)}{1 - .45^2}}$$

$$= \sqrt{\frac{.27 + .42 - .30}{.80}}$$

$$= \sqrt{\frac{.39}{.80}} = .70$$

Multiple R tells us to what extent variable I (marks in Class X Examination) is determined by the combined effect of variable 2 and variable 3.

14.8.5 The Phi Coefficient (ϕ)

When the data on the two variables being correlated falls into genuine dichotomies, then phi coefficient may be calculated. *For example*, when the dichotomies are Pass-Fail, True-False or Right-Wrong with no intrmediate responses or answers, phi coefficient may be calculated the formula for which is

$$\phi = \frac{AD - BC}{(A + B)(C + D)(A + C)(B + D)} \quad \text{...(14.15)}$$

where A, B, C and D are the frequencies or the number of cases. This formula is useful when we wish to find out correlation between two items on a test.

Suppose we have a four-fold frequency table of the right and wrong responses on two test items Question 1 and Question 2 of the test as follows:

		Question 1	
		Right	Wrong
Question 2	Right	60^A	50^B
	Wrong	45^D	65^D

Applying the formula (14.15) we get

$$\phi = \frac{60 \times 65 - 50 \times 45}{\sqrt{(100)(100)(105)(115)}}$$

$$\phi = \frac{3900 - 2250}{12068.16} = .14$$

14.8.6 Contingency Correlation Coefficient (C)

When two variables have been split into two or more categories, contingency correlation coefficient may be employed.

Suppose we have frequencies of B.Ed. students who have obtained marks in theory (X) and skill in teaching (Y) as follows:

		X			
		> 70%	60.69%	> 60%	
Y	> 70%	60 (56.55)	45 (41.47)	10 (16.96)	115
	60-69%	70 (59.01)	30 (43.27)	20 (17.70)	120
	< 60%	20 (34.42)	35 (25.24)	15 (10.32)	70

Steps:

- Calculate independence values or expected frequencies for the cells. These would be:

$$\frac{150\times115}{305}=56.55 \quad \frac{110\times115}{305}=41.47 \quad \frac{45\times115}{305}=16.96$$

$$\frac{150\times120}{305}=59.01 \quad \frac{110\times120}{305}=43.27 \quad \frac{45\times120}{305}=17.70$$

$$\frac{150\times70}{305}=34.42 \quad \frac{110\times70}{305}=25.24 \quad \frac{45\times70}{305}=10.32$$

- **Calculate C values.** Each observed value is squared and then divided by its expected or chance value. The sum of these values yields S.

$$\frac{60^2}{56.55}=63.66 \quad \frac{45^2}{41.47}=48.83 \quad \frac{10^2}{16.96}=5.89$$

$$\frac{70^2}{59.01}=83.03 \quad \frac{30^2}{43.27}=20.79 \quad \frac{20^2}{16.96}=5.89$$

$$\frac{20^2}{34.42}=11.62 \quad \frac{35^2}{25.24}=48.53 \quad \frac{15^2}{10.32}=21.80$$

S = 63.66 + 83.03 + ... + 21.80 = 326.74

$$C=\sqrt{\frac{S-N}{S}}$$

$$=\sqrt{\frac{326.74-305}{326.74}}=.26$$

- **Sign of the Contingency Coefficient:** In the diagonal cells, beginning from the top left hand corner of the contingency table, if $f_e < f_o$, then the contingency coefficient is +ve. If in the diagonal cells $f_e > f_0$ and in others $f_e < f_o$, then the contingency coefficient has –ve sign.

14.9 ANALYSIS OF COVARIANCE

Analysis of covariance is an extension of analysis of variance. When groups being compared for the effect of the experimental treatment, have not been matched or equated before the treatment, then analysis of covariance enables us to make adjustments in the final scores which will allow for the initial differences in the groups.

	Group A		*Group B*		*Group C*	
	X_1	Y_1	X_2	Y_2	X_3	Y_3
	6	9	7	8	8	9
	5	7	5	7	8	10
	8	10	9	9	7	7
	10	13	8	9	8	8
	11	13	6	8	12	12
Sums	40	52	35	41	43	46
Means	8	10.4	7	8.2	8.6	9.2

Step 1. Calculate the values ΣX, ΣY, ΣXY, ΣX^2 and ΣY^2. These are $\Sigma X = 118$, $\Sigma Y = 139$, $\Sigma XY = 1143$, $\Sigma X^2 = 987$ and $\Sigma Y^2 = 1345$.

Step 2. Calculate the correction terms:

$$C_X = \frac{118^2}{15} = 928.27, \; C_Y = \frac{139^2}{15} = 1288.07,$$

$$C_{XY} = \frac{(118)(139)}{15} = 1093.47$$

Step 3. Calculate Total Sum of Squares:

For $\quad X = \Sigma X^2 - C_X$

$$= 987\text{-}928.27 = 58.73$$

$$Y = 1345\text{-}1288.07 = 56.93$$

$$XY = 1143\text{-}1093.47 = 49.53$$

Step 4. Calculate Among Groups SS:

For $X = \frac{40^2 + 35^2 + 43^2}{5} - 928.27 = 6.53$

$Y = \frac{52^2 + 41^2 + 46^2}{5} - 1288.07 = 12.13$

$XY = \frac{(40 \times 42) + (35 \times 41) + (43 \times 46)}{5} - 1093.47 = 5.13$

Step 5. Calculate Within groups SS:

Total – Among

For $X = 58.73 - 6.53 = 52.20$

$Y = 56.93 - 12.13 = 44.80$

$XY = 49.53 - 5.13 = 44.40$

Step 6. Summary of ANOVA (X and Y taken separately):

Source of Variation	*df*	SS_X	SS_Y	MS_X	MS_Y
Among Means	2	6.53	12.13	3.27	6.07
Within Groups	12	52.20	44.80	4.38	3.73
Total	14	58.73	56.93		

$$F_X = \frac{3.27}{4.38} = .75$$

$$F_Y = \frac{6.07}{3.73} = 1.63$$

From table of F we find that both the values .75 and 1.63 fail to reach the table value of $F = 3.88$ at the .05 level for The three groups are not significantly different from one another on initial testing as our obtained $F_X = .75$. The value for within groups is 1.63 which is not significant but moves toward table *F* value=3.88.

Step 7. Calculate Adjusted *SS* for $Y\left(SS_{Y.X}\right)$

Total $$SS_{Y.X} = SS_Y - \frac{(SS_{XY})^2}{SS_X}$$

$$= 56.93 - \frac{49.53^2}{58.73} = 15.16$$

Within $$SS_{Y.X} = SS_Y - \frac{(SS_{XY})^2}{SS_X}$$

$$= 44.80 - \frac{(44.40)^2}{52.20} = 7.03$$

Among Groups = Total – Within
= 15.16 – 7.03 = 8.13

Step 8. Summary of Analysis of Covariance

Source of Variation	*df*	SS_X	SS_Y	SS_{XY}	MS_X	MS_Y
Among Means	2	6.53	12.13	5.13	8.13	4.07
Within Groups	11*	52.20	44.80	44.40	7.03	.64
Total	13	58.73	56.93	49.53	15.16	

(* One *df* is lost in the calculation of adjusted Y value)

$$F_{YX} = \frac{\text{Among Means}}{\text{Within Groups}}$$

$$\frac{4.07}{.64} = 6.36 \left(\text{significant at .05 level, df 2, 11}\right)$$

The three groups significantly differ from one another on the posttest scores.

Step 9. Calculate correlation and regression for working out adjusted Y means of the three groups:

$$r_{total} = \frac{SS_{XY}}{\sqrt{(Among\ SS_t)(Within\ SS_W)}}$$

$$= \frac{49,53}{\sqrt{(58.73)(56.93)}} = .86$$

$$r_{among} = \frac{5.13}{\sqrt{(6.53)(44.80)}} = .58$$

$$r_{within} = \frac{44.40}{\sqrt{(52.20)(44.80)}} = .93$$

$$b_{total} = \frac{SS_{XY}}{SS_X} = \frac{49.53}{58.73} = .84 \quad \text{(See Chapter 15)}$$

$$b_{among} = \frac{SS_{XY}}{SS_X} = \frac{5.13}{6.53} = .79$$

$$b_{within} = \frac{SS_{XY}}{SS_X} = \frac{44.40}{52.20} = .86$$

Step 10. Calculation of Adjusted Y means:

Group	*N*	M_X	M_Y
A	5	8	10.4
B	5	7	8.2
C	5	8.6	9.2
Combined General Means		7.67	9.27

$M_{Y.X} = M_Y - b(M_X - GM_X)$ (From the Regression Equation in Chapter 15)

Adjusted Y Mean for Group A = 10.4 – .84(8 – 7.67) = 10.68

Adjusted Y Mean for Group B = 8.2 – .84 (7 – 7.67) = 8.76

Adjusted Y Mean for Group C = 9.2 – .84 (8.6 – 7.67) = 8.42

Step 11. SD of the differences Among Adjusted Y Means:

$$SD_{Y.X} = \sqrt{\text{Within Groups } MS_{Y.X}}$$

$$= \sqrt{.64} = .80$$

Step 12. Standard Error of the Difference between any two Adjusted Y Means:

$$SE_{dm} = SD_{Y.X}\sqrt{\frac{1}{N_1} + \frac{1}{N_2}}$$

$$= .80\sqrt{\frac{1}{5} + \frac{1}{5}}$$

$$= .80 \times .63 = .50$$

Step 13. Comparisons of the three Adjusted Y Means:

Groups	*Mean Diff.*	*t*	*Significance*
A and B	1.92	3.84	$p < .01$
A and C	2.26	4.52	$p < .01$
B and C	0.34	0.68	(NS)

(* Table Value for t = 3.11 for *df* 11, at .01 level)

CONCLUSION

Performance after immediate feedback is superior to both no feedback and delayed feedback.

There is no significant difference in performance after delayed feedback and no feedback.

EXERCISES

1. Following are the data for two groups. Determine the mean of the group B.

Group	Mean	N
A	15	20
B		16

Combined Mean = 12.78 (**Ans.** 10)

2. Calculate SD and QD for the following data

Scores	*f*
80-84	1
75-79	1
70-74	1
65-69	4
60-64	4
55-59	7
50-54	6
45-49	6
40-44	6
35-39	3
30-34	0
25-29	1

(**Ans.** SD=11.60
Q=8.12)

3. Following are the scores of 10 students on two tests. Compute and compare Pearson r and Spearman.

Test X	*Test Y*
15	12
14	14
10	9
9	10
8	8
8	7
7	8
6	4
4	6
2	4

(**Ans.** $r = .92$,
$\rho = .93$)

4. Responses of 200 students on two test items are as follows. Calculate Phi Coefficient for the data.

		Item X	
		Agree	Disagree
Item Y	Agree	70	30
	Disagree	30	70

(**Ans.** .40)

5. Given as follows:

   $r_{12} = .80$ $\quad r_{23} = .50$ and $r_{13} = .60$

   Work out correlation coefficient with the effect of variable 1 ruled out. (**Ans.** .04)

6. Calculate point biserial for the following data.

   $M_p = 22.33 \quad M_q = 20.33 \quad \sigma_{total} = 1.82$ (**Ans.** .54)

7. Explain with an example the concept of the standard error of mean.

8. Given $r_{12} = .50$, $r_{13} = 60$ and $r_{23} = .40$ Calculate $R_{1.23}$ (**Ans.** .66)

15

Simple Regression and Prediction

15.1 SIMPLE REGRESSION ANALYSIS

Regression analysis is used to predict or determine one variable from another variable or variables.

Simple or bivariate regression involves two variables in which the predicted variable Y is the dependent variable. The predictor variable X is the independent variable. In simple regression analysis only a straight line relationship between the two variables is examined. Can we predict class X Board examination achievement using regression analysis? The answer is in affirmative. What are the variables related to academic achievement in the class X Board examination? Of the many variables, a few variables could be intelligence, study habits, motivation and adjustment.

The first step in regression analysis involves construction of a scatterplot of the scores on the two variables. This gives preliminary information about the shape and spread of data. Suppose we have achievement marks and IQ scores of a group of pupils (N=10), which are given in table 15.1. Figure 15.1 gives a scatter-plot of this data.

Table 15.1 Achievement Marks and IQs of Pupils

IQ(X)	90	85	100	105	110	120	115	95	112	116
Ach.(Y)	50	55	52	54	58	65	56	48	52	70

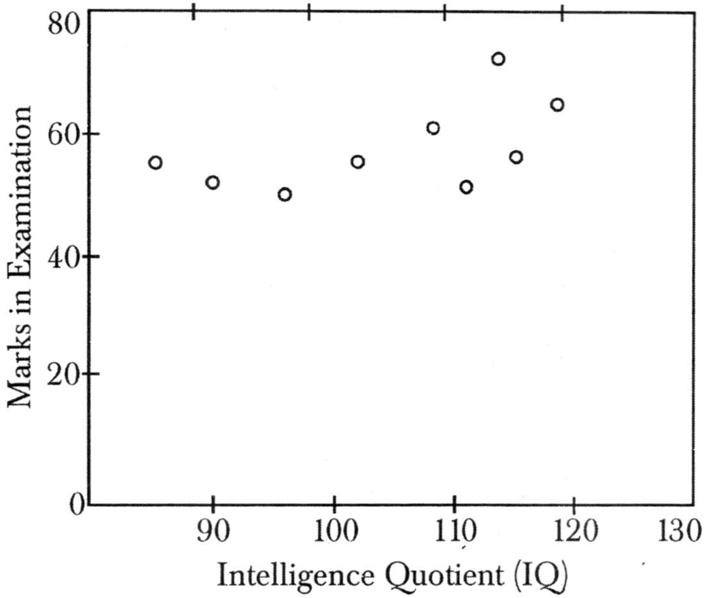

Fig. 15.1: Scatter plot of IQ and Marks

Imagine a line passing through these points. This plot gives an idea of how well a regression line fits the data. The first step in determining the equation of the regression line through these points is to establish the form of the equation. In regression analysis, the slope-intercept equation of a line is used. The equation of a line in the slope-intercept form is

$$Y = a + bX$$

where b = the slope of the line

a = Y intercept

In statistics, the equation of regression line in the slope-intercept form is

$$Y' = \beta_0 + \beta X$$

where $Y' =$ the predicted value of Y

$\beta_0 =$ Y intercept for the population

$\beta_1 =$ the population slope

For any specific dependent variable value Y_1

$$Y_i = \beta_0 + \beta_1 X_i + \beta_i X_i + E_i$$

where $X_i =$ the value of the independent variable for the *i*th value

$Y_i =$ the value of the dependent variable for the *i*th value

$\beta_0 =$ the population Y interpcept

$\beta_1 =$ the population slope

$E_1 =$ the error of prediction for the *i*th value

If the points being fitted by the regression equation are not aligned (in straight line), the regression equation will miss some of the points. In the preceding formula, E_i represents the error of regression line in fitting these points. When a point falls on the regression line, $E_i = 0$.

Suppose the equation of a regression line is

$$Y = 2 + 2.5X$$

For a given value of $X = 5$, the exact predicted value of Y is

$$Y = 2+2.5(5)$$

$= 14.5$

This is an example of an exact prediction of Y for a given input $X = 5$. However, most of the time, the values of Y will not be exactly the same as the values obtained through the regression equation. Random errors will occur in the prediction of Y values because the variable X does not explain all the variability of the Y variable. In our example of academic achievement and IQ, though the variable academic achievement is related to the independent variable IQ, other factors related to academic achievement are not explained by IQ. Therefore, prediction of academic achievement from IQ probably involves some error. As such, in regression analysis we may use probabilistic model which includes an error term that allows for variation in Y values for any given value of X.

The probabilistic regression equation is

$$Y = \beta_o + \beta_1 X + E \qquad ...(15.1)$$

In the above equation $\beta_o + \beta_1 X$ is deterministic, error free prediction. In a determinisitic model all points are assumed to be on the regression line, and in all cases E = 0.

Since for regression analysis we make use of data of a sample and not the population parameters, therefore, β_o and β_1 are estimated by sample statistics $b_o + b_1$. The equation of the regression line becomes

$$Y' = +b_0 + b_1 X \qquad ...(15.2)$$

where b_0 = the intercept of the sample

b_1 = the sample slope

For determining the equation of the regression for a given sample data, $b_0 + b_1$ are calculated. This is called least squares analysis. A regression model is developed by producing a minimum sum of the squared error values. The value of the sample slope (b_1), when Y is to be predicted, is calculated by the formula

$$b_1 = \frac{\Sigma(X-\overline{X})(Y-\overline{Y})}{\Sigma(X-\overline{X})^2} \quad ...(15.2.1)$$

or $$b_1 = \frac{\Sigma XY - (\Sigma X)(\Sigma Y)/n}{\Sigma X^2 - (\Sigma X)^2/n}$$

or $$b_1 = \frac{SS_{XY}}{SS_{XX}}$$

For calculating Y intercept of the sample, the formula is

$$b_0 = \overline{Y} - b_1\overline{X}$$

$$= \frac{\Sigma Y}{n} - b_1\frac{\Sigma X}{n} \quad ...(15.2.2)$$

For the data in the table 15.1, the least squares equation of the regression line is worked out as follows:

X	Y	X^2	Y^2	XY
90	50	8100	2500	4500
85	55	7225	3025	4675
100	52	10000	2704	5200
105	54	11025	2916	5670
110	58	12100	3364	6380
120	65	14400	4225	7800
115	56	13225	3136	6440

95	48	9025	2304	4560
112	52	12544	2704	5824
116	70	13456	4900	8120
1048= ΣX	560= ΣY	111100= ΣX^2	31778= ΣY^2	59159= ΣXY

Steps:

- Calculate the values $\Sigma X, \Sigma Y, \Sigma X^2, \Sigma Y^2$ and ΣXY
- Calculate the slope (b_1) of the regression line using the formula (15.2.1)

$$b_1 = \frac{\Sigma XY - \frac{(\Sigma X)(\Sigma Y)}{n}}{\Sigma X^2 - \frac{(\Sigma X)^2}{n}}$$

$$= \frac{59169 - \frac{(1048)(560)}{10}}{111100 - \frac{(1048)^2}{10}}$$

$$= \frac{481}{1269.6} = .378$$

- Calculate the Y intercept (b_0) using the formula (15.2.2)

$$b_0 = \frac{\Sigma Y}{n} - b_1 \frac{\Sigma X}{n}$$

$$= \frac{560}{10} - .378\left(\frac{1048}{10}\right)$$

$$= 56 - 39.61$$

$$= 16.39$$

• Substituting the values

which is $Y' = b_0 + b_1X$

we get $Y' = 16.39 + .378X$

The interpretation of the slope of this equation is that for every unit increase in IQ(X), there is an increase of .378 in academic achievement (Y). *For example*, if the IQ score of a pupil is 104, his predicted academic achievement marks would be

$$Y' = 16.39 + .378(104)$$
$$= 55.70$$

If we wish to predict IQ score from academic achievement, that is, X from Y, then the slope b_1 and the X intercept b_0 would be

$$b_1 = \frac{SS_{XY}}{SS_{YY}} = \frac{\Sigma XY - \frac{(\Sigma X)(\Sigma Y)}{n}}{\Sigma Y^2 - \frac{(\Sigma Y)^2}{n}}$$

$$= \frac{59169 - \frac{(1048)(560)}{10}}{31778 - \frac{(560)^2}{10}}$$

$$= \frac{481}{418} = 1.15$$

$$b_0 = \frac{X}{n} - b_1 \frac{\Sigma Y}{n}$$

$$= \frac{1048}{10} - 1.15\left(\frac{560}{10}\right)$$

$$= 40.4$$

Substituting b_1 and b_0 in the formula

$$X' = b_0 + b_1 Y$$

we get $$X' = 40.4 + 1.15Y$$

If the academic achievement marks of a pupil are 61, then his predicted IQ score will be

$$X' = 1.15(61) + 40.40$$

$$X' = 110.55$$

$$= 111$$

15.2 ACCURACY OF PREDICTION

Values of X and Y predicted from their regression equations are probabilistic in nature. How accurate is the estimated value of the dependent (predicted) variable for a given value of the independent (predictor) variable? This is determined through the standard error of estimate. When Y scores are predicted from X scores

$$\sigma_{(estY)} = \sigma_Y \left(\sqrt{1 - r_{XY}^2}\right) \qquad ...(15.3)$$

where σ_Y = standard deviation of the Y distribution

r_{XY} = correlation coefficient between X and Y scores

When X scores are to be predicted from Y scores

$$\sigma_{(estX)} = \sigma_X \left(\sqrt{1 - r_{XY}^2}\right) \qquad ...(15.3.1)$$

$$\sigma_X = 11.88;\ \sigma_Y = 6.82; \text{and } r_{XY} = .66$$

$$\sigma_{(estY)} = 6.82 \quad \sqrt{1 - .66^2} = 5.10$$

$$\sigma_{(estX)} = 11.88 \ \sqrt{1 - .66^2} = 8.89$$

Therefore, for a pupil whose IQ is 104 and the predicted achievement marks are 55.70, the probability is 68 times out of 100 that his true achievement marks would lie within the range $55.70 \pm 1\sigma_{(estY)}$ which is 50.60 to 60.80. There are 95 chances out of 100 that his true score will lie within the range $55.70 \pm 2\sigma_{(estY)} = 45.50$ to 65.90.

15.3 REGRESSION EQUATIONS IN SCORE FORM

Another way of establishing regression equations is in the score form the formulas for which are

$$Y - M_y = r\frac{\sigma_y}{\sigma_x}(X - Mx)$$

or

$$Y' = r\frac{\sigma_y}{\sigma_x}(X - M_x) + M_y \qquad \text{...(15.4)}$$

and

$$X - M_x = r\frac{\sigma_x}{\sigma_y}(Y - M_y)$$

$$X' = r\frac{\sigma_x}{\sigma_y}(Y - M_y) + M_x \qquad \text{...(15.4.1)}$$

Problem: An investigator reported that the number of teachers in a school can be estimated by the number of pupils enrolled. Twelve schools were surveyed and the following data were obtained. Set-up a regression equation for the number of teachers for a school by the number of pupil enrolled in the school.

School	*No. of Pupils(X)*	*No. of Teachers(Y)*
A	20	1
B	30	1
C	40	2

D	50	2
E	60	2
F	80	3
G	100	3
H	120	4
I	150	4
J	160	4
K	180	5
L	200	5

Steps:

- The values ΣX, ΣX^2, ΣY^2 and ΣXY are determined.
- $\Sigma X = 1190$; $\Sigma Y = 36$. The column X values are squared to obtain X^2 values whose sum $\Sigma X^2 = 160300$. The sum of the XY values is $\Sigma XY = 4510$.
- $$SS_{XY} = \Sigma XY - \frac{(\Sigma X)(\Sigma Y)}{n}$$
$$= 4510 - \frac{(1190)(36)}{12} = 940$$
- $$SS_{XX} = \Sigma X^2 - \frac{(\Sigma X)^2}{n}$$
$$= 160300 - \frac{(1190)^2}{12} = 42291.67$$
$$\therefore \ b_1 = \frac{SS_{XY}}{SS_{XX}} = \frac{940}{42291.67} = .022$$
$$b_0 = \frac{\Sigma Y}{n} - b_1 \frac{\Sigma X}{n} = \frac{36}{12} - .022\left(\frac{1190}{12}\right) = 3 - 2.18 = .82$$

The formula for a simple regression equation is $Y = b_0 + b_1 X$

$$Y = .82 + .022X$$

For every unit (pupil) increase in X, the number of teachers(Y) is predicted to increase by .022.

The solution of this problem in the score form would be

$$Y = r\frac{\sigma_y}{\sigma_x}(X - M_x) + M_y$$

and the value of r for the two variables *X* and *Y* will be

$$r = \frac{(N\Sigma XY) - (\Sigma X)(\Sigma Y)}{\sqrt{\left[N\Sigma X^2 - (\Sigma X)^2\right]\left[N\Sigma Y^2 - (\Sigma Y)^2\right]}}$$

$$= \frac{12(4510) - (1190)(36)}{\sqrt{\left[12(160300) - 1190^2\right]\left[12(130) - 36^2\right]}}$$

$$= \frac{11280}{(712.39)(16.25)} = .974$$

σ_y, σ_x, M_x and M_y would be

$$\sigma_y = \sqrt{\frac{\Sigma Y^2 - \frac{(\Sigma Y^2)}{n}}{n}}$$

$$= \sqrt{\frac{130 - \frac{(36)^2}{12}}{12}} = 1.35$$

$$\sigma_x = \sqrt{\frac{\Sigma X^2 - \frac{(\Sigma X)^2}{n}}{n}}$$

$$= \sqrt{\frac{16300 - \frac{(1190)^2}{12}}{12}} = 59.37$$

$M_x = 9.17; M_y = 3$

Substituting the values of r, σ_x, σ_y, M_x and M_y in the score form regression equation we get

$$Y' = .974\left(\frac{1.35}{59.37}\right)(X - 99.17) + 3$$

$$Y' = .022(X - 99.17) + 3$$

$$Y' = .022X + .82$$

We get the same results whether we use the deviation form or the score form of the regression equations.

EXERCISES

1. Calculate Y' for each of the following:

   $X = 6, \quad a = 3, \quad b = 2$

   $X = -7, \quad a = 4, \quad b = -3$

   $X = 8, \quad a = -2, \quad b = 5$

   (**Ans.** $Y' = 15$, $Y' = 25$, $Y' = 38$)

2. Data for two tests are as follows. Work out regression equations in score form.

	Test X	Test Y	
M	60	65	$r_{xy} = .50$
σ	5	4	

   (**Ans.** $Y' = .4X + 41$, $X' = .63Y + 19.37$)

3. From the data in exercise 2, predict the probable score of a student on Test X whose score on the Test Y is 55. Also find σ_{est} of this prediction.

   (**Ans.** 54.02, $\sigma_x = 4.33$)

4. Work out the regression equation for the prediction of Y from X for the following data.

X	Y
10	8
12	11

5	8
8	6
9	5

What will be the predicted Y score for an individual whose score on the X variable is 6?

(**Ans.** $Y' = .395X + 4.12$, $Y' = 6.49$)

5. Calculate standard error of estimate for the variable Y from the data in exercise 4.

(**Ans.** 1.85)

Appendix–I

Table A. Areas and Ordinates of the Normal Distribution Curve in terms of x/σ

(1) z	(2) A	(3) B	(4) C	(5)
Standard Score $\left(\frac{x}{\sigma}\right)$	*Area from Mean to* $\frac{x}{\sigma}$	*Area in Larger Portion*	*Area in Smaller Portion*	y *Ordinate at* $\frac{x}{\sigma}$
0.00	.000	.5000	.5000	.3989
0.01	.0040	.5040	.4960	.3989
0.02	.0080	.5080	.4920	.3989
0.03	.0120	.5120	.4880	.3988
0.04	.0160	.5160	.4840	.3986
0.05	.0199	.5199	.4801	.3984
0.06	.0239	.5239	.4761	.3982
0.07	.0279	.5279	.4721	.3980
0.08	.0319	.5319	.4681	.3977

0.09	.0359	.5359	.4641	.3973
0.10	.0398	.5398	.4602	.3970
0.11	.0438	.5438	.4562	.3965
0.12	.0478	.5478	.4522	.3961
0.13	.0517	.5517	.4483	.3956
0.14	.0557	.5557	.4443	.3951
0.15	.0596	.5596	4404	.3945
0.16	.0636	.5636	.4364	.3939
0.17	.0675	.5675	.4325	.3932
0.18	.0714	.5714	.4286	.3925
0.19	.0753	.5753	.4247	.3918
0.20	.0793	.5793	.4207	.3910
0.21	.0832	.5832	.4168	.3902
0.22	.0871	.5871	.4129	.3894
0.23	.0910	.5910	.4090	.3885
0.24	.0948	.5948	.4052	.3876
0.25	.0987	.5987	.4013	.3867
0.26	.1026	.6026	.3974	.3857
0.27	.1064	.6064	.3936	.3847
0.28	.1103	.6103	.3897	.3836
0.29	.1141	.6141	.3859	.3825
0.30	.1179	.6179	.3821	.3814
0.31	.1217	.6217	.3783	.3802
0.32	.1255	.6255	.3745	.3790
0.33	.1293	.6293	.3707	.3778
0.34	.1331	.6331	.3669	.3765

0.35	.1368	.6368	.3632	.3752
0.36	.1406	.6406	.3594	.3739
0.37	.1443	.6443	.3557	.3725
0.38	.1480	.6480	.3520	.3712
0.39	.1517	.6517	.3483	.3697
0.40	.1554	.6554	.3446	.3683
0.41	.1591	.6591	.3409	.3668
0.42	.1628	.6628	.3372	.3653
0.43	.1664	.6664	.3336	.3637
0.44	.1700	.6700	.3300	.3621
0.45	.1736	.6736	.3264	.3605
0.46	.1772	.6772	.3228	.3589
0.47	.1808	.6808	.3192	.3572
0.48	.1844	.6844	.3156	.3555
0.49	.1879	.6879	.3121	.3538
0.50	.1915	.6915	.3085	.3521
0.51	.1950	.6950	.3050	.3503
0.52	.1985	.6985	.3015	.3485
0.53	.2019	.7019	.2981	.3467
0.54	.2054	.7054	.2946	.3448
0.55	.2088	.7088	.2912	.3429
0.56	.2123	.7123	.2877	.3410
0.57	.2157	.7157	.2843	.3391
0.58	.2190	.7190	.2810	.3372
0.59	.2224	.7224	.2776	.3352
0.60	.2257	.7257	.2743	.3332

0.61	.2291	.7291	.2709	.3212
0.62	.2324	.7324	.2676	.3292
0.63	.2357	.7357	.2643	.3271
0.64	.2389	.7389	.2611	.3251
0.65	.2422	.7422	.2578	.3230
0.66	.2454	.7454	.2546	.3209
0.67	.2486	.7486	.2514	.3187
0.68	.2517	.7517	.2483	.3166
0.69	.2549	.7549	.2451	.3144
0.70	.2580	.7580	.2420	.3123
0.71	.2611	.7611	.2389	.3101
0.72	.2642	.7642	.2358	.3079
0.73	.2673	.7673	.2327	.3056
0.74	.2704	.7704	.2296	.3034
0.75	.2734	.7734	.2266	.3011
0.76	.2764	.7764	.2236	.2989
0.77	.2794	.7794	.2206	.2966
0.78	.2823	.7823	.2177	.2943
0.79	.2852	.7852	.2148	
0.80	.2881	.7881	.2119	.2897
0.81	.2910	.7910	.2090	.2874
0.82	.2939	.7939	.2061	.2850
0.83	.2967	.7967	.2033	.2827
0.84	.2995	.7995	.2005	.2803
0.85	.3023	.8023	.1977	.2780
0.86	.3051	.8051	.1949	.2756

0.87	.3078	.8078	.1922	.2732
0.88	.3106	.8106	.1894	.2709
0.89	.3133	.8133	.1867	.2685
0.90	.3159	.8159	.1841	.2661
0.91	.3186	.8186	.1814	.2637
0.92	.3212	.8212	.1788	.2613
0.93	.3228	.8238	.1762	.2589
0.94	.3264	.8264	.1736	.2565
0.95	.3289	.8289	.1711	.2541
0.96	.3315	.8315	.1685	.2516
0.97	.3340	.8340	.1660	.2492
0.98	.3365	.8365	.1635	.2468
0.99	.3389	.8389	.1611	.2444
1.00	.3413	.8413	.1587	.2420
1.01	.3438	.8438	.1562	.2396
1.02	.3461	.8461	.1539	.2371
1.03	.3485	.8485	.1515	.2347
1.04	.3508	.8508	.1492	.2323
1.05	.3531	.8531	.1469	.2299
1.06	.3554	.8554	.1446	.2275
1.07	.3577	.8577	.1423	.2251
1.08	.3599	.8599	.1401	.2227
1.09	.3621	.8621	.1379	.2203
1.10	.3643	.8643	.1357	.2179
1.11	.3665	.8665	.1335	.2155
1.12	.3686	.8686	.1314	.2131

1.13	.3708	.8708	.1292	.2107
1.14	.3729	.8729	.1271	.2083
1.15	.3749	.8749	.1251	.2059
1.16	.3770	.8770	.1230	.2036
1.17	.3790	.8790	.1210	.2012
1.18	.3810	.8810	.1190	.1989
1.19	.3830	.8830	.1170	.1965
1.20	.3849	.8849	.1151	.1942
1.21	.3869	.8869	.1131	.1919
1.22	.3888	.8888	.1112	.1895
1.23	.3907	.8907	.1093	.1872
1.24	.3925	.8925	.1075	.1849
1.25	.3944	.8944	.1056	.1826
1.26	.3962	.8962	.1038	.1804
1.27	.3980	.8980	.1020	.1781
1.28	.3997	.8997	.1003	.1758
1.29	.4015	.9015	.0985	.1736
1.30	.4032	.9032	.0968	.1714
1.31	.4049	.9049	.0951	.1691
1.32	.4066	.9066	.0934	.1669
1.33	.4082	.9082	.0918	.1647
1.34	.4099	.9099	.0901	.1626
1.35	.4115	.9115	.0885	.1604
1.36	.4131	.9131	.0869	.1582
1.37	.4147	.9147	.0853	.1561
1.38	.4162	.9162	.0838	.1539

1.39	.4177	.9177	.0823	.1518
1.40	.4192	.9192	.0808	.1497
1.41	.4207	.9207	.0793	.1476
1.42	.4222	.9222	.0778	.1456
1.43	.4236	.9236	.0764	.1435
1.44	.4251	.9251	.0749	.1415
1.45	.4265	.9265	.0735	.13943
1.46	.4279	.9279	.0721	.1374
1.47	.4292	.9292	.0708	.1354
1.48	.4306	.9306	.0964	.1334
1.49	.4319	.9319	.0681	.1315
1.50	.4332	.9332	.0668	.1295
1.51	.4345	.9345	.0655	.1276
1.52	.4357	.9357	.0643	.1257
1.53	.4370	.9370	.0630	.1238
1.54	.4382	.9382	.0618	.1219
1.55	.4394	.9394	.0606	.1200
1.56	.4406	.9406	.0594	.1182
1.57	.4418	.9418	.0582	.1163
1.58	.4429	.9429	.0571	.1145
1.59	.4441	.9441	.0559	.1127
1.60	.4452	.9452	.0548	.1109
1.61	.4463	.9463	.0537	.1092
1.62	.4474	.9474	.0526	.1074
1.63	.4484	.9484	.0516	.1057
1.64	.4495	.9495	.0505	.1040

1.65	.4505	.9505	.0495	.1023
1.66	.4515	.9515	.0485	.1006
1.67	.4525	.9525	.0475	.0989
1.68	.4535	.9535	.0465	.0973
1.69	.4545	.9545	.0455	.0957
1.70	.4554	.9554	.0446	.0940
1.71	.4564	.9564	.0436	.0925
1.72	.4573	.9573	.0427	.0909
1.73	.4582	.9582	.0418	.0893
1.74	.4591	.9591	.0409	.0878
1.75	.4599	.9599	.0401	.0863
1.76	.4608	.9608	.0392	.0848
1.77	.4616	.9616	.0384	.0833
1.78	.4625	.9625	.0375	.0818
1.79	.4633	.9633	.0367	.0804
1.80	.4641	.9641	.0359	.0790
1.81	.4649	.9649	.0351	.0775
1.82	.4656	.9656	.0344	.0761
1.83	.4664	.9664	.0336	.0748
1.84	.4671	.9671	.0329	.0734
1.85	.4648	.9678	.0322	.0721
1.86	.4686	.9686	.0314	.0707
1.87	.4693	.9693	.0307	.0694
1.88	.4699	.9699	.0301	.0681
1.89	.4706	.9706	.0294	.0669
1.90	.4713	.9713	.0287	.0656

1.91	.4719	.9719	.0281	.0644
1.92	.4726	9726	.0274	.0632
1.93	.4732	.9732	.0268	.0620
1.94	.4738	.9738	.0262	.0608
1.95	.4744	.9744	.0256	.0596
1.96	.4750	.9750	.0250	.0584
1.97	.4756	.9756	.0244	.0573
1.98	.4761	.9761	.0239	.0562
1.99	.4767	.9767	.0233	.0551
2.00	.4772	.9772	.0228	.0540
2.01	.4778	.9778	.0222	.0529
2.02	.4783	.9783	.0217	.0519
2.03	.4788	.9788	.0212	.0508
2.04	.4793	.9793	.0207	.0498
2.05	.4798	.9798	.0202	.0488
2.06	.4803	.9803	.0197	.0478
2.07	.4808	.9808	.0192	.0468
2.08	.4812	.9812	.0188	.0459
2.09	.4817	.9817	.0183	.0449
2.10	.4821	.9821	.0179	.0440
2.11	.4826	.9826	.0174	.0431
2.12	.4830	.9830	.0170	.0422
2.13	.4834	.9834	.0166	.0413
2.14	.4838	.9838	.0162	.0404
2.15	.4842	.9842	.0158	.0396
2.16	.4846	.9846	.0154	.0387
2.17	.4850	.9850	.0150	.0379

2.18	.4854	.9854	.0146	.0371
2.19	.4857	.9857	.0143	.0363
2.20	.4861	.9861	.0139	.0355
2.21	.4864	.9864	.0136	.0347
2.22	.4868	.9868	.0132	.0339
2.23	.4871	.9871	.0129	.0332
2.24	.4875	.9875	.0125	.0325
2.25	.4878	.9878	.0122	.0317
2.26	.4881	.9881	.0119	.0310
2.27	.4884	.9884	.0116	.0303
2.28	.4887	.9887	.0113	.0297
2.29	.4890	.9890	.0110	.0290
2.30	.4893	.9893	.0107	.0283
2.31	.4896	.9896	.0104	.0277
2.32	.4898	.9898	.0102	.0270
2.33	.4901	.9901	.0099	.0264
2.34	.4904	.9904	0.096	.0258
2.35	.4906	.9906	.0094	.0252
2.36	.4909	.9909	.0091	.0246
2.37	.4911	.9911	.0089	.0241
2.38	.4913	.9913	.0087	.0235
2.39	.4916	.9916	.0084	.0229
2.40	.4918	.9918	.0082	.0224
2.41	.4920	.9920	.0080	.0219
2.42	.4922	.9922	.0078	.0213
2.43	.4925	.9925	.0075	.0208

2.44	.4927	.9927	.0073	.0203
2.45	.4929	.9929	.0071	.0198
2.46	.4931	.9931	.0069	.0194
2.47	.4932	.9932	.0068	.0189
2.48	.4934	.9934	.0066	.0184
2.49	.4936	.9936	.0064	.0180
2.50	.4938	.9938	.0062	.0175
2.51	.4940	.9940	.0060	.0171
2.52	.4941	.9941	.0059	.0167
2.53	.4943	.9943	.0057	.0163
2.54	.4945	.9945	.0055	.0158
2.55	.4946	.9946	.0054	.0154
2.56	.4948	.9948	.0052	.0151
2.57	.4949	.9949	.0051	.0147
2.58	.4951	.9951	.0049	.0143
2.59	.4952	.9952	.0048	.0139
2.60	.4953	.9953	.0047	.0136
2.61	.4955	.9955	.0045	.0132
2.62	.4956	.9956	.0044	.0129
2.63	.4957	.9957	.0043	.0126
2.64	.4959	.9959	.0041	.0122
2.65	.4960	.9960	.0040	.0119
2.66	.4961	.9961	.0039	.0116
2.67	.4962	.9962	.0038	.0113
2.68	.4963	.9963	.0037	.0110
2.69	.4964	.9964	.0036	.0107

2.70	.4965	.9965	.0035	.0104
2.71	.4966	.9966	.0034	.0101
2.72	.4967	.9967	.0033	.0099
2.73	.4968	.9968	.0032	.0096
2.74	.4969	.9969	.0031	.0093
2.75	.4970	.9970	.0030	.0091
2.76	.4971	.9971	.0029	.0088
2.77	.4972	.9972	.0028	.0086
2.78	.4973	.9973	.0027	.0084
2.79	.4974	.9974	.0026	.0081
2.80	.4974	.9974	.0026	.0079
2.81	.4975	.9975	.0025	.0077
2.82	.4976	.9976	.0024	.0075
2.83	.4977	.9977	.0023	.0073
2.84	.4977	.9977	.0023	.0071
2.85	.4978	.9978	.0022	.0069
2.86	.4979	.9979	.0021	.0067
2.87	.4979	.9979	.0021	.0065
2.88	.4980	.9980	.0020	.0063
2.89	.4981	.9981	.0019	.0061
2.90	.4981	.9981	.0019	.0060
2.91	.4982	.9982	.0018	.0058
2.92	.4982	.9982	.0018	.0056
2.93	.4983	.9983	.0017	.0055
2.94	.4984	.9984	.0016	.0053
2.95	.4984	.9984	.0016	.0051
2.96	.4985	.9985	.0015	.0050
2.97	.4985	.9985	.0015	.0048
2.98	.4986	.9986	.0014	.0047

2.99	.4986	.9986	.0014	.0046
3.00	.4987	.9987	.0013	.0044
3.01	.4987	.9987	.0013	.0043
3.02	.4987	.9987	.0013	.0042
3.03	.4988	.9988	.0012	.0040
3.04	.4988	.9988	.0012	.0039
3.05	.4989	.9989	.0011	.0038
3.06	.4989	.9989	.0011	.0037
3.07	.4989	.9989	.0011	.0036
3.08	.4990	.9990	.0010	.0035
3.09	.4990	.9990	.0010	.0034
3.10	.4990	.9990	.0010	.0033
3.11	.4991	.9991	.0009	.0032
3.12	.4991	.9991	.0009	.0031
3.13	.4991	.9991	.0009	.0030
3.14	.4992	.9992	.0008	.0029
3.15	.4992	.9992	.0008	.0028
3.16	.4992	.9992	.0008	.0027
3.17	.4992	.9992	.0008	.0026
3.18	.4993	.9993	.0007	.0025
3.19	.4993	.9993	.0007	.0025
3.20	.4993	.9993	.0007	.0024
3.21	.4993	.9993	.0007	.0023
3.22	.4994	.9993	.0006	.0022
3.23	.4994	.9994	.0006	.0022
3.24	.4994	.9994	.0006	.0021
3.30	.4995	.9995	.0005	.0017
3.40	.4997	.9997	.0003	.0012
3.50	.4998	.9998	.0002	.0009

3.60	.4998	.9998	.0002	.0006
3.70	.4999	.9999	.0001	.0004

Table B. Significant values of *t* for given Probabilities (Abridged Table)

df	*Probability*		*df*	*Probability*	
	.05	*.01*		*.05*	*.01*
1	12.71	63.66	18	2.10	2.88
2	4.30	9.92	19	2.09	2.86
3	3.18	5.84	20	2.09	2.84
4	2.78	4.60	21	2.08	2.83
5	2.57	4.03	22	2.07	2.82
6	2.45	3.71	23	2.07	2.81
7	2.36	3.50	24	2.06	2.80
8	2.31	3.36	25	2.06	2.79
9	2.26	3.25	26	2.06	2.78
10	2.23	3.17	27	2.05	2.77
11	2.20	3.11	28	2.05	2.76
12	2.18	3.06	29	2.05	2.76
13	2.16	3.01	30	2.04	2.75
14	2.14	2.98	.	.	.
15	2.13	2.95	50	2.01	2.68
16	2.12	2.92	100	1.98	2.63
17	2.11	2.90	00	1.96	2.58

For a given *df*, if the obtained t-value reaches or exceeds the table *t*-value under .01 level, then the obtained *t* is significant at the .01 level. A *t*-value which is significant at the .01 level (for a given *df*) will always be significant at the corresponding .05 level.

Table C. 5 Per cent (in lightface) and 1 Per cent (in boldface) Values for Significance of F

f_1 Degrees of Freedom (for Greater Mean Square)

f_2	1	2	3	4	5	6	7	8	9	10	11	12
1	161	200	216	225	230	234	237	239	241	242	243	244
	4052	**4999**	**5403**	**5625**	**5764**	**5859**	**5928**	**5981**	**6022**	**6056**	**6082**	**6106**
2	18.51	19.09	19.16	19.25	19.30	19.33	19.36	19.37	19.38	19.39	19.40	19.41
	98.49	**99.00**	**99.17**	**99.25**	**99.30**	**99.33**	**99.34**	**99.36**	**99.38**	**99.40**	**99.41**	**99.42**
3	10.13	9.55	9.28	9.12	9.01	8.94	8.88	8.84	8.8!	8.78	8.76	8.74
	34.12	**30.82**	**29.46**	**28.71**	**28.24**	**27.91**	**29.67**	**27.49**	**27.34**	**27.23**	**27.13**	**27.05**
4	7.71	6.94	6.59	6.39	6.26	6.16	6.09	6.04	**6.00**	5.96	5.93	5.91
	21.20	**18.00**	**16.69**	**15.98**	**15.52**	**15.21**	**14.98**	**14.80**	**14.66**	**14.54**	14.45	14.37
5	6.61	5.79	5.41	5.19	5.05	4.95	4.88	4.82	4.78	4.74	4.70	4.68
	16.26	**13.27**	**12.06**	**11.39**	**10.97**	**10.67**	**10.45**	**10.27**	**10.15**	**10.05**	**9.96**	**9.89**
6	5.99	5.14	4.76	4.53	4.39	4.28	4.21	4.15	4.10	4.06	4.03	4.00
	13.74	**10.92**	**9.78**	**9.15**	**8.75**	**8.47**	**8.26**	**8.10**	**7.98**	**7.87**	**7.79**	**7.72**
7	5.59	4.74	4.35	4.12	3.97	3.87	3.79	3.73	**3.68**	3.63	3.60	3.57
	12.25	**9.55**	**8.45**	**7.85**	**7.46**	**7.19**	**7.00**	**6.84**	**6.71**	**6.62**	**6.54**	**6.67**
8	5.32	4.46	4.07	3.84	3.69	3.58	3.50	3.44	3.39	3.34	3.31	3.28
	11.26	**8.65**	**7.59**	**7.01**	**6.63**	**6.37**	**6.19**	**6.03**	**5.91**	**5.82**	**5.74**	**5.67**
9	5.12	4.26	3.86	3.63	3.48	3.37	3.29	3.23	3.18	3.13	3.10	3.07
	10.56	**8.02**	**6.99**	**6.42**	**6.06**	**5.80**	**5.62**	**5.47**	**5.35**	**5.26**	**5.18**	**5.11**
10	4.96	4.10	3.71	3.48	3.33	3.22	3.14	3.07	**3.02**	2.97	2.94	2.91
	10.04	**7.56**	**6.55**	**5.99**	**5.64**	**5.39**	**5.21**	**5.06**	**4.95**	**4.85**	**4.78**	**4.71**
11	4.84	3.98	3.59	3.36	3.20	3.09	3.01	2.95	2.90	2.86	2.82	2.79
	9.65	**7.20**	**6.22**	**5.67**	**5.32**	**5.07**	**4.88**	**4.74**	**4.63**	**4.54**	**4.46**	**4.40**
12	4.75	3.88	3.49	3.26	3.11	3.00	2.92	2.85	2.80	2.76	2.72	2.69
	9.33	**6.93**	**5.95**	**5.41**	**5.06**	**4.82**	**4.65**	**4.50**	**4.39**	**4.30**	**4.22**	**4.16**
13	4.67	3.80	3.41	3.18	3.02	2.92	2.84	2.72	2.77	2.63	2.63	2.60
	9.07	**6.70**	**5.74**	**5.20**	**4.86**	**4.62**	**4.44**	**4.30**	**4.19**	**4.10**	**4.02**	**3.96**
14	4.60	3.74	3.34	3.11	2.96	2.85	2.77	2.70	2.65	2.60	2.56	2.53
	8.86	**6.51**	**5.56**	**5.03**	**4.69**	**4.46**	**4.28**	**4.14**	**4.03**	**3.94**	**3.86**	**3.80**
15	4.54	3.68	3.29	3.06	2.90	2.79	2.70	2.64	2.59	2.55	2.51	2.48
	8.68	**6.36**	**5.42**	**4.89**	**4.56**	**4.32**	**4.14**	**4.00**	**3.89**	**3.80**	**3.73**	**3.67**
16	4.49	3.63	3.24	3.01	2.85	2.74	2.66	2.59	2.54	2.49	2.45	2.42
	8.53	**6.23**	**5.29**	**4.77**	**4.44**	**4.20**	**4.03**	**3.89**	**3.78**	**3.69**	**3.61**	**3.55**
17	4.45	3.59	3.20	2.96	2.81	2.70	2.62	2.55	2.50	2.45	2.41	2.38
	8.40	**6.11**	**5.18**	**4.67**	**4.34**	**4.10**	**3.93**	**3.79**	**3.68**	**3.59**	**3.52**	**3.45**
18	4.41	3.55	3.16	2.93	2.77	2.66	2.58	2.51	2.46	2.41	2.37	2.34
	8.28	**6.01**	**5.09**	**4.58**	**4.25**	**4.01**	**3.85**	**3.71**	**3.60**	**3.51**	**3.44**	**3.37**

14	16	20	24	30	40	50	75	100	200	500	∞	f_2
245	246	248	249	250	251	252	253	253	254	254	254	1
6142	**6169**	**6208**	**6234**	**6258**	**6286**	**6302**	**6323**	**6334**	**6352**	**6361**	**6366**	
19.42	19.43	19.44	19.45	19.46	19.47	19.47	19.48	19.49	19.49	19.49	19.50	2
99.43	**99.44**	**99.45**	**99.46**	**99.47**	**99.48**	**99.48**	**99.49**	**99.49**	**99.49**	**99.50**	**99.50**	
8.71	8.69	8.66	8.64	8.62	8.60	8.58	8.57	8.56	8.54	8.54	8.53	3
26.92	**26.83**	**26.69**	**26.60**	**26.50**	**26.41**	**26.35**	**26.27**	**26.23**	**26.18**	**26.14**	**36.12**	
5.87	5.84	5.80	5.77	5.74	5.71	5.70	5.68	5.66	5.65	5.64	5.63	4
14.24	**14.15**	**14.02**	**13.93**	**13.83**	13.74	13.69	**13.61**	**13.57**	**13.52**	**13.48**	**13.46**	
4.64	4.60	4.56	4.53	4.50	4.46	4.44	4.42	4.40	4.38	4.37	4.36	5
9.77	**9.68**	**9.55**	**9.47**	**9.38**	**9.29**	**9.24**	**9.17**	**9.13**	**9.07**	**9.04**	**9.02**	
3.96	3.92	3.87	3.84	3.81	3.77	3.75	3.72	3.71	3.69	3.68	3.67	6
7.60	**7.52**	**7.39**	**7.31**	**7.23**	**7.14**	**7.09**	**7.02**	**6.99**	**6.94**	**6.90**	**6.88**	
3.52	3.49	3.44	3.41	3.38	3.34	3.32	3.29	3.28	3.25	3.24	3.23	7
6.35	**6.27**	**6.15**	**6.07**	**5.98**	**5.90**	**5.85**	**5.78**	**5.75**	**5.70**	**5.67**	**5.65**	
3.23	3.20	3.15	3.12	3.08	3.05	3.03	3.00	2.98	2.96	2.94	2.93	8
5.56	**5.48**	**5.36**	**5.28**	**5.20**	**5.11**	**5.06**	**5.00**	**4.96**	**4.91**	**4.88**	**4.86**	
3.02	2.98	2.93	2.90	2.86	2.82	2.80	2.77	2.76	2.73	2.72	2.71	9
5.00	**4.92**	**4.80**	**4.73**	**4.64**	**4.56**	**4.51**	**4.45**	**4.41**	**4.36**	**4.33**	**4.31**	
2.86	2.82	2.77	2.74	2.70	2.67	2.64	2.61	2.59	2.56	2.55	2.54	10
4.60	**4.52**	**4.41**	**4.33**	**4.25**	**4.17**	**4.12**	**4.05**	**4.01**	**3.96**	**3.93**	**3.91**	
2.74	2.70	2.65	2.61	2.57	2.53	2.50	2.47	2.45	2.42	2.41	2.40	11
4.29	**4.21**	**4.10**	**4.02**	**3.94**	**3.86**	**3.80**	**3.74**	**3.70**	**3.66**	**3.62**	**3.60**	
2.64	2.60	2.54	2.50	2.46	2.42	2.40	2.36	2.35	2.32	2.31	2.30	12
4.05	**3.98**	**3.86**	**3.78**	**3.70**	**3.61**	**3.56**	**3.49**	**3.46**	**3.41**	**3.38**	**3.36**	
2.55	2.51	2.46	2.42	2.38	2.34	2.32	2.28	2.26	2.24	2.22	2.21	13
3.85	**3.78**	**3.67**	**3.59**	**3.51**	**3.42**	**3.37**	**3.30**	**3.27**	**3.21**	**3.18**	**3.16**	
2.48	2.44	2.39	2.35	2.31	2.27	2.24	2.21	2.19	2.16	2.14	2.13	14
3.70	**3.62**	**3.51**	**3.43**	**3.34**	**3.26**	**3.21**	**3.14**	**3.11**	**3.06**	**3.02**	**3.00**	
2.43	2.39	2.33	2.29	2.25	2.21	2.18	2.15	2.12	2.10	2.08	2.07	15
3.56	**3.48**	**3.36**	**3.29**	**3.20**	**3.12**	**3.07**	**3.00**	**2.97**	**2.92**	**2.89**	**2.87**	
2.37	2.33	2.28	2.24	2.20	2.16	2.13	2.09	2.07	2.04	2.02	2.01	16
3.45	**3.37**	**3.25**	**3.18**	**3.10**	**3.01**	**2.96**	**2.89**	**2.86**	**2.80**	**2.77**	**2.75**	
2.33	2.29	2.23	2.19	2.15	2.11	2.08	2.04	2.02	1.99	1.97	1.96	17
3.35	**3.27**	**3.16**	**3.08**	**3.00**	**2.92**	**2.86**	**2.79**	**2.76**	**2.70**	**2.67**	**2.65**	
2.29	2.25	2.19	2.15	2.11	2.07	2.04	2.00	1.98	1.95	1.93	1.92	18
3.27	**3.19**	**3.07**	**3.00**	**2.91**	**2.83**	**2.78**	**2.71**	**2.68**	**2.62**	**2.59**	**2.57**	

f_2	1	2	3	4	5	6	7	8	9	10	11	12
19	4.38	3.52	3.13	2.90	2.74	2.63	2.55	2.48	2.43	2.38	2.34	2.31
	8.18	**5.93**	**5.01**	**4.50**	**4.17**	**3.94**	**3.77**	**3.63**	**3.52**	**3.43**	**3.36**	**3.30**
20	4.35	3.49	3.10	2.87	2.71	2.60	2.52	2.45	2.40	2.35	2.31	2.28
	8.10	**5.85**	**4.94**	**4.43**	**4.10**	**3.87**	**3.71**	**3.56**	**3.45**	**3.37**	**3.30**	**3.23**
21	4.32	3.47	3.07	2.84	2.68	2.57	2.49	2.42	2.37	2.32	2.28	2.25
	8.02	**5.78**	**4.87**	**4.37**	**4.04**	**3.81**	**3.65**	**3.51**	**3.40**	**3.31**	**3.24**	**3.17**
22	4.30	3.44	3.05	2.82	2.66	2.55	2.47	2.40	2.35	2.30	2.26	2.23
	7.94	**5.72**	**4.82**	**4.31**	**3.99**	**3.76**	**3.59**	**3.45**	**3.35**	**3.26**	**3.18**	**3.12**
23	4.28	3.42	3.03	2.80	2.64	2.53	2.45	2.38	2.32	2.28	2.24	2.20
	7.88	**5.66**	**4.76**	**4.26**	**3.94**	**3.71**	**3.54**	**3.41**	**3.30**	**3.21**	**3.14**	**3.07**
24	4.26	3.40	3.01	2.78	2.62	2.51	2.43	2.36	2.30	2.26	2.22	2.18
	7.82	**5.61**	**4.72**	**4.22**	**3.90**	**3.67**	**3.50**	**3.36**	**3.25**	**3.17**	**3.09**	**3.03**
25	4.24	3.38	2.99	2.76	2.60	2.49	2.41	2.34	2.28	2.24	2.20	2.16
	7.77	**5.57**	**4.68**	**4.18**	**3.86**	**3.63**	**3.46**	**3.32**	**3.21**	**3.13**	**3.05**	**2.99**
26	4.22	3.37	2.98	2.74	2.59	2.47	2.39	2.32	2.27	2.22	2.18	2.15
	7.72	**5.53**	**4.64**	**4.14**	**3.82**	**3.59**	**3.42**	**3.29**	**3.17**	**3.09**	**3.02**	**2.96**
27	4.21	3.35	2.96	2.73	2.57	2.46	2.37	2.30	2.25	2.20	2.16	2.13
	7.68	**5.49**	**4.60**	**4.11**	**3.79**	**3.56**	**3.39**	**3.26**	**3.14**	**3.06**	**2.98**	**2.93**
28	4.20	3.34	2.95	2.71	2.56	2.44	2.36	2.29	2.24	2.19	2.15	2.12
	7.64	**5.45**	**4.57**	**4.07**	**3.76**	**3.53**	**3.36**	**3.23**	**3.11**	**3.03**	**2.95**	**2.90**
29	4.18	3.33	2.93	2.70	2.54	2.43	2.35	2.28	2.22	2.18	2.14	2.10
	7.60	**5.42**	**4.54**	**4.04**	**3.73**	**3.50**	**3.33**	**3.20**	**3.08**	**3.00**	**2.92**	**2.87**
30	4.17	3.32	2.92	2.69	2.53	2.42	2.34	2.27	2.21	2.16	2.12	2.09
	7.56	**5.39**	**4.51**	**4.02**	**3.70**	**3.47**	**3.30**	**3.17**	**3.06**	**2.98**	**2.90**	**2.84**
32	4.15	3.30	2.90	2.67	2.51	2.40	2.32	2.25	2.19	2.14	2.10	2.07
	7.50	**5.34**	**4.46**	**3.97**	**3.66**	**3.42**	**3.25**	**3.12**	**3.01**	**2.94**	**2.86**	**2.80**
34	4.13	3.28	2.88	2.65	2.49	2.38	2.30	2.23	2.17	2.12	2.08	2.05
	7.44	**5.29**	**4.42**	**3.93**	**3.61**	**3.38**	**3.21**	**3.08**	**2.97**	**2.89**	**2.82**	**2.76**
36	4.11	3.26	2.86	2.63	2.48	2.36	2.28	2.21	2.15	2.10	2.06	2.03
	7.39	**5.25**	**4.38**	**3.89**	**3.58**	**3.35**	**3.18**	**3.04**	**2.94**	**2.86**	**2.78**	**2.72**
38	4.10	3.25	2.85	2.62	2.46	2.35	2.26	2.19	2.14	2.09	2.05	2.02
	7.35	**5.21**	**4.34**	**3.86**	**3.54**	**3.32**	**3.15**	**3.02**	**2.91**	**2.82**	**2.75**	**2.69**
40	4.08	3.23	2.84	2.61	2.45	2.34	2.25	2.18	2.12	2.07	2.04	2.00
	7.31	**5.18**	**4.31**	**3.83**	**3.51**	**3.29**	**3.12**	**2.99**	**2.88**	**2.80**	**2.73**	**2.66**
42	4.07	3.22	2.83	2.59	2.44	2.32	2.24	2.17	2.11	2.06	2.02	1.99
	7.27	**5.15**	**4.29**	**3.80**	**3.49**	**3.26**	**3.10**	**2.96**	**2.86**	**2.77**	**2.70**	**2.64**
44	4.06	3.21	2.82	2.58	2.43	2.31	2.23	2.16	2.10	2.05	2.01	1.98
	7.24	**5.12**	**4.26**	**3.78**	**3.46**	**3.24**	**3.07**	**2.94**	**2.84**	**2.75**	**2.68**	**2.62**

14	16	20	24	30	40	50	75	100	200	500	∝	f_2
2.26 **3.19**	2.21 **3.12**	2.15 **3.00**	2.11 **2.92**	2.07 **2.84**	2.02 **2.76**	2.00 **2.70**	1.96 **2.63**	1.94 **2.60**	1.91 **2.54**	1.90 **2.51**	1.88 **2.49**	19
2.23 **3.13**	2.18 **3.05**	2.12 **2.94**	2.08 **2.86**	2.04 **2.77**	1.99 **2.69**	1.96 **2.63**	1.92 **2.56**	1.90 **2.53**	1.87 **2.47**	1.85 **2.44**	1.84 **2.42**	20
2.20 **3.07**	2.15 **2.99**	2.09 **2.88**	2.05 **2.80**	2.00 **2.72**	1.96 **2.63**	1.93 **2.58**	1.89 **2.51**	1.87 **2.47**	1.84 **2.42**	1.82 **2.38**	1.81 **2.36**	21
2.18 **3.02**	2.13 **2.94**	2.07 **2.83**	2.03 **2.75**	1.98 **2.67**	1.93 **2.58**	1.91 **2.53**	1.87 **2.46**	1.84 **2.42**	1.81 **2.37**	1.80 **2.33**	1.78 **2.31**	22
2.14 **2.97**	2.10 **2.89**	2.04 **2.78**	2.00 **2.70**	1.96 **2.62**	1.91 **2.53**	1.88 **2.48**	1.84 **2.41**	1.82 **2.37**	1.79 **2.32**	1.77 **2.28**	1.76 **2.26**	23
2.13 **2.93**	2.09 **2.85**	2.02 **2.74**	1.98 **2.66**	1.94 **2.58**	1.89 **2.49**	1.86 **2.44**	1.82 **2.36**	1.80 **2.33**	1.76 **2.27**	1.74 **2.23**	1.73 **2.21**	24
2.11 **2.89**	2.06 **2.81**	2.00 **2.70**	1.96 **2.62**	1.92 **2.54**	1.87 **2.45**	1.84 **2.40**	1.80 **2.32**	1.77 **2.29**	1.74 **2.23**	1.72 **2.19**	1.71 **2.17**	25
2.10 **2.86**	2.05 **2.77**	1.99 **2.66**	1.95 **2.58**	1.90 **2.50**	1.85 **2.41**	1.82 **2.36**	1.78 **2.28**	1.76 **2.25**	1.72 **2.19**	1.70 **2.15**	1.69 **2.13**	26
2.08 **2.83**	2.03 **2.74**	1.97 **2.63**	1.93 **2.55**	1.88 **2.47**	1.84 **2.38**	1.80 **2.33**	1.76 **2.25**	1.74 **2.21**	1.71 **2.16**	1.68 **2.12**	1.67 **2.10**	27
2.06 **2.80**	2.02 **2.71**	1.96 **2.60**	1.91 **2.52**	1.87 **2.44**	1.81 **2.35**	1.78 **2.30**	1.75 **2.22**	1.72 **2.18**	1.69 **2.13**	1.67 **1.09**	1.65 **2.06**	28
2.05 **2.77**	2.00 **2.68**	1.94 **2.57**	1.90 **2.49**	1.85 **2.41**	1.80 **2.32**	1.77 **2.27**	1.73 **2.19**	1.71 **2.15**	1.68 **2.10**	1.65 **2.06**	1.64 **2.03**	29
2.04 **2.74**	1.99 **2.66**	1.93 **2.55**	1.89 **2.47**	1.84 **2.38**	1.79 **2.29**	1.76 **2.24**	1.72 **2.16**	1.69 **2.13**	1.66 **2.07**	1.64 **2.03**	1.62 **2.01**	30
2.02 **2.70**	1.97 **2.62**	1.91 **2.51**	1.86 **2.42**	1.82 **2.34**	1.76 **2.25**	1.74 **2.20**	1.69 **2.12**	1.67 **2.08**	1.64 **2.02**	1.61 **1.98**	1.59 **1.96**	32
2.00 **2.66**	1.95 **2.58**	1.89 **2.47**	1.84 **2.38**	1.80 **2.30**	1.74 **2.21**	1.71 **2.15**	1.67 **2.08**	1.64 **2.04**	1.61 **1.98**	1.59 **1.94**	1.57 **1.91**	34
1.98 **2.62**	1.93 **2.54**	1.87 **2.43**	1.82 **2.35**	1.78 **2.26**	1.72 **2.17**	1.69 **2.12**	1.65 **2.04**	1.62 **2.00**	1.59 **1.94**	1.56 **1.90**	1.55 **1.87**	36
1.96 **2.59**	1.92 **2.51**	1.85 **2.40**	1.80 **2.32**	1.76 **2.22**	1.71 **2.14**	1.67 **2.08**	1.63 **2.00**	1.60 **1.97**	1.57 **1.90**	1.54 **1.86**	1.53 **1.84**	38
1.95 **2.56**	1.90 **2.49**	1.84 **2.37**	1.79 **2.29**	1.74 **2.20**	1.69 **2.11**	1.66 **2.05**	1.61 **1.97**	1.59 **1.94**	1.55 **1.88**	1.53 **1.84**	1.51 **1.81**	40
1.94 **2.54**	1.89 **2.46**	1.82 **2.35**	1.78 **2.26**	1.73 **2.17**	1.68 **2.08**	1.64 **2.02**	1.60 **1.94**	1.57 **1.91**	1.54 **1.85**	1.51 **1.80**	1.49 **1.78**	42
1.92 **2.52**	1.88 **2.44**	1.81 **2.32**	1.76 **2.24**	1.72 **2.15**	1.66 **2.06**	1.63 **2.00**	1.58 **1.92**	1.56 **1.88**	1.52 **1.82**	1.50 **1.78**	1.48 **1.75**	44

f_2	1	2	3	4	5	6	7	8	9	10	11	12
46	4.05	3.20	2.81	2.57	2.42	2.30	2.22	2.14	2.09	2.04	2.00	1.97
	7.21	**5.10**	**4.24**	**3.76**	**3.44**	**3.22**	**3.05**	**2.92**	**2.82**	**2.73**	**2.66**	**2.60**
48	4.04	3.19	2.80	2.56	2.41	2.30	2.21	2.14	2.08	2.03	1.99	1.96
	7.19	**5.08**	**4.22**	**3.74**	**3.42**	**3.20**	**3.04**	**2.90**	**2.80**	**2.71**	**2.64**	**2.58**
50	4.03	3.18	2.79	2.56	2.40	2.29	2.20	2.13	2.07	2.02	1.98	1.95
	7.17	**5.06**	**4.20**	**3.72**	**3.41**	**3.18**	**3.02**	**2.88**	**2.78**	**2.70**	**2.62**	**2.56**
55	4.02	3.17	2.78	2.54	2.38	2.27	2.18	2.11	2.05	2.00	1.97	1.93
	7.12	**5.01**	**4.16**	**3.68**	**3.37**	**3.15**	**2.98**	**2.85**	**2.75**	**2.66**	**2.59**	**2.53**
60	4.00	3.15	2.76	2.52	2.37	2.25	2.17	2.10	2.04	1.99	1.95	1.92
	7.08	**4.98**	**4.13**	**3.65**	**3.34**	**3.12**	**2.95**	**2.82**	**2.72**	**2.63**	**2.56**	**2.50**
65	3.99	3.14	2.75	2.51	2.36	2.24	2.15	2.08	2.02	1.98	1.94	1.90
	7.04	**4.95**	**4.10**	**3.62**	**3.31**	**3.09**	**2.93**	**2.79**	**2.70**	**2.61**	**2.54**	**2.47**
70	3.98	3.13	2.74	2.50	2.35	2.23	2.14	2.07	2.01	1.97	1.93	1.89
	7.01	**4.92**	**4.08**	**3.60**	**3.29**	**3.07**	**2.91**	**2.77**	**2.67**	**2.59**	**2.51**	**2.45**
80	3.96	3.11	2.72	2.48	2.33	2.21	2.12	2.05	1.99	1.95	1.91	1.88
	6.96	**4.88**	**4.04**	**3.56**	**3.25**	**3.04**	**2.87**	**2.74**	**2.64**	**2.55**	**2.48**	**2.41**
100	3.94	3.09	2.70	2.46	2.30	2.19	2.10	2.03	1.97	1.92	1.88	1.85
	6.90	**4.82**	**3.98**	**3.51**	**3.20**	**2.99**	**2.82**	**2.69**	**2.59**	**2.51**	**2.43**	**2.36**
125	3.92	3.07	2.68	2.44	2.29	2.17	2.08	2.01	1.95	1.90	1.86	1.83
	6.84	**4.78**	**3.94**	**3.47**	**3.17**	**2.95**	**2.79**	**2.65**	**2.56**	**2.47**	**2.40**	**2.33**
150	3.91	3.06	2.67	2.43	2.27	2.16	2.07	2.00	1.94	1.89	1.85	1.82
	6.81	**4.75**	**3.91**	**3.44**	**3.14**	**2.92**	**2.76**	**2.62**	**2.53**	**2.44**	**2.37**	**2.30**
200	3.89	3.04	2.65	2.41	2.26	2.14	2.05	1.98	1.92	1.87	1.83	1.80
	6.76	**4.71**	**3.88**	**3.41**	**3.11**	**2.90**	**2.73**	**2.60**	**2.50**	**2.41**	**2.34**	**2.28**
400	3.86	3.02	2.62	2.39	2.23	2.12	2.03	1.96	1.90	1.85	1.81	1.78
	6.70	**4.66**	**3.83**	**3.36**	**3.06**	**2.85**	**2.69**	**2.55**	**2.46**	**2.37**	**2.29**	**2.23**
1000	3.85	3.00	2.61	2.38	2.22	2.10	2.02	1.95	1.89	1.84	1.80	1.76
	6.66	**4.62**	**3.80**	**3.34**	**3.04**	**2.82**	**2.66**	**2.53**	**2.43**	**2.34**	**2.26**	**2.20**
∞	3.84	2.99	2.60	2.37	2.21	2.09	2.01	1.94	1.88	1.83	1.79	1.75
	6.64	**4.60**	**3.78**	**3.32**	**3.02**	**2.80**	**2.64**	**2.51**	**2.41**	**2.32**	**2.24**	**2.18**

14	16	20	24	30	40	50	75	100	200	500	∝	f_2
1.91	1.87	1.80	1.75	1.71	1.65	1.62	1.57	1.54	1.51	1.48	1.46	46
2.50	**2.42**	**2.30**	**2.22**	**2.13**	**2.04**	**1.98**	**1.90**	**1.86**	**1.80**	**1.76**	**1.72**	
1.90	1.86	1.79	1.74	1.70	1.64	1.61	1.56	1.53	1.50	1.47	1.45	48
2.48	**2.40**	**2.28**	**2.20**	**2.11**	**2.02**	**1.96**	**1.88**	**1.84**	**1.78**	**1.73**	**1.70**	
1.90	1.85	1.78	1.74	1.69	1.63	1.60	1.55	1.52	1.48	1.46	1.44	50
2.46	**2.39**	**2.26**	**2.18**	**2.10**	**2.00**	**1.94**	**1.86**	**1.82**	**1.76**	**1.71**	**1.68**	
1.88	1.83	1.76	1.72	1.67	1.61	1.58	1.52	1.50	1.46	1.43	1.41	55
2.43	**2.35**	**2.23**	**2.15**	**2.06**	**1.96**	**1.90**	**1.82**	**1.78**	**1.71**	**1.66**	**1.64**	
1.86	1.81	1.75	1.70	1.65	1.59	1.56	1.50	1.48	1.44	1.41	1.39	60
2.40	**2.32**	**2.20**	**2.12**	**2.03**	**1.93**	**1.87**	**1.79**	**1.74**	**1.68**	**1.63**	**1.60**	
1.85	1.80	1.73	1.68	1.63	1.57	1.54	1.49	1.46	1.42	1.39	1.37	65
2.37	**2.30**	**2.18**	**2.09**	**2.00**	**1.90**	**1.84**	**1.76**	**1.71**	**1.64**	**1.60**	**1.56**	
1.84	1.79	1.72	1.67	1.62	1.56	1.53	1.47	1.45	1.40	1.37	1.35	70
2.35	**2.28**	**2.15**	**2.07**	**1.98**	**1. 88**	**1.82**	**1.74**	**1.69**	**1.62**	**1.56**	**1.53**	
1.82	1.77	1.70	1.65	1.60	1.54	1.51	1.45	1.42	1.38	1.35	1.32	80
2.32	**2.24**	**2.11**	**2.03**	**1.94**	**1.84**	**1.78**	**1.70**	**1.65**	**1.57**	**1.52**	**1.49**	
1.79	1.75	1.68	1.63	1.57	1.51	1.48	1.42	1.39	1.34	1.30	1.28	100
2.26	**2.19**	**2.06**	**1.98**	**1.89**	**1.79**	**1.73**	**1.64**	**1.59**	**1.51**	**1.46**	**1.43**	
1.77	1.72	1.65	1.60	1.55	1.49	1.45	1.39	1.36	1.31	1.27	1.25	125
2.23	**2.15**	**2.03**	**1.94**	**1.85**	**1.75**	**1.68**	**1.59**	**1.54**	**1.46**	**1.40**	**1.37**	
1.76	1.71	1.64	1.59	1.54	1.47	1.44	1.37	1.34	1.29	1.25	1.22	150
2.20	**2.12**	2.00	**1.91**	**1.83**	**1.72**	**1.66**	**1.56**	**1.51**	**1.43**	**1.37**	**1.33**	
1.74	1.69	1.62	1.57	1.52	1.45	1.42	1.35	1.32	1.26	1.22	1.19	200
2.17	**2.09**	**1.97**	**1.88**	**1.79**	**1.69**	**1.62**	**1.53**	**1.48**	**1.39**	**1.33**	**1.28**	
1.72	1.67	1.60	1.54	1.49	1.42	1.38	1.32	1.28	1.22	1.16	1.13	400
2.12	**2.04**	**1.92**	**1.84**	**1.74**	**1.64**	**1.57**	**1.47**	**1.42**	**1.32**	**1.24**	**1.19**	
1.70	1.65	1.58	1.53	1.47	1.41	1.36	1.30	1.26	1.19	1.13	1.08	1000
2.09	**2.01**	**1.89**	**1.81**	**1.71**	**1.61**	**1.54**	**1.44**	**1.38**	**1.28**	**1.19**	**1.11**	
1.69	1.64	1.57	1.52	1.46	1.40	1.35	1.28	1.24	1.17	1.11	1.00	∞
2.07	**1.99**	**1.87**	**1.79**	**1.69**	**1.59**	**1.52**	**1.41**	**1.36**	**1.25**	**1.15**	**1.00**	

Table D. Significant Values of Chi-Square χ^2 (Abridged Table)

df	*Probability* .05	*Probability* .01
1	3.84	6.64
2	5.99	9.21
3	7.82	11.35
4	9.49	13.28
5	11.07	15.09
6	12.59	16.81
7	14.07	18.48
8	15.51	20.09
9	16.92	21.67
10	18.31	23.21
11	19.68	24.73
12	21.03	26.22
13	22.36	27.69
14	23.69	29.14
15	25.00	30.58
16	26.30	32.00
17	27.59	33.41
18	28.87	34.81
19	30.14	36.19
20	31.41	37.57

Testing significance of obtained χ^2 : Suppose our obtained χ^2 value for 4 *df* is $= 9.54$. In the above table, under column *df* for 4 *df*, the corresponding χ^2 value under .05 level is 9.49. Obtained value of 9.54 exceeds this table value. Therefore, the obtained $\chi^2 = 9.54$ is significant at the .05 level.

Table E. Conversion of a Pearson *r* into corresponding Fisher coefficient (Abridged Table)

*r**	*z*	*r*	*z*	*r*	*z*
.25	.26	.51	.56	.77	1.02
.26	.27	.52	.58	.78	1.05
.27	.28	.53	.59	.79	1.07
.28	.29	.54	.60	.80	1.10
.29	.30	.55	.62	.81	1.13
.30	.31	.56	.63	.82	1.16
.31	.32	.57	.65	.83	1.19
.32	.33	.58	.66	.84	1.22
.33	.34	.59	.68	.85	1.26
.34	.35	.60	.69	.86	1.29
.35	.37	.61	.71	.87	1.33
.36	.38	.62	.73	.88	1.38
.37	.39	.63	.74	.89	1.42
.38	.40	.64	.76	.90	1.47
.39	.41	.65	.78	.905	1.50
.40	.42	.66	.79	.910	1.53
.41	.44	.67	.81	.915	1.56
.42	.45	.68	.83	.920	1.59
.43	.46	.69	.85	.925	1.62
.44	.47	.70	.87	.930	1.66
.45	.48	.71	.89	.935	1.70
.46	.50	.72	.91	.940	1.74
.47	.51	.73	.93	.945	1.78
.48	.52	.74	.95	.950	1.83
.49	54	.75	.97	.975	2.18
.50	.55	.76	1.00	.995	2.99

**r* under .25 may be taken as equivalent to *z*

Table F. Significant value of *r* (Abridged Table)

df (N–2)	*Probability* .05	.01	*df* (N–2)	*Probability* .05	.01
1	.997	1.000	35	.325	.418
2	.950	.990	40	.304	.393
3	.878	.959	45	.288	.372
4	.811	.917	50	.273	.354
5	.754	.874	60	.250	.325
6	.707	.834	70	.232	.302
7	.666	.798	80	.217	.283
8	.632	.765	90	.205	.267
9	.602	.735	100	.195	.254
10	.576	.708	125	.174	.228
11	.553	.684	150	.159	.208
12	.532	.661	200	.138	.181
13	.514	.641	300	.113	.148
14	.497	.623	400	098	.128
15	.482	.606	500	.088	.115
16	.468	.590	1000	.062	.081
17	.456	.575			
18	.444	.561			
19	.433	.549			
20	.423	.537			
21	.413	.526			
22	.404	.515			
23	.396	.505			
24	.388	.496			
25	.381	.487			
26	.374	.478			
27	.367	.470			
28	.361	.463			
29	.355	.456			
30	.349	.449			

Appendix–II

SUPPLEMENTARY EXERCISES

1. Calculate mean, median and mode for the following distributions.

(*i*)

Scores	*f*
10-12	4
13-15	6
16-18	8
19-21	5
22-24	4

(*ii*)

Scores	*f*
42-45	4
39-42	5
36-39	3
33-36	2
30-33	1

2. Calculate median for the following distribution.

20-21	18-19	16-17	14-15	12-13	10-11	8-9	6-7	4-5	2-3	0-1
2	1	0	0	2	0	0	2	1	1	1

3. Calculate SD and QD for the following data.

70-79	60-69	50-59	40-49	30-39	20-29	10-19
5	4	8	6	5	3	2

4. Calculate Pearson *r* for the following set of scores from (*i*) original scores and (*ii*) deviation scores.

X	10	8	9	6	8
Y	9	10	11	5	8

5. Calculate Spearman *rho* for the above data and interpret your result.

6. The means and standard deviations of a class (N=25) on two subjects science and social science are as follows. What will be the sigma (z) scores of a student whose scores are 40 and 50 on these subjects? In which subject he performs better?

	Science	Social Science
M	55	60
SD	10	5

7. Convert the obtained sigma scores in example 6 into T-scores.
8. In a class of 125 students, a student is ranked 30th from the top. What is his Percentile Rank?
9. For a normal distribution, determine the following:
   (*i*) Out of 200, number of cases between $-.75\sigma$ and $+.50\sigma$,
   (*ii*) Value of the ordinate (u) at a distance of 1.22σ from the mean.
10. The means and standard deviations on a biology test for two independent groups are as follows. Do the groups differ on achievement in biology?

	N	M	SD
Group A	45	65	10
Group B	55	70	8

11. Two groups which have been matched pairwise for intelligence have their marks on a mathematics test as follows. Do the groups differ on maths achievement?

Group					
A	40	50	32	55	46
B	42	52	36	54	45

12. For a group of students, the data on a science test is as follows. Determine the .95 and .99 confidence intervals within which the mean is expected to fall.

M	SD	N
55	6	30

13. Two hundred and ten college students were asked to express their opinion about usefulness of Anna Hazare's crusade against corruption in public places. The responses of students were categorised as follows. Do the responses indicate a significant trend of opinion?

Favourable	Unfavourable	Undecided
100	60	50

14. Fifty teachers have been classified as competent, average and poor on teaching ability by their students. Does this distribution of ratings differ significantly from that to be expected if teaching ability is normally distributed?

Good	Average	Poor
10	25	15

15. The correlation coefficient (r) between science and mathematics achievement of group A ($N = 25$) is $= 0.70$. For the group B ($N = 36$), the value of r is $= 0.80$. Do the groups differ from each other on the relationship between science and maths achievement?

16. Group A studies science 6 hours a week and the Group B studies it for 4 hours a week. The scores on a science test administered to the two groups are as follows. Is there a relationship between study hours and science achievement?

Scores	Group A	Group B
70-79	3	1
60-69	6	3
50-59	7	4
40-49	2	6
30-39	1	4
20-29	1	2

17. Calculate biserial correlation coefficient for the data in exercise 16.
18. Determine F-ratio for the following data and test for significance at the .05 level.

Group A	Group B	Group C
6	5	4
5	7	4
4	8	5
8	9	5
2	4	2
	3	

19. SE_{dm} for two large groups is 2.55. What should be the difference between the two means to be significant at the .05 level?
20. Given as follows:

    $MS_{among\ groups} = 6.50, \qquad df = 3(f_1), 5(f_2)$

    What is the value of MS_{within} for the F-ratio to be significant at the .05 level?
21. Summary of an ANOVA is as follows. Calculate F-ratio and test its significance.

Source of Variance	*df*	Sum of Squares
Total	19	41
Among	3	21

22. For three variables 1, 2 and 3, given as follows:

    $r_{12} = .60, \qquad r_{23} = .50, \qquad r_{13} = 5.8$

    Find out the correlation coefficient between variables 2 and 3 with the effects of variable 1 ruled out.

23. For two variables *X* and *Y* data are given as follows: Work out the regression equation for the *Y* variable on *X*.

    $\Sigma X = 15 \qquad \Sigma Y = 20 \qquad \Sigma XY = 63$

    $\Sigma X^2 = 49 \qquad \Sigma Y^2 = 90 \qquad N = 5$

24. In the above exercise if $\sigma_y = 1.41$, then work out the *SE* of estimate for predicting *Y* from *X*.

ANSWERS

1. (*i*) 16.65, 16.63, 16.59 (*ii*) 39.30, 39.90, 41.01
2. 9.5
3. 17.40, 12.69
4. .76
5. .68(*NS*, $df = 3$)
6. $-1.5z$, $-2z$, science
7. 35, 30
8. 98th
9. $N = 92.98(93)$, $U = .1895$
10. $t = 2.71$ (*Sig.*, $p < .01$)
11. $t = .75$ (*NS*, $p > .05$)
12. 52.86–57.14, 52.19–57.81

13. $\chi^2 = 20$ (*Sig.*, $p < .01$)
14. $\chi^2 = 10.50(Sig., p < .01)$
15. $t = .89(NS, p > .05)$
16. $r_{pbis} = .45(NS, p < .01, df = 38)$
17. $r_{pbis} = .36(Sig., p < .05, df = 38)$
18. $F = 1.32(NS, p > .05, df\,2{,}13)$
19. $M_d = 5$
20. $MS_w = 1.20$
21. $F = 5.6(Sig., p < .01, df\ 3{,}16)$
22. $r_{23} = .23$
23. $Y' = 1.75 + .75X$
24. $\sigma_{Y.X} = 1.24$

Appendix–III

Questions asked by Begining Researchers

It is not uncommon to find students asking questions and seeking clarifications when they are deciding about opting for dissertation work. Some of the frequently asked questions and their answers are as follows. These brief answers provide some guidance for research activity.

Q. Which method of research is the easiest and the best?

A. There are no such criteria as would distinguish between an easy and a difficult method or between the best and the worst method of research. Suitability of the research method depends on the nature of the problem.

Q. What points should I keep in mind while choosing a topic?

A. Without being under the spell of misplaced idealism, the following points should be kept in mind:

Knowledge (reasonable) about the area/topic of research, methodology of research; computational and writing skills. Doability of research in terms of time, financial and material support together with availability of sample, that is, feasibility of research should be examined. Last but not the least is the interest and motivation of the researcher.

Q. How do I identify problem for research?

A. Discuss with your friends, teachers and seniors. Examine popular literature, newspapers and technical literature pertaining to the area of interest; search on the Internet.

Q. What points should I keep in view while reviewing literature?

A. It should be relevant to your study. Collect studies, both for and against for your hypotheses. Prepare summaries of studies with reference to purpose, sample, tools, techniques and major findings including delimitations and limitations, and duly supported by the information regarding the source (Journal, volume, no., page, author and title) of the study. Try to tap as many primary sources as possible. Information should be put up in a chronological order, with recent studies in the beginning. At least, studies of last 10 years must be reviewed.

Q. Should I write hypotheses of the study after literature review in my dissertation?

A. Definitely it would be a better way. However, follow the guidelines of your university/department. Quite often, for the convenience of the reader, the objectives and hypotheses are placed in the first chapter and before review of literature which is taken up as the second chapter.

Q. What should be the sample size of my study?

A. It depends on a number of factors which may include the purpose, method of study and the size of the population. A case study may be based on a single case and a survey research on a sample of 400 or more. A sample size below 30 is considered small. If the population size is 30, then a sample of 28 would be needed. When the population size is 10,000 a sample size of 370 is needed. As population goes on increasing, the sample size increases with diminishining magnitude.

Q. Should the sample of my study be large or representative?

A. It should be representative. *For example*, a population of 10,000 adults has an equal number of men and women. Picking up 4000 men would make the sample large but not representative because women have not been included.

Q. Which sampling procedure and technique should be preferred?

A. It depends on the nature of the study, population, sampling frame and resourcs such as time, money, energy, etc. Probability sampling procedure is preferred because every member of the population has an equal chance of making it to the sample. When population is finite (limited) and sampling frame is available, simple random sampling is preferred. When the population is heterogeneous and large, stratified random sampling is preferred. When list of population (sampling frame) is not available, prefer systematic sampling. When the population is spread over a wide area, places rather than people are sampled through multistage sampling. Cluster sampling is the final stage of multistage sampling when naturally occurring similar units or group are taken intact.

Q. When should I prefer non-probability sampling techniques?

A. When you have some specific purpose in mind. *For example*, you are studying food preferences of hyperactive children. Purposive sampling would be preferred because your objective is hyperactive children.

Q. How do I deal with non-response of the individuals in the sample?

A. Try to keep a bigger sample in the beginning as some subjects would drop out due to varying reasons. Try to keep non-response rate under 20 per cent. If many people do not respond, finding of the study may become invalid because non-response may be from people who feel differently and therefore have not responded.

Q. When are parametric tests preferred?

A. When data has been obtained from a normally distributed population, on interval or ratio scale.

Q. Is statistical significance different from practical significance?

A. Yes. A statistically significant result may have no practical significance. *For example*, on an anxiety scale, children of working mothers score two points signifcantly higher than children of non-working mothers. Recalling working-mothers because of this significant difference of 2 scores on anxiety would have no practical significance or meaningfulness.

Q. What does "significant at the .05 level" mean?

A. It means that the probability of the obtained statistics occurring due to chance is less than 5 times out of hundred.

Q. t-ratio for difference between means of two groups has been found to be significant at the .01 level ($t = 3$, $df = 100$). How do I write it?

A. The obtained t value is = 3.00 which is significant at the .01 level for df = 100. Therefore, the null hypothesis of no significant difference between the means of the two groups is rejected at the .01 level of significance. The two groups signifcantly differ from one other. The direction of the difference favours the first/or the second group (whatever the case may be).

Q. What is the difference between delimitations and limitations of the research study?

A. Delimitations imply the boundaries of research with reference to variables, sample size and geographical area. Limitations refer to factors beyond the control of the researcher, weaknesses and shortcomings in the study.

Q. Is it necessary to formulate hypotheses of the study?

A. Not necessary.

Q. What style should be followed while I write my dissertation?

A. In education, the present style is the one prescribed by the American Psychological Association (2001). Other desciplines prescribe their own styles. Modern Languages Association (MLA) and the Chicago style are other popular styles. Universities also prescribe their style manuals.

Q. How many pages should my disseration have?

A. This is irrelevant. More important is the content coverage, in an orderly sequence and free from unnecessary repetition. Not so important, but relevant information should find place in appendices. Commonly used formulas should not be printed in the text. Whatever is written in the text should be self-explanatory. Plagiarism is a criminal offence. The contents should be written in third person.

Q. When is a one-tailed test used?

A. When we have a basis for specifying in advance that one treatment or condition is superior to the other on the dependent variable, then one-tailed test may be employed, for which the cut-off values are 1.65 (.05 level) and 2.33 (.01 level) for large samples.

Q. What is random assignment?

A. In experimental studies, the samples are randomly assigned to treatment groups with the help of generated random numbers or tables of random numbers.

Q. How do I decide whether a test is reliable or not?

A. Reliability of a test is understood in terms of its dependability which may be across time (stability) and across the items (internal consistency). Test-retest gives stability measure and inter items correlation (Cronbach alpha) gives internal consistency. An achievement test should have a test-retest reliability of .90 and more, whereas for personality and related measures it could be .60 and above. Cronbach alpha of .70 and above is considered to be reliable enough measure of internal consistency.

Q. What is the relationship between reliability and validity?

A. A highly reliable test may be a valid test for some purpose, but not for our purpose. A highly reliable test of achievement in science is not a valid test of motor ability. A valid test is also a reliable test.

Q. What is Sampling Error?

A. Sampling error is not the error in taking a sample. The extent to which a sample taken from a population differs from the population parameter, is called sampling error.

Appendix-IV

Publishers and Suppliers of Psychological Tests in India

National Psychological Corporation
4/230, Kacheri Ghat, AGRA-282004
www.npcindia.com

Rupa Psycho Centre
B-19/60B Deoriabir
Bhelpur, VARANASI-221010

Psy Com Services
B-4, 80/2 Safdarjang Enclave
NEW DELHI-110029

Prasad Psycho Corp.
B-39, Guru Nank Pura
Laxmi Nagar, NEW DELHI
(www.prasad.psycho.com)

Manasayan
Aggarwal Complex
S-524, School Block
Shakarpur, DELHI-110092

Ankur Psychological Agency
22/481, Indira Nagar
Lucknow-226016

Glossary

A posteriori: coming after; after experience.

A priori: coming before; before experience.

Attribute independent variable: an independent variable on which subjects differ before a study begins.

Bias: the conscious or subconscious influence of researcher's beliefs, attitudes, convictions and value on the research process.

Biased sample: a sample which knowingly includes or excludes unit, groups or individuals in the sample.

Canonical correlation: a statistical procedure for determining the relationship between several independent variables and more than one dependent variable.

Categorical variable: a variable that differs in kind, not in amount or degree, *e.g.*, male-female.

Causal relationship: a relationship in which changes in one variable produce changes in the other.

Ceiling effect: an effect which occurs when the range of performance on a measure is so limited on the upper end that subjects cannot perform to their maximum ability.

Census: a survey that includes the entire population of interest.

Coefficient of determination: the square of the correalation coefficient. It indicates the percentage of variance in one variable common with the other.

Cohen's d: a measure of effect size found by dividing the difference between two sample means by the weighted average of their standard deviations.

Confounding variable: an uncontrolled extraneous variable whose effect on the dependent variable may be incorrectly attributed to the independent variable.

Construct: an abstraction at a higher level than a concept used to explain, interpret or summarize observations.

Control: steps undertaken to remove the effects of variable(s) other than the independent variables which may influence the dependent variable.

Degrees of freedom (*df*): The number of observations free to vary around a constant parameter.

Directional hypothesis: a hypothesis that specifies the direction of the expected findings.

Double blind experiment: an experiment in which neither the observers nor the subjects know which is the experimental and which is the control group.

Double-dipped sample: a sample drawn from the non-respondents to a survey, who are interviewed to determine whether they differ significantly from the respondents.

Ecological validity: a finding is ecologically valid when it is applicable to real life situations.

Factor analysis: a statistical procedure for analysing intercorrelations among three or more measures that reduces the set to a smaller number of underlying factor.

Factor loading: in factor anlysis, the correlation between a variable and a factor. The higher the loading, the more is the contribution of the variable to a particular factor.

Grounded theory: a methodological approach to social science that a researcher should approach a research problem without a preconceived theory. Theory should gradually emerge from the data collected in a research study, through the process of induction.

Hypothesis: a statement of the researcher's expectations about the relationship among the variables of a study.

Internal validity: the extent to which observed differences on the dependent variable, in an experiment are the result of the independent variable, not some uncontrolled extraneous variable(s).

Level of significance: the largest probability error acceptable for rejection of the null hypothesis in educational research, usually p=.05 or p=.01.

Meta analysis: a systematic combination of quantitative data from a number of studies investigating the relationship between the same variables.

Multiple regression: the prediction of a criterion using two or more predictor variables in combination. Each predictor is weighted in proportion to its contribution to prediction accuracy. The equation showing the weights assigned to each predictor is the multiple regression equation.

Operational definition: a definition which specifies the procedure that will be followed in producing or measuring a concept.

Phenomenology: an approach which tries to understand how participants experience and give meaning to an event, phenomenon or a concept.

Power: the ability of a test of significance to find significant differences when they truly exist. It is also the ability to avoid type II error.

Quasi-experimental research: research in which the treatment and measurement of the dependent variable can be controlled, but not the assignment of subjects to treatment(s).

Reflexivity: use of self-reflection by the researcher to look for his own biases.

Regression (statistical): the statistical tendency of extreme scores on first measurement to move closer to the mean on second measurement.

Sampling error: the difference between a sample statistics and a population parameter

Target population: the total population to which the results of a study are to be generalized.

Theory: a set of interrelated propositions or hypotheses which tries to explain why of a phenomenon.

Triangulation: giving strength and support to findings by drawing evidence from other sources.

True experimental design: an experimental design in which the researcher controls the treatment and subjects are randomly assigned to treatment groups.

T Score: a standard score with a mean of 50 and a standard deviation of 10.

Type I error: rejecting a null hypothesis that is in fact true.

Type II error: failing to reject a null hypothesis which is in fact false.

Validity: in psychometry it means whether a particular test or procedure measures what it claims to measure.

Variability: the spread or dispersion in a distribution of scores.

***z* score**: a standard score that indicates how far a score is above or below the mean score in terms of standard deviation units.

References

Anastasi, A. and Urbina, S.(1997). *Psychological Testing.* Delhi:Pearson.

Anderson, G. (1998). *Introduction to Educational Research.* London: Routledge Falmer.

Ary, D., Jacobs, L., Razavieh, A. and Sorenson, C. (2006). *Introduction to Research in Education* (7th ed.). CA: Thomson Wadsworth.

Best, J.W. and Kahn,J.V. (2008). *Research in Education.* Delhi:Pearson.

Bryman, A. (2008). *Social Research Methods.* NY: OUP.

Burnaford,G. Fischer, J. and Hobson, D. (2001). *Teachers Doing Research: The Power of Action Through Inquiry* (2nd ed.). Mahawa, NJ: Erlbaum.

Campbell, D.T. and Stanley, J.(1963). Experimental and Quasi-experimental Designs for Research on Teaching. In N. Gage (ed.) *Handbook of Research on Teaching.* Chicago: Rand McNally.

Downie, N.M. and Heath, R.W. (1970). *Basic Statistical methods* (3rd ed.). NY: Harper International.

Garrett, H.E. and Woodworth, R.S. (1966). *Statistics in Psychology and Education* (9th Indian Reprint, 1979). Bombay: Vakils, Feffer and Simons.

Jena, S.P.K. (2013). *Learning Disability*. New Delhi: Sage.

Kerlinger, F.N. (1970). *Foundations of Behavioural Research*. NY: Holt, Rinehart & Winston.

Kerlinger, F.N. (1986). *Foundations of Behavioural Research* (3rd ed.) NY: Holt, Rinehart & Winston.

Kline, P. (1992). *The Handbook of Psychological Testing*. London: Routledge.

Kline, T.J.B. (2005). *Psychological Testing*. New Delhi: Sage.

Koul, L.(1997). *Methodology of Educational Research* (3rd ed.). New Delhi: Vikas.

Kumar, R. (2005). *Research methods: A Step-by-step Guide for Beginners* (2nd ed.). Delhi: Pearson.

Oppenheim, A.N. (1966/1992). *Questionnaire Design, Interviewing and Attitude Measurement*. London: Continuum.

Sixth Survey of Research in Education (1993-2000). (2006). New Delhi: NCERT.

Wallinman, N. (2005). *Your Research Project* (2nd ed.). New Delhi: Sage.

Wiersma, W. and Jurs, S.G. (2009). *Research Methods in Education: An Introduction* (9th ed.). Delhi: Dorling Kindersley (India).

Index

NAME INDEX

SUBJECT INDEX